THEORIZING ABOUT MYTH

THEORIZING
ABOUT MYTH

Robert A. Segal

UNIVERSITY OF MASSACHUSETTS PRESS
Amherst

Copyright © 1999 by Robert A. Segal
All rights reserved
Printed in the United States of America
LC 98-52004
ISBN 1-55849-194-5
Designed by Milenda Nan Ok Lee
Printed and bound by BookCrafters, Inc.
Set in Bembo
Typeset by Graphic Composition

Library of Congress Cataloging-in-Publication Data
Segal, Robert Alan.
Theorizing about myth / Robert A. Segal.
p.   cm.
Includes bibliographical references and index.
ISBN 1-55849-194-5 (alk. paper)—ISBN 155849-191-0 (paper : alk. paper)
1. Myth.   I. Title.
BL311.S43   1999
291.1'3'01—dc21   98-52004
                                                                        CIP
This book is published with the support and cooperation of the
University of Massachusetts Boston.

British Library Cataloguing in Publication data are available.

The chapters in this book are revisions of previously published essays and are included with
permission of the original publishers. Acknowledgments appear after the notes.

In memory of my mother and father

CONTENTS

INTRODUCTION

THE ESSAYS COLLECTED in this book offer a comparison of many of the leading modern theories of myth. Some of the essays are themselves comparative, but even the ones that focus on a single theory present it vis-à-vis others. Though a number of the essays are critical of the theories presented, the aim of the book is less to evaluate the theories considered than, more modestly, to work out the distinctiveness of each.

The main theories discussed are those of Edward Tylor, William Robertson Smith, James Frazer, Jane Harrison, S. H. Hooke, Mircea Eliade, Rudolf Bultmann, Hans Jonas, Sigmund Freud, C. G. Jung, Joseph Campbell, Claude Lévi-Strauss, and Hans Blumenberg. Other theories, including those of Bronislaw Malinowski, René Girard, and Walter Burkert, get mentioned briefly. Some of the essays concentrate on disciples of the original theorists—for example, on the Frazerians Jessie Weston and Lord Raglan; on the Lévi-Straussian Marcel Detienne; on the Freudians Otto Rank and Bruno Bettelheim; and, when taken as a Jungian, on Joseph Campbell.

Theories of myth are hard to compare, and for many reasons. To begin with, myth is an applied subject. Theories of myth are always theories of something broader that is applied to the case of myth. To compare theories of myth is ineluctably to compare theories of the broader categories, themselves as varied as the physical world, the mind, society, culture, literature, and religion.

Second, the most conventional kind of comparison—by discipline—proves tenuous. Differences among disciplines are often blurry, and similarities among theories within disciplines are often hazy. For example, it is far from clear that the theories of Tylor, Frazer, and Lévi-Strauss belong under anthropology rather than under psychology. And in whatever discipline one puts these theories, the similarities among them do not self-evidently outweigh the differences.

As an alternative, one might compare theories by the positions they hold on key issues in the study of myth. Take, for example, the relationship between myth and religion. For many theorists, myth is a subset of religion. For Tylor, Smith, Frazer, Harrison, and Hooke, religion is the primitive counterpart to modern science, and myth is part of the religious explanation of the world or part of the religious means of controlling the world. For Bultmann, myth is part of the religious worldview, itself eternal rather than merely primitive. For other theorists, myth stands opposed to religion. For Campbell, who is the most extreme, religion perverts the psychological and mystical meaning of myth by interpreting its own myths literally and historically. Yet for other theorists the issue of the relationship between myth and religion is either hazy or, worse, irrelevant. For Eliade, primitive myth falls wholly under religion, but modern myth is secular. Freud and Jung alike allow for secular as well as religious myths, but they are concerned far more with the relationship between myth and dream than with the relationship between myth and religion.

Take, as another example, the issue of the dispensability of myth. For some theorists, myth is entirely replaceable. For Tylor and Frazer, myth has already been replaced by science. For Eliade and Campbell, by contrast, myth is irreplaceable. It is panhuman. Yet for other theorists the situation is less straightforward. For Harrison, myth as part of fertility rituals has long been succeeded by science, but myth as part of initiation rituals has likely not been. And myth detached from ritual has become literature, which is not the same as myth and which has hardly been superseded. For Lévi-Strauss, myth as primitive science has been succeeded by modern science, but primitive science, the science of the concrete, is different from modern science, the science of the abstract, and so has not really been duplicated. Similarly for Lévi-Strauss, myth as the resolution of contradictions in experience seems likewise to be a merely primitive possession, but what can be said to have taken its place in the modern world? For Bultmann and Jonas, the message of myth may be indispensable, but myth may not be indispensable to conveying that message. For other theorists as well, such as Jung, the indispensability of the function served by myth need not mean the indispensability of myth to the serving of it.

A sturdier way of comparing theories might be by the answers they give to the fundamental questions about myth: what is its origin, what is its function, what is its subject matter? Certainly theories present an array of answers to these questions. The subject matter, or referent, of myth can range from the literal subject matter, which is most often gods, to a symbolic one, such as gods as symbols of natural phenomena or of human traits. For most theorists, myth originates and functions to satisfy a need, but that need can be for anything—for example, for rain, for information, or for purpose in life. The need can be on the part of individuals or on the part of the community.

Yet even this seemingly fail-safe way of comparing theories falls short, for it turns out that by no means all theories answer all three questions. Most answer only one or two. Blumenberg, for example, dismisses the question of the origin of myth. Bultmann and Jonas confine themselves to the question of subject matter. They translate the outdated, literal, prescientific meaning of myth into an eternal, existentialist one, but they supply no origin or function for the conveying of that meaning. Malinowski restricts himself to the question of function. He rejects the question of origin as unknowable and is simply indifferent to the question of subject matter.

If all of these possible means of comparison fail, how, then, to compare theories of myth? While not foolproof, the way employed in this book is, one might say, "argumentative": determining whom each theorist is arguing against. The comparisons will, then, prove to be contrasts. In the first chapter Tylor presents his theory of myth as a rejoinder to those contemporaries who make myth either a metaphorical, magnified description of merely human heroes—the euhemerists—or an equally metaphorical prescription for how human beings ought to behave—the moral allegorizers. For Tylor, myth is meant literally, not metaphorically; it is about gods, not human beings; and it is an explanation of how gods act to control the physical world, not an evaluation of their actions. Tylor writes to defend what he deems the integrity of myth against those who would cheapen it in making it palatable to moderns.

In the second chapter it is Tylor himself who, if not in name then in view, is being argued against—here by four theorists. Where for Tylor myth, as an explanation of the physical world, is doomed by science, for Eliade, Bultmann, Jonas, and Jung myth is compatible with science, the authority of which is not in question. These theorists recast either the function of myth, so that myth is not explaining the physical world, or the subject matter of myth, so that myth is not even referring to the physical world. Each of the four strives to preserve myth in the face of the death sentence that, according to Tylor, science pronounces.

The third chapter traces the history of the myth-ritualist theory, the theory that ties myth to ritual. The pioneering myth-ritualist, William Robertson Smith, argues against the view, epitomized by Tylor, that myth is a primitive explanation of the world. For Smith, myth is indeed a primitive explanation—but of ritual, not the world. To take myth as an explanation of the world is, for Smith, to conflate myth with creed and thereby to conflate primitive religion with modern. James Frazer, who develops the myth-ritualist theory far beyond Smith and gives it its classic formulation, does turn myth back into primitive science. But still breaking with Tylor, he makes myth only secondarily an explanation of the world and makes it primarily a ritualistic means of controlling the world. Myth for him is closer to applied science—to technology—than to scientific theory.

The fourth chapter presents Jessie Weston's faithful application of Frazer's myth-ritualism to the Grail legend. Weston is not, to be sure, arguing against another theory of myth. Rather, she is arguing against another interpretation of the legend—the Christian one and, to a lesser extent, the Celtic one. She employs Frazer's theory of myth to make her case. When applied to the Grail, Frazer's theory turns the concern for the fate of the ethereal Fisher King and in turn of the land into an instance of the practical primitive concern for food, which depends on the fate of the land, which itself depends on the fate of the king. The quest for the Grail thereby loses any uniquely Christian spin.

The fifth chapter presents Bruno Bettelheim's Freudian interpretation of not only myths but also fairy tales. Like Weston, Bettelheim is arguing less against another theory than against another interpretation of, primarily, fairy tales. That interpretation spurns fairy tales as sheer escapist fantasies. On the contrary, contends Bettelheim, fairy tales help children face, not evade, everyday problems. Fairy tales help children grow up. Bettelheim is really defending Freudian theory against the staid charge that it reduces all folklore to the mere expression of Oedipal and other childhood wishes lingering in the minds of adult neurotics. Yet Bettelheim simultaneously interprets myths, which he pits against fairy tales, in precisely this regressive fashion. More precisely, he reads myths as expressions of the impossibility of growing up, so overwhelming are the demands that adulthood imposes. Bettelheim is thereby arguing against fellow Freudians, who nowadays read myths in exactly the way that Bettelheim reads fairy tales: as aids to growing up.

Chapter six offers a systematic overview of Jung's theory of myth. While Jung is continually obsessed with refuting Freud, in his theorizing about myth he recognizes that he must first refute nonpsychological theories. His nemeses here are Frazer and Tylor, or at least the views they espouse. Jung seeks to refute their assumption that myth is about the external world. Myth, he argues, is really about the human mind, which simply projects itself onto the world, typically in the form of gods. Not until Jung has established that, despite appearances, the subject matter of myth is not gods or even forces of nature can he turn to establishing that its psychological subject matter is archetypes and not, as for Freud, parents and siblings. Jung challenges Frazer's, Tylor's, and Freud's views of the origin and function as well as the subject matter of myth.

The seventh chapter juxtaposes three rival interpretations of the myth of Adonis: Frazer's, Lévi-Strauss's, and Jung's. Marcel Detienne, a Lévi-Straussian at the time, is explicitly writing to refute Frazer's classic analysis of the myth. A Jungian approach, while admittedly not directed against either a Frazerian or a Lévi-Straussian one, can be taken as a corrective to the analyses of both—analyses which skew the character of the figure of Adonis.

Like chapter seven, chapter eight juxtaposes three theories of myth—here theories applied to hero myths in particular. Otto Rank, originally a fervently orthodox Freudian, presents what is still the classic Freudian interpretation of hero myths and really of myths per se. Joseph Campbell, though never a full-fledged

Jungian, nevertheless provides what remains the classic Jungian, or largely Jungian, interpretation of hero myths and, again, of myths per se. Lord Raglan, a follower of Frazer's, offers a myth-ritualist interpretation of hero myths and of myths as a whole. Each follower is writing to advocate, not merely to apply, his master's theory. While Rank, coming first, is not writing against Campbell or Raglan, the Jungian Campbell is in effect writing against the Freudian Rank; and Raglan, ever dismissive of psychology, is in effect writing against both Rank and Campbell, even if his direct attack is against those who take myth historically.

The ninth chapter suggests that the popularity of Campbell's theory lies in its romantic approach to myth. Campbell can be taken as railing against the relentlessly rationalist theory of Tylor. Where for Tylor myth is an outdated, merely primitive attempt to do what today science does so much better, for Campbell myth is an indispensable source of eternal wisdom about the nature of both human beings and ultimate reality. Campbell's passion for myth exceeds that of any other theorist, even Eliade and Jung.

Hans Blumenberg, the subject of the tenth chapter, is explicitly arguing against both rationalist and romantic views of myth—views epitomized by Tylor and Campbell. Contrary to Tylor, Blumenberg maintains that myth is other than primitive science; contrary to Campbell, he contends that myth is other than perennial wisdom. What, then, is left for myth to do is the question posed by this last chapter.

I · TYLOR'S THEORY OF MYTH AS PRIMITIVE SCIENCE

MYTH AND SCIENCE

IT IS FASHIONABLE to say that whatever else myth is, it is compatible with science. For if myth is incompatible with science, it is unacceptable to moderns, who, it is taken for granted, accept science. At least two ways of reconciling myth with science are regularly proposed. Sometimes it is argued that myth and science serve different functions and so run askew. Other times it is declared, more boldly, that science itself is mythic.

While the view that myth and science are incompatible has contemporary defenders, its staunchest exponent remains the Victorian anthropologist Edward Tylor.[1] By no coincidence present-day proponents of this view like Robin Horton are commonly labeled "neo-Tyloreans." Tylor himself never actually *argues* that myth and science are incompatible. Rather, he takes their incompatibility for granted. He does argue that the two are redundant—with both functioning to explain events in the physical world. But redundancy does not mean incompatibility. Why for him are myth and science outright incompatible?

The answer must be that the explanations they give are. Myth for Tylor attributes events to the wills of personalities—above all to gods but sometimes to humans and even to animals. Science ascribes events to mechanical forces. Myth and science are incompatible because both offer direct explanations of the same events. Gods operate not behind or through mechanical forces but in place of them. Tylor thus notes the gradual displacement of the personal causes of religion, or "animism," by the mechanical ones of science: "But just as mechanical astronomy gradually superseded the animistic astronomy of the lower races, so biological pathology gradually supersedes animistic pathology, the immediate operation of personal spiritual beings in both cases giving place to the operation of natural processes" (*Primitive Culture* [hereafter *PC*], 2:229).

But even if myth and science are incompatible, why for Tylor is myth unscientific? The answer must be that personal causes are unscientific. But why? Tylor never says, and one must reconstruct his view. There are various possibilities.[2]

1. Perhaps for Tylor personal causes are mental—the decisions of divine, human, or animal agents—whereas mechanical causes are material. But Tylor himself contrasts the "primitive" religious conception of the soul as *material* to the modern religious conception of it as immaterial (see, for example, *PC*, 2:41, 85). From the primitive conception of souls comes the conception of gods, who are therefore material as well: ". . . the lower races are apt to ascribe to spirits in general that kind of ethereal materiality which we have seen they attribute to souls" (*PC*, 2:284). Primitive religion is for him no less materialist than science (see *PC*, 2:85). He even states that "the later metaphysical notion of immateriality could scarcely have conveyed any meaning to a savage" (*PC*, 2:41).

Tylor's own view aside, any automatic equation of science with materialism is debatable. At least some present-day scientists and philosophers of science are dualists,[3] and the relationship of the mind to the body remains an open scientific question. Tylor's reason for deeming personal causation unscientific therefore not only cannot but should not necessarily be that gods are immaterial entities.

2. Perhaps for Tylor personal causes are neither predictable nor testable, whereas mechanical ones are both predictable and testable. For example, while it is predictable that lightning will cause thunder, it is not predictable that the god of thunder will decide to send thunder. But the events that, according to Tylor, primitives most want explained are regular, hence predictable, ones like the daily course of the sun, not irregular ones like thunder.

Moreover, many scientific explanations are merely probabilistic, yet they are not thereby less scientific than deductive explanations. The predictability of events in fields like medicine is often much less than even fifty-fifty. Weather predictions are notoriously fallible, yet meteorology is still a science. Some currently probabilistic explanations may eventually become deductive ones, but others may not— not because the information required to make them deductive will still be missing but because they will turn out to be inherently probabilistic. Many contemporary physicists believe that the *ultimate* explanations of physics will prove to be merely probabilistic.[4]

Tylor does contrast the testability of science to the untestability of myth, but he does not specify the nature of the test: "We are being trained to the facts of physical science, which we can test and test again, and we feel it a fall from this high level of proof when we turn our minds to the old records which elude such testing, and are even admitted on all hands to contain statements not to be relied on" (*PC*, 1:280). Perhaps Tylor is referring not merely to "experimental tests," to which, he says, "progressive races have been learning to submit their opinions" (*PC*, 1:112–13), but, more broadly, to a critical attitude—a willingness to entertain and even to seek alternative hypotheses.[5] Certainly he attributes at least the origin of myth to the childlike naïveté of primitives, who adopt the first hypothesis that comes to mind: "To the human intellect in its early childlike state may be assigned the origin and first development of myth. . . . The first beings that children learn to understand something of are human beings, and especially their own selves; and the first explanation of all events will be the human explanation, as though chairs and sticks and wooden horses were actuated by the same sort of personal will as nurses and children and kittens" (*PC*, 1:284–85). Yet even Tylor must grant primitives sufficient self-criticism to be able to account for the eventual abandonment of myth for science.

3. Perhaps for Tylor personal causes are particularistic, whereas mechanical ones are generalizable. For example, myth, like history and literature, describes the actions of specific gods and not of gods per se. But the events that, according to Tylor, primitives most want explained are, again, recurrent, not singular, ones: not the origin of the sun but its daily rising and setting. Unlike such theorists of myth as Mircea Eliade, Tylor thus downplays creation myths. Moreover, the cause of recurrent events in myth is for him always the same: whenever the sun rises and sets, it does so because the sun god has decided to make it rise and set, and the god's reason never changes. Insofar as for Tylor the causes of all events in the physical world are the decisions of gods, myths collectively might even be said to provide a uniform explanation of all events. Still, individual myths explain only individual events, albeit recurrent ones. In explaining recurrent events, myth for Tylor is more like science than like history, so that personal causation cannot for him be unscientific because it explains only one-time events.

4. Perhaps for Tylor personal causes are final, or teleological, whereas mechanical ones are efficient. Gods act not just in response to something but also for some end; mechanical forces like atoms behave merely in response to something. But science was partly teleological until Newton, and biology remained teleological until Darwin. Much human behavior continues to be explained teleologically. The difference between myth and science is that myth explains the *whole world* teleologically. There is no disjunction between the nature of the explanations of human behavior and the nature of the explanations of the behavior of everything else. Indeed, gods for Tylor are postulated on analogy to human beings. Still, for Tylor the counterpart to myth is not social science but natural science, so that the retention of teleological explanations in social science is beside the point. Tylor need only observe that the course of natural science from Aristotle to today has been from teleological to mechanistic explanations. Even so, it would be going too far to pronounce teleological explanations inherently unscientific rather than ever less scientific.

In short, it is not easy to see how Tylor either does defend or could defend his conviction that myth is unscientific. Because he never questions this conviction, he takes for granted not merely that primitives have only myth but, even more, that moderns have only science. Not coincidentally, Tylor refers to the "myth-making stage" of culture (see, for example, *PC*, 1:283, 392). Rather than an eternal phenomenon, as for Eliade, C. G. Jung, and Joseph Campbell, myth for Tylor is merely a passing one. Humans have myth only until they discover science. There are but two stages: the mythic and the scientific.[6] Moderns who still have myth have simply failed either to recognize or to concede its incompatibility with science. While Tylor does not date the beginning of the scientific stage, it is recent: it is synonymous with the beginning of modernity. Dying in 1917, Tylor never quite envisioned a stage post the modern one.

MYTH TAKEN LITERALLY

One reason Tylor pits myth against science is that he reads myth literally. He opposes those who read myth poetically, metaphorically, or symbolically—for him, interchangeable terms. Tylor assumes that the explanatory function of myth *requires* a literal reading. To read myth nonliterally is automatically to cede any explanatory function, and to cede the explanatory function is automatically to trivialize myth. He thus says that "the basis on which such [mythic] ideas . . . are built is not to be narrowed down to poetic fancy and transformed metaphor. They rest upon a broad philosophy of nature, early and crude indeed, but thoughtful, consistent, and quite really and seriously meant" (*PC*, 1:285). Tylor even assumes that modern theorists who take myth nonliterally do so because they project their own incredulity onto primitives. Never taking myth seriously themselves, these moderns cannot conceive that anyone else has ever done so.

It is not self-evident that myth must be taken literally to be taken seriously. Such theorists as Campbell and Rudolf Bultmann argue the opposite: that myth must be taken nonliterally to be taken seriously. Where Tylor argues that myth is credible to primitives only because they take it literally, Campbell argues that myth is credible to primitives only because they take it nonliterally. Where Tylor argues that myth is incredible to moderns precisely because they rightly take it literally, Campbell and Bultmann alike argue that myth is credible to moderns only insofar as they rightly take it nonliterally. Tylor objects not to those theorists who read myth nonliterally for themselves but to those who read it nonliterally for primitives. He would thus berate Campbell far more for what Campbell says of primitives than for what Campbell and Bultmann say of moderns.

According to Tylor, moderns who interpret myth nonliterally for primitives are anachronistically interpreting it as poetry: "Poetry has so far kept alive in our minds the old animative [i.e., mythic] theory of nature, that it is no great effort to us to fancy the [inanimate] waterspout a huge giant or sea-monster, and to depict in what we call appropriate metaphor its march across the fields of ocean. But where such forms of speech are current among less educated races, they are underlaid by a distinct prosaic [i.e., literal] meaning of [actual] fact" (*PC*, 1:292). In contrast above all to Friedrich Max Müller, Tylor regards primitives as scientists rather than poets.[7]

At the same time Tylor says that *modern* poets like Wordsworth best grasp the primitive disposition to personify nature because they can best imagine the sea, for example, as literally raging:

> Just so the civilized European may contrast his own stiff orderly prosaic thought with the wild shifting poetry and legend of the old myth-maker, and may say of him that everything he saw gave birth to [mere] fancy. Wanting the power of transporting himself into this imaginative atmosphere, the [nonpoetically inclined] student occupied with the analysis of the mythic world may fail so pitiably in conceiving its depth and intensity of meaning, as to convert it into stupid fiction. Those can see more justly who have the poet's gift of throwing their minds back into the world's older life, like the actor who for a moment can forget himself and become what he pretends to be. (*PC*, 1:305)

Nevertheless, Tylor says that modern *theorists* of myth misunderstand the primitive disposition to personify nature either because, as in the quotation, they dismiss the literal personification as silly or, worse, because, like Campbell, they transform literal personification into poetry.[8]

There is a double respect in which Tylor, in the name of primitives, interprets myth literally: not only is myth, according to him, really about the physical world rather than about either society or human beings, but it is really about the divine causes of events in the physical world rather than about the physical world itself. For Tylor's nonliteralist nemeses, it is about neither.

One group of nonliteralists singled out by Tylor, the euhemerists, contend that myths are really about human heroes, who subsequently get magnified into gods (see *PC*, 1:278–82). Heroes neither are gods nor control the physical world. Euhemerists grant that the *apparent* subject matter of myth is gods and the world. They simply deny that the real one is. Myth for them does not just *originate* out of the biography of heroes—a possibility that Tylor allows—but actually *remains* a merely hyperbolic version of that human biography: "legendary wonders" are "treated [by euhemerists] . . . as being matter-of-fact disguised in metaphor" (*PC*, 1:279). For example, the myth of Helius' driving his chariot daily across the sky proves to be only a colorful way of describing the life of a local or national hero. Similarly, "already in classic times [according to euhemerists] men were declaring that Atlas was a great astronomer who taught the use of the sphere, and was therefore [merely] represented with the world resting on his shoulders" (*PC*, 1:279).[9]

The other group of nonliteralists named by Tylor, the moral allegorizers, assert that myths are really prescriptions for proper human behavior (see *PC*, 1:277–78,

408–15). The myth of Helius becomes a clever technique for promoting self-discipline: "Helius daily drives his chariot across the sky" means "One should work hard." Likewise the myth of Memnon, who is killed by Achilles at Troy, "depicts the destinies of rash young men of promise." Perseus "symbolizes war, and when of the three Gorgons he attacks only the mortal one, this means that only practicable wars are to be attempted" (*PC,* 1:277).

For the euhemerists, myth cannot be primitive science because its subject is human beings rather than gods or the world. For the moral allegorizers—Tylor limits himself to allegorizers for whom the allegory is moral—myth cannot be primitive science because, in addition, it says how humans ought to behave rather than how they do behave. Tylor assumes that myth, as part of primitive religion, is not only nonnormative but also amoral (see *PC,* 2:11, 402–17, 445–47, 459–60; *Anthropology,* 221–23). For two reasons, then, myth cannot be moral allegory.[10]

Since Tylor denies the reality of the gods, he himself might seem to be taking them as mere personifications of natural phenomena and thereby be taking myth nonliterally. But he is not. Unlike both the euhemerists and the moral allegorizers, he assumes that primitives themselves take the gods literally. Also unlike his antagonists, so does he.

The difference between Tylor and, notably, James Frazer is that while Frazer, like Tylor, assumes that primitives take gods and myths literally, he himself interprets both symbolically. For Frazer, myths about the death and rebirth of the god of vegetation, for him the chief god of the pantheon, are merely symbolic descriptions of the annual death and rebirth of vegetation itself. For Tylor, by contrast, the myths are literal descriptions of the death and rebirth of the god believed responsible for the course of vegetation.

More than descriptions, myths for Tylor are explanations, explanations less of the lives of gods than of the effect of their lives or, better, their decisions on the natural phenomena they control. The ultimate subject matter of myth for Tylor is not physical events themselves, as it is for Frazer, but the divine causes of those events. As mere descriptions of events, myths would be unnecessary. Ever observant, primitives for Tylor notice events on their own. They invent myths to account for their observations, not to record them. For Tylor, gods originate out of the personification of nature, but once conjured up, gods are more than mere personifications. They are the causes—the professed literal causes—of the origin and operation of the world.

Tylor's most telling argument for a literal reading of myth is the otherwise inexplicable beliefs of primitives. Only persons who took myth literally would think the way they do: "When the Aleutians thought that if anyone gave offence to the moon, he [i.e., moon] would fling down stones on the offender and kill him, or when the moon came down to an Indian squaw, appearing in the form of a beautiful woman with a child in her arms, and demanding an offering of tobacco and fur robes, what conceptions of personal life could be more distinct [i.e., real] than these?" (*PC,* 1:289–90). While for Tylor taking the gods literally does not entail taking them as real, taking them as real does presuppose taking them literally.

MYTH AND RELIGION

Another reason Tylor pits myth against science is that he subsumes myth under religion. For him, there is no myth outside religion, even though modern religion is without myth. Because religion for Tylor is primitive science, myth must be so as well. Because religion for him is to be taken literally, so must myth be.

On the one hand myth for Tylor arises last within primitive religion and pre-supposes the rest of it. Hence he says that the "first and foremost" cause of myth is the "doctrine of Animism," or the belief in gods, itself (*PC,* 1:285). On the other hand myth for him supplements the rest of religion. There is no primitive religion without myth. Without myth, believers would still know who their gods are, what phenomena individual gods control, and what the hierarchy of the gods is. But they would not know the biographies of their gods, the past behavior of the gods, and the relationship between gods and humans. Without myth, believers would know the operation but not the origin of the world. They would know the causes of only recurrent, not initial, events in the world. Myth completes the explanation of the world provided by the rest of religion.

HERO MYTHS

Despite Tylor's subsumption of myth under religion, he allows for at least one variety of secular myths: hero myths. While some heroes are gods, many are not (see *PC,* 1:281–82). Tylor divides myths into "nature myths," which one would have assumed were for him identical with myths per se, and a host of other, often overlapping kinds: "myths philosophical or explanatory; myths based on real descriptions misunderstood, exaggerated, or perverted; myths attributing inferred events to legendary or historical personages [i.e., heroes]; myths based on realiza-tion of fanciful metaphor; and myths made or adapted to convey moral or social or political instruction" (*PC,* 1:368).[11] For all Tylor's denunciation of euhemerists and moral allegorizers, he thus apparently grants them some place, just not the whole place, in the study of myth.

In recognizing hero stories as myths, Tylor makes myth more than primitive science. First, the events attributed to heroes affect the social condition of human beings more than the physical one. Adam and Eve's misdeeds may make their descendants' lives mortal, painful, and wearying, but the accomplishments of Abraham, Isaac, and Jacob shape the customs, values, and institutions of Jews rather than their physical state. Tylor himself includes social phenomena in saying that "When the attention of a man in the myth-making stage of intellect is drawn to any [natural] phenomenon or *custom* which to him has no obvious reason, he invents and tells a story to account for it" (*PC*, 1:392 [italics added]).

Second, if hero stories qualify as myths, then there can be modern as well as primitive myths. Tylor might reply that modern hero stories are less than full-fledged myths, but he would have to defend this position.

Third, if hero stories qualify as myths, then myths can be normative as well as explanatory. To the extent that heroes serve as models for subsequent behavior, Tylor becomes a moral allegorizer. In short, Tylor, for the sake of his theory of myth, would be wiser to classify hero myths as legends rather than as myths—the way folklorists do.

REASON IN MYTH

For Tylor, myth stems from innate intellectual curiosity, which is as strong in primitives as in moderns: "Man's craving to know the causes at work in each event he witnesses, the reasons why each state of things he surveys is such as it is and no other, is no product of high civilization, but a characteristic of his race down to its lowest stages" (*PC*, 1:368–69). More than idle curiosity, the quest for knowledge among even primitives "is already an intellectual appetite whose satisfaction claims many of the moments not engrossed by war or sport, food or sleep" (*PC*, 1:369). Tylor acknowledges an emotional as well as an intellectual side of religion, but he deems the intellectual side paramount (see *PC*, 2:444–45).

For Tylor, the postulation of first souls and then gods is a rational inference from the data: "the primitive animistic doctrine is thoroughly at home among savages, who appear to hold it on the very evidence of their senses, interpreted on the biological principle which seems to them most reasonable" (*PC*, 2:83–84; see also, for example, 29–31, 62, 194). Rather than transforming heretofore dead and inert phenomena into living and mobile ones, primitives hypothesize souls and gods to account for the life and activity—the data—that they already experience around them:

> The sense of an absolute psychical distinction between man and beast, so prevalent in the civilized world, is hardly to be found among the lower races. Men to whom the cries of beasts and birds seem like human language, and their actions guided as it were by human thought, logically enough allow the existence of souls to beasts, birds, and reptiles, as to men. The lower psychology cannot but recognize in beasts the very

characteristics which it attributes to the human soul, namely, the phenomena of life and death, will and judgment, and the phantom seen in vision or in dream. (*PC*, 2:53)

We moderns consider even more madcap the postulation of souls and gods in inanimate objects like "stocks and stones, weapons, boats, food, clothes, ornaments, and other objects," for to us these objects "are not merely soulless but [underlying it] lifeless" (*PC*, 2:61). But "if we place ourselves by an effort in the intellectual position of an uncultured tribe, and examine the theory of object-souls from their point of view, we shall hardly pronounce it irrational" (*PC*, 2:61). A stone over which one trips can seem to have placed itself there. Plants as well as animals do seem to be exercising their wills in their varying responses to human effort. Animals, plants, and inanimate objects do appear as agents in dreams and visions.

Because moderns no less than primitives see humans in their dreams, hear the humanlike cries of beasts and birds, and trip over stones, Tylor is not distinguishing primitive senses from modern ones. He is distinguishing primitive *trust* in the senses from modern wariness. Less critical than moderns, primitives accept unquestioningly not only their normal, waking impressions but even their dream and hallucinatory ones: "Even in healthy waking life, the savage or barbarian has never learnt to make that rigid distinction between subjective and objective, between imagination and reality, to enforce which is one of the main results of scientific education. Still less, when disordered in body and mind he sees around him phantom human forms, can he distrust the evidence of his very senses" (*PC*, 2:29). Religion partly *originates* from the primitive attempt to explain the appearance of humans in dreams and visions, which are therefore taken as real.

Tylor faults primitives for failing to check not only their sense impressions but also their inferences from those impressions. Primitives automatically take as speech the noises made by beasts and birds, in which case animals must for them possess not only life and motion but also intellect, for which additional reason animals must harbor souls and then gods. Because primitives never question the inferences they draw from sense impressions, ordinary or abnormal, they invent myth and religion rather than science.

Once primitives hypothesize souls and gods as the causes of natural events, they *experience*, not just *explain*, the world as filled with souls and gods: "They [primitives] could see the flame licking its yet undevoured prey with tongues of fire, or the serpent gliding along the waving sword from hilt to point; they could feel a live creature gnawing within their bodies in the pangs of hunger; they heard the voices of the hill-dwarfs answering in the echo, and the chariot of the Heaven-god rattling in thunder over the solid firmament" (*PC*, 1:297). But unlike such theorists as Lucien Lévy-Bruhl, Ernst Cassirer, and Henri Frankfort, for all of whom primitive religion shapes experience from the outset, Tylor maintains that primitives initially experience the world no differently from moderns. Primitives see and hear what moderns do. They merely trust their eyes and ears and on the basis of them reason out, not assume or project, the existence of souls and gods. Primitives may be uncritical, but they are not illogical. Like moderns, they work scrupulously inductively—from observations to inferences to generalizations. Tylor thus preserves the parallel between primitive religion and modern science, or his conception of modern science.

IMAGINATION IN MYTH

As much as Tylor stresses the role of reason in myth and religion, he accords a place to imagination, at least in myth. Like the rest of religion, myth functions to explain the world, but unlike the rest of religion, myth does so in the form of stories, which are in part the product of imagination.

It is imagination which transforms the rational belief in Helius as the sun god into the fantastic story of Helius' daily driving a chariot across the sky. Undeniably, Tylor vigorously decries the view that myth stems from *unrestrained* imagination: "Among those opinions which are produced by a little knowledge, to be dispelled by a little more, is the belief in an almost boundless creative power of the human imagination. The superficial student, mazed in a crowd of seemingly wild and lawless fancies, which he thinks to have no reason in nature nor pattern in this material world, at first concludes them to be new births from the imagination of the poet, the tale-teller, and the seer" (*PC*, 1:273). Tylor even maintains that both the euhemerists and the moral allegorizers fail to take myth seriously *because* they attribute it to unbridled imagination, which he equates with "poetic fancy" (see, for example, *PC*, 1:285, 289–90). For Tylor, to attribute myth to imagination is invariably to make its subject other than the physical world, is thereby to make its function other than explanatory, and is thereby to cease to take myth seriously.

Still, Tylor accords a commodious place to *restrained* imagination—imagination restrained by reason. The comparative approach, which he takes for granted neither the euhemerists nor the moral allegorizers employ (see *PC*, 1:280–82), "makes it possible to trace in mythology the operation of imaginative processes recurring with the evident regularity of mental law" (*PC*, 1:282; see also 274–75). Tylor assumes that untethered imagination would never yield the patterns he finds in myths, so that regularities constitute *ipso facto* evidence of the subordination of imagination to reason. The stories may be fantastic, but they are fantastic in uniform ways. Tylor asks rhetorically, "What would be popularly thought more indefinite and uncontrolled than the products of the imagination in myths and fables?" (*PC*, 1:18). Here he anticipates Claude Lévi-Strauss. For both, the demonstration of uniformity in myth, the seemingly least orderly of artifacts, proves that not only it but also its primitive creators are rational.[12] For both Tylor and Lévi-Strauss as well, the rational function of myth must be scientificlike.

ASSESSMENT

Tylor's subordination of imagination to reason is symptomatic of the central limitation of his overall theory of myth: his overemphasis on myth as akin to science and his underemphasis on it as akin to literature. Myth for him is a scientificlike hypothesis that merely happens to take the form of a narrative. Like Lévi-Strauss, he downplays the format in order to uphold the content. He assumes that myth, like the rest of religion, is an explanation of the physical world, is taken seriously only when it is taken as an explanation of the physical world, and is taken as an explanation of the physical world only when the form is taken as merely a colorful way of presenting the content. Form and content are separable, and content alone counts. To treat the form as anything more than a medium is to reduce a set of would-be truth-claims about the world to fiction.

Tylor views myth the way Karl Popper and Carl Hempel, among many others, view history: as a causal explanation of events. For Popper and Hempel, a historical account may take the form of a narrative, but the form is irrelevant to the purpose of the account, which is to explain why something happened. Other philosophers maintain that history is more or even other than explanation and that the narrative form is central to the purpose of history. Narrative for them is not merely a literary device but a way of thinking. Someone of a Tylorean bent would reply that to regard history as more, let alone other, than a causal explanation is to trivialize it.[13]

Tylor's attempt at minimizing both narrative and imagination fails. First, he simply cannot confine the subject of myth to the physical world or even the human one. He cannot disregard the divine world. Even if gods are postulated in order to explain the physical world, surely they become of interest in their own right, if only for their power over the physical world. Surely the intellectual inquisitiveness that Tylor is so zealous to credit to primitives would not abate with the postulation of gods as the causes of events in the world. Exactly insofar as myths for Tylor are narratives about gods, there must be interest in gods in themselves. The Hebrew Bible may present God only in relation to humans and the world, but Homer and Hesiod, for example, also depict the gods amongst themselves. Certainly in science the microscopic world, even if initially postulated to account for the macroscopic world, becomes of interest in itself.

Second, descriptions of the divine world are surely the work of imagination. Gods may be postulated on analogy to human beings, but they are more than human beings. Whatever qualities make gods gods and make heaven heaven surely are the product of imagination. Far from constricting the exercise of imagination, the belief in gods spurs it.

Third, the content of myth does not evince "the operation of imaginative processes recurring with the evident regularity of mental law" (*PC*, 1:282). Strikingly, Tylor barely discusses the content of myth—beyond stipulating that myth presents a divine explanation of natural phenomena. What form that explanation takes, he never says. He provides no common pattern for myths. The sole myths for which he provides any regularity are hero myths, in which, according to him, the subjects are exposed at birth, are saved, and grow up to become national heroes (see *PC*, 1:281–82). But this pattern is neither universal nor detailed. And hero myths for Tylor are secondary. He offers no comparable pattern for creation myths, flood myths, or myths of recurrent natural processes.

It is hardly clear that Tylor could if he tried. While it may be facile to say, as both ancients (Plato, Plotinus) and moderns (Hans Blumenberg) do, that in myth anything can happen, in myth a grand array of things does happen. Any limits on the plot are likely to be set by the scope of imagination, whether imagination is envisioned as something running free or as something rigidly checked by cognitive processes. Literary critics like Richard Chase may go too far in reducing myth to literature,[14] but Tylor doubtless goes too far in ignoring the literary character of myth. Tylor sees myth as sheer plot. He ignores other standard literary considerations such as point of view, character, diction, narrative technique, reader reaction, and (wherever allowed by Tylor) symbolism.[15]

In the light of postmodernism, Tylor's approach doubtless seems not simply one-sided but also hopelessly out of date. Where postmodernists would view myth as a mere story and not an explanation, Tylor views myth as an explanation and only incidentally a story. What is needed is not the replacement of myth as explanation by myth as story but instead the integration of the two: the working out of how form and content, story and explanation, operate together.

The continuing importance of Tylor lies in his insistence on the intellectual content of myth. He refuses to pay the price of reconciling myth with science: giving up the explanatory function of myth. For Tylor, myth is either explanation or nothing.

II • DOES MYTH HAVE A FUTURE?

WHETHER MYTH has a future depends on its capacity to meet the challenge posed by modern science. As Marcel Detienne and many others have shown, the challenge to myth does not begin in the modern era.[1] It goes back to at least Plato, who rejected Homeric myth as trivial and immoral. The Stoics defended myth against these charges by reinterpreting it as metaphysical and moral allegory.

Modern challenges to myth have been made on intellectual, theological, and political grounds. The chief modern challenge, however, has come from natural science, which does so well what myth had long been assumed to do: explain the origin and operation of the physical world. Where myth attributes events in the world to the decisions of gods, science ascribes events to impersonal, mechanical processes. To accept the scientific explanation of the world is to render the mythic one both superfluous and outright false—superfluous because superseded by the scientific account, false because incompatible with the scientific one. Science does not challenge the *origin* of myth. How and why myth arises does not matter. Science challenges the assumed *function* of myth by usurping that function.

The most facile response to the gauntlet thrown down by science has been to ignore science. An only slightly less facile response has been to pronounce science itself mythic. A more credible response has accepted science as the reigning explanation of the world and has then either "surrendered" or "regrouped." Surrendering means simply replacing myth with science. Myth is here conceded to be an outdated and incorrect explanation of the world. Regrouping means altering either the function or the subject matter of myth in order to make myth compatible with science. Myth here becomes other than a *literal explanation* of the world. Either the function of myth becomes other than that of explanation, or the subject matter of myth becomes other than the literal one.

THE SURRENDER OF MYTH TO SCIENCE: TYLOR

The exemplars of the surrendering response to science are the pioneering anthropologists Edward Tylor and James Frazer. Tylor represents a purer case than Frazer, whose views on the function of myth are muddled and contradictory.[2] According to Tylor, myth arises and functions solely to explain events in the physical world. Like science, myth serves neither to endorse nor to condemn the world but only to account for it. Myth does not moralize, sanction, or emote. It explains.

Tylor's surrender of myth to science presupposes not only that the exclusive function of myth is explanatory but also that mythic explanations are unscientific. Tylor assumes that myth is unscientific because it employs personal rather than impersonal causes.[3] Tylor also assumes that personal explanations are inferior to impersonal ones. He therefore takes for granted that the rise of science spells the fall of myth. "Primitives" have myth; moderns have science. Yet the rise of science somehow does not also dictate the end of religion. Even though for Tylor religion and myth operate in tandem to explain the world—religion identifies which god causes an event; myth tells how and why that god causes the event—religion can survive the rise of science where myth cannot. True, religion can survive only by ceding explanation to science and by becoming instead a mere espousal of ethics—a view epitomized by Matthew Arnold. But at least religion can change and thereby survive. For some unstated reason myth cannot.

In fact, Tylor rails against those theorists of myth who dare to make myth other than an explanation, including those who turn myth into moral allegory.[4] According to this group of theorists, Perseus, for instance, "symbolizes war, and when of the three Gorgons he attacks only the mortal one, this means that only practicable wars are to be attempted." A present-day moral allegorizer might take the story of Perseus as "an allegory of trade: Perseus himself is Labour, and he finds Andromeda, who is Profit, chained and ready to be devoured by the monster Capital; he rescues her and carries her off in triumph."[5] For the moral allegorizers, myth is compatible with science both because it is really about human beings rather than about gods and because it says how human beings ought to behave rather than how they do behave. The function of myth becomes normative rather than explanatory, and the subject matter of myth becomes symbolic rather than literal.

Tylor denounces the moral allegorizers not because they alter the function or subject matter of myth for themselves but because they do so for primitives. For Tylor, to cede the explanatory function of myth is to trivialize myth, and the explanatory function requires a literal reading. He thus says that "the basis on which such [mythic] ideas as these are built is not to be narrowed down to poetic fancy and transformed metaphor. They rest upon a broad philosophy of nature, early and crude indeed, but thoughtful, consistent, and quite really and seriously meant."[6] Tylor assumes that the allegorizers anachronistically project their own incredulity onto primitives. Scarcely taking myth seriously themselves, these theorists cannot imagine that anyone else ever has.

It is, then, in the *name* of myth that Tylor denies myth a future. For him, to take myth seriously is to take it as an explanation of the world. That that explanation has been vanquished by the scientific one does not, for Tylor, demean it. On the contrary, myth remains a competitor, albeit a losing competitor, in the grandest intellectual enterprise.

THE REGROUPING OF MYTH IN THE WAKE OF SCIENCE: ELIADE, BULTMANN, JONAS, AND JUNG

As common as the strategy of surrendering myth to science has been, even more popular has been the strategy of regrouping. Conceding to science only the explanatory function and the literal subject matter of myth, this strategy seeks alternative functions and subjects beyond the ken of science. Regrouping has taken several forms. One form has been to credit myth with one or more nonexplanatory functions, in which case myth runs askew to science and can therefore coexist with it. The exemplar of this response is Mircea Eliade. A second form of response has been to interpret myth symbolically, in which case myth does not even refer to the physical world and so can likewise coexist with science. The exemplars of this response are Rudolf Bultmann and Hans Jonas. The boldest form of response has been to alter both the function and the subject matter of myth, so that on neither count does myth compete with science. The exemplars of this two-pronged rejoinder to science are C. G. Jung and Joseph Campbell.

Mircea Eliade

Mircea Eliade does not reject the explanatory function of myth. For him, as for Tylor, myth serves to explain how gods created and control the world: "Myth narrates a sacred history; it relates an event that took place in primordial Time, the fabled time of the 'beginnings.' In other words, myth tells how, through the deeds of Supernatural Beings, a reality came into existence, be it the whole of reality, the Cosmos, or only a fragment of reality—an island, a species of plant, a particular kind of human behavior, an institution."[7] Indeed, Eliade goes beyond Tylor in crediting myth with explaining not only natural phenomena but also social ones: "Myths, that is, narrate not only the origin of the World, of animals, of plants, and of man, but also all the primordial events in consequence of which man became what he is today—mortal, sexed, organized in a society, obliged to work in order to live, and working in accordance with certain rules."[8]

How, then, does Eliade meet the challenge of science? By proposing functions served by myth in addition to the explanatory one. Myth for Eliade justifies as well as explains phenomena. Myth does not, to be sure, pronounce phenomena good. But it does pronounce them inevitable and in that sense seeks to reconcile humanity to them. For example, myth justifies death less by postulating an after-life, though Eliade notes myths that do, than by rooting death in an event in primordial time, when the world was still malleable but when any action made permanent whatever it effected. In primordial, or mythic, time the cosmic clay is soft; by subsequent, historical, ordinary time it has hardened. According to myth, human beings die because "a mythical Ancestor stupidly lost immortality, or be-cause a Supernatural Being decided to deprive him of it, or because a certain mythical event left him endowed at once with sexuality and mortality, and so on."[9] Myth makes the present less arbitrary and therefore more tolerable by locat-ing its origin in the hoary past.

Myth for Eliade does more than explain and justify. It regenerates. To hear, to read, and especially to reenact a myth is magically to return to the time when the myth took place, the time of the origin of whatever phenomenon it explains and justifies: "But since ritual recitation of the cosmogonic myth implies reactualiza-tion of that primordial event, it follows that he for whom it is recited is magically projected *in illo tempore,* into the 'beginning of the World'; he becomes contem-porary with the cosmogony."[10] In returning one to primordial time, myth reunites one with the gods, for it is then when they are nearest, as the biblical case of "the Lord God['s] walking in the garden in the cool of the day" typifies (Genesis 3:8). That "reunion" reverses the postlapsarian separation from the gods, a separation that is equivalent to the fall, and renews one spiritually: "What is involved is, in short, a return to the original time, the therapeutic purpose of which is to begin life once again, a symbolic rebirth."[11] The ultimate payoff of myth is experiential: encountering divinity.

Clearly, science offers no regenerative or even justificatory function. Science simply explains. Myth, then, has a future: it can do things that science cannot.

But Eliade offers another argument in favor of the future—in fact, the eter-nality—of myth. Myth not only serves functions that transcend the function served by science; it also serves them for moderns as well as for primitives. Mod-erns for Eliade fancy themselves scrupulously rational, intellectual, unsentimental, and forward-looking—in short, scientific. Nothing could veer farther from their collective self-image than adherence to myth, which they dismiss as egregiously outdated. Yet even they, according to Eliade, cannot dispense with myth:

A whole volume could well be written on the myths of modern man, on the mytholo-gies camouflaged in the plays that he enjoys, in the books that he reads. The cinema, that "dream factory," takes over and employs countless mythical motifs—the fight between hero and monster, initiatory combats and ordeals, paradigmatic figures and images (the maiden, the hero, the paradisal landscape, hell, and so on). Even reading includes a mythological function . . . because, through reading, the modern man succeeds in obtaining an "escape from time" comparable to the "emergence from time" effected by myths. Whether modern man "kills" time with a detective story or enters such a foreign temporal universe as is represented by any novel, reading projects him out of his personal duration and incorporates him into other rhythms, makes him live in another "history."[12]

Plays, books, and movies are mythiclike because they reveal the existence of another world alongside the everyday one—a world of extraordinary figures and events akin to those found in earlier, superhuman myths. Furthermore, the actions of those figures account for the present state of the everyday world. Most of all, moderns get so absorbed in plays, books, and movies that they imagine themselves to be back in the world before their eyes. Identifying themselves with the characters of the stories, they experience the same hopes and fears. If, argues Eliade, even self-professed atheists ineluctably have their own myths, then surely myth is panhuman, in which case it has a boundless future.

However appealing, Eliade's dual counterargument to Tylor—that myth serves functions that science cannot duplicate and that even moderns cherish myth—is dubious. First, the nonexplanatory functions of myth depend on the explanatory one, as Eliade himself recognizes in always characterizing myth as at least an explanation. But then myth can serve its other functions only if it can fend off science in serving its explanatory function. How it can do so, Eliade never says. Perhaps he is assuming that the phenomena explained by modern myths are entirely social—for example, the origin of tools, marriage, government, and nationalities—and not at all natural—for example, the origin of the sun and the moon. But *social* science seeks to account for social phenomena, so what is left for myth alone to explain?

Second, modern myths do not return one to the time of the gods. They may not even go backward in time but may instead go forward, as in science fiction, or go sideways, such as to other cultures around the world. Even myths that do move backward rarely go as far back as the time of the gods. They take one back to only "post-primordial" time. These myths may provide escape from the present, but how much renewal can they provide? A hagiographical biography of George Washington may attribute the establishment of twentieth-century American laws and mores to the accomplishments of this larger-than-life hero, but a human being he remains. Reliving the American Revolution might be inspiring, but would it provide cosmic regeneration?

Third, moderns travel back in time only in their imaginations, not in reality. Americans may feel *as if* they are present at the Revolution, but they hardly claim actually to be back there, whisked on a mythic time machine. Once the play, book, movie, or other vehicle is over, so is the myth. One may remember a stirring story long afterward, but as a memory or an inspiration only. As affecting as Eliade's effort to confer a future on myth is, it is unconvincing.

Rudolf Bultmann

The second main regrouping response to the challenge of science has come from the existentialist camp: from the New Testament scholar and theologian Rudolf Bultmann and from his one-time student, the philosopher Hans Jonas. Both were students of Martin Heidegger. For both Bultmann and Jonas, myth does not explain the world because myth is not about the world. The true subject matter of myth is the place of human beings in the world, and the function of myth is to describe that place. As Bultmann puts it, "The real purpose of myth is not to present an objective picture of the world as it is, but to express man's understanding of himself in the world in which he lives. Myth should be interpreted not cosmologically, but anthropologically, or better still, existentially."[13]

Bultmann acknowledges that, read literally, myth is about the world itself. But unlike Eliade and Tylor, both of whom retain a literal interpretation of myth, Bultmann, together with Jonas, offers a symbolic one. In Bultmann's celebrated, if excruciatingly confusing, phrase, one must "demythologize" myth, by which he means not eliminating, or "demythicizing," the mythology but instead extricating the true, existential subject matter of the mythology.

Taken literally, myth for Bultmann is exactly as it is for Tylor: a prescientific explanation of the world, an explanation rendered not merely superfluous but plainly false by science. Were myth to harbor no other subject matter, Bultmann no less than Tylor would spurn it altogether as primitive.

Demythologized, however, myth ceases to be an explanation at all and becomes an expression, an expression not of the nature of the world but of the nature of the human experience of the world. Myth ceases to be merely primitive and becomes universal. It ceases to be false and becomes true. It becomes a statement of the human condition.

Read literally, the New Testament in particular describes a cosmic battle between good and evil anthropomorphic gods and angels for control of the physical world. These beings intervene not only in the operation of nature, as for Tylor, but also in the lives of human beings. The beneficent beings direct humans to do good; the malevolent ones compel them to do evil. Taken literally, the New Testament describes a prescientific outlook:

The world is viewed as a three-storied structure, with the earth in the centre, the heaven above, and the underworld beneath. Heaven is the abode of God and of celestial beings—the angels. The underworld is hell, the place of torment. Even the earth is more than the scene of natural, everyday events, of the trivial round and common task. It is the scene of the supernatural activity of God and his angels on the one hand, and of Satan and his daemons on the other. These supernatural forces intervene in the course of nature and in all that men think and will and do. Miracles are by no means rare. Man is not in control of his own life. Evil spirits may take possession of him. Satan may inspire him with evil thoughts. Alternatively, God may inspire his thought and guide his purposes. He may grant him heavenly visions. He may allow him to hear his word of succour or demand. He may give him the supernatural power of his Spirit.[14]

Demythologized, the New Testament still refers in part to the physical world, but now to a world ruled by a single, nonanthropomorphic, transcendent God. Because God does not act directly in the world and because no evil powers exist, human beings are free rather than controlled like puppets:

Mythology expresses a certain understanding of human existence. It believes that the world and human life have their ground and their limits in a power which is beyond all that we can calculate or control. Mythology speaks about this power inadequately and insufficiently because it speaks about it as if it were a worldly [i.e., physical] power. It [rightly] speaks of gods who represent the power beyond the visible, comprehensible world. [But] it speaks of gods as if they were men and of their actions as human actions. . . . Again, the conception of Satan as ruler over the world expresses a deep insight, namely, the insight that evil is not only to be found here and there in the world, but that all particular evils make up one single power which in the last analysis grows from the very actions of men, which form an atmosphere, a spiritual tradition, which overwhelms every man. The consequences and effects of our sins become a power dominating us, and we cannot free ourselves from them.[15]

Demythologized, God still exists, but Satan does not. Sin becomes one's own doing, and Satan symbolizes only one's own evil inclinations. Damnation refers not to a future place but to one's present state of mind, which exists as long as one rejects God. Similarly, salvation refers to one's state of mind once one accepts God. Hell symbolizes despair over the absence of God; heaven, joy in his presence. The eschatology refers not to the coming end of the physical world but to the personal acceptance or rejection of God in one's daily life.

Because a literal interpretation of the New Testament reduces human beings to the pawns of cosmic forces, a literal reading focuses on those forces themselves, which means on the world itself. Because a symbolic interpretation pronounces humanity free, it concentrates on the actions humans choose in response to the world.

Taken literally, myth, as a supernatural explanation of the physical world, is incompatible with science and is therefore unacceptable to moderns:

> Man's knowledge and mastery of the world have advanced to such an extent through science and technology that it is no longer possible for anyone seriously to hold the New Testament view of the world—in fact, there is no one who does. What meaning, for instance, can we attach to such phrases in the creed as "descended into hell" or "ascended into heaven"? We no longer believe in the three-storied universe which the creeds take for granted. . . . No one who is old enough to think for himself supposes that God lives in a local heaven. There is no longer any heaven in the traditional sense of the word. The same applies to hell in the sense of a mythical underworld beneath our feet. . . . Now that the forces and the laws of nature have been discovered, we can no longer believe in spirits, whether good or evil.[16]

Once demythologized, however, myth is compatible with science because it now refers both to the transcendent, nonphysical world and, even more, to humans' experience of the physical one.

Like Eliade, Bultmann urges moderns to accept myth. But where Eliade neglects to show how moderns can accept myth, Bultmann translates myth into existentialist terms in order to make it acceptable. At the same time he justifies his translation not on the pragmatic grounds that otherwise moderns could not accept it but on the grounds that its true subject matter *is* human existence: "If the truth of the New Testament proclamation is to be preserved, the only way is to demythologize it. But our motive in so doing must not be to make the New Testament relevant to the modern world at all costs. The question is simply whether the New Testament message consists exclusively of mythology, or whether it [itself] actually demands the elimination of myth [at the literal level] if it is to be understood as it is meant to be."[17] The incompatibility of literally read myth with science provides the opportunity to extricate the symbolic meaning of myth intended all along.

To say that myth is acceptable to scientifically minded moderns is not, however, to say why myth should be accepted. In providing a modern *subject matter* of myth, Bultmann provides no modern *function*. Perhaps for him the function is self-evident: myth serves to express the human condition. But why is it necessary to express that condition, and why is it necessary to express that condition through myth? Perhaps for Bultmann myth does not merely express but outright reveals the human condition, and perhaps for Bultmann myth alone does so. Still, what is the function served by that revelation? Why do humans need to know their condition? Bultmann never says.

Moreover, myth, even when demythologized, is acceptable to moderns only when the existence of God is. For as a religious existentialist rather than, like

Jonas, a secular one, Bultmann takes myth to be preserving the reality of God, simply of a nonphysical god. Bultmann saves myth from science only insofar as moderns can accept even a sophisticated conception, not to mention a specifically Christian conception, of God. Where Eliade saves myth from science by appealing to the existence of distinctively modern myths—myths without gods in them—Bultmann retains an ancient myth with its God. Furthermore, at least Eliade tries to demonstrate that moderns, however avowedly atheistic, actually espouse myth. Bultmann merely leaves myth as something worthy of espousal. He does say that the message of myth need not be conscious: "It goes without saying that this existential self-understanding need not be conscious."[18] But he nowhere establishes that this message is commonly espoused.

Hans Jonas

In proposing a demythologization of the New Testament, Bultmann declares his debt to Hans Jonas, who had already (1934) offered a demythologization of Gnosticism: "A good example of such treatment [i.e., demythologization] is to be found in Hans Jonas's book on Gnosticism. Our task is to produce an existentialist interpretation of . . . the New Testament along similar lines."[19]

Jonas argues that ancient Gnosticism touts the same fundamental view of the human condition as modern existentialism. Both philosophies stress the radical alienation of human beings from the world. Taking the roots of existentialism all the way back to the seventeenth century, Jonas describes Pascal's depiction of the human situation:

> "Cast into the infinite immensity of spaces of which I am ignorant, and which know me not, I am frightened." "Which know me not": more than the overawing infinity of cosmic spaces and times, more than the quantitative disproportion, the insignificance of man as a magnitude in this vastness, it is the "silence," that is, the indifference of this universe to human aspirations . . . which constitutes the utter loneliness of man in the sum of things. As a part of this sum, as an instance of nature, man is only a reed, liable to be crushed at any moment by the forces of an immense and blind universe in which his existence is but a particular blind accident, no less blind than would be the accident of his destruction. As a thinking reed, however, he is no part of the sum, not belonging to it, but radically different, incommensurable: for the *res extensa* does not think, so Descartes had taught, and nature is nothing but *res extensa*—body, matter, external magnitude. If nature crushes the reed, it does so unthinkingly, whereas the reed—man—even while crushed, is aware of being crushed.[20]

While Pascal, unlike Sartre and Camus, is a religious existentialist, his God "is essentially an unknown God, an *agnostos theos,* and is not discernible in the evidence of his creation."[21] The result is human estrangement from God as well as from the world.

For Jonas, ancient Gnosticism presents an outlook as forlorn as that of modern existentialism. For here, too, lies an uncompromising divide between human beings and the world:

> And, like Pascal, he [the Gnostic] is frightened. His solitary otherness, discovering itself in this forlornness, erupts in the feeling of dread. Dread . . . is the self's reaction to the discovery of its situation, actually itself an element in that discovery: it marks the awakening of the inner self from the slumber or intoxication of the world. . . . Becoming aware of itself, the self also discovers that it is not really its own, but is rather the involuntary executor of cosmic designs. Knowledge, *gnosis,* may liberate man from this servitude; but since the *cosmos* is contrary to life and to spirit, the saving knowledge cannot aim at integration into the cosmic whole. . . . For the Gnostics, on the contrary, man's alienation from the world is to be deepened and brought to a head, for the extrication of the inner self which only thus can gain itself.[22]

The Gnostic and existentialist worldviews are far from identical, as Jonas certainly grants. In Gnosticism one is presently separated from one's true, divine self, which itself is separated from both the true god and the true world. One finds oneself trapped in an alien, material self that is part of an alien world under the control of an alien god. In secular existentialism the true self from which one is separated is the absence of any fixed nature or essence. One is presently severed from the true self exactly insofar as one deems one's nature determined by heredity or the environment rather than freely created and re-created. There beckons no higher world beyond the present world. And there looms no god of any kind, lower or higher.

In Gnosticism one's false self is not just the body but worldly values. In existentialism one's false self is the role with which one identifies oneself—for example, that of professor, student, lawyer, parent, child, or sibling. One has no essence because no god created humanity. In Gnosticism one's true self is consubstantial with the true world: the spark is part of the immaterial world. The alien world is the material world ruled by the Demiurge, the nemesis of the true god. In existentialism the sole world that exists is antithetical to oneself: human consciousness stands over against inert, dead matter, which is amoral rather than demonic. The world is meaningless. It has no essence, or purpose, precisely because no god created it. In Gnosticism one's true self is consubstantial with the true god: the spark is a split-off piece of the godhead, which strives for reunification. In the ideal state one is reunited with the godhead and loses all individual identity. In existentialism belief in any god is false hope and, like the identification of oneself with a single role, is an attempt to avoid responsibility for one's life. It is what Sartre calls "bad faith."

In Gnosticism the state of alienation is temporary. To heed the revelation of the true nature of things from the savior is automatically to begin the process of overcoming that state—a process that culminates in the severance of the spark from the body at death. In existentialism the state of alienation from the world is permanent. It is the human condition. Alienation from one's true self is overcome the moment one recognizes that one has chosen to forge one's present identity. No savior from outside is required for that recognition. No world or god has deceived one. To evade responsibility for one's actions, one has deceived oneself.

Despite these not inconsiderable divergences between ancient Gnosticism and modern existentialism, Jonas demonstrates the even keener similarities. Like Bultmann, Jonas translates ancient myth into contemporary parlance. While Jonas himself is captivated as much by the way ancient Gnosticism sheds light on modernity as by the way modernity sheds light on ancient Gnosticism, it is the light that modern existentialism sheds on ancient Gnosticism which gives myth a future.

For Jonas, as for Bultmann, myth, rightly deciphered, refers not to the world but to the experience of the world. Gnostic myths no longer describe the god-head, the emanations, the creator god, or the material world. They now describe the state of alienation from the material world. Gnostic myths no longer explain the origin of the material world from or through the immaterial world. They now describe the way human beings comport themselves in the material world. Gnostic myths cease to offer any escape from the material world and instead condemn one to life in that world.

More accurately, Jonas, like Bultmann, ignores those aspects of ancient myths that are cosmogonic or eschatological and concentrates on those aspects that are existential. The *fact* of human alienation from the world, not the source of it or the solution to it, is the demythologized subject of myth. The residue is mere mythology—to be discarded, just like *all* mythology for Tylor.

Yet no more than Bultmann does Jonas offer any function of myth for moderns. Even if myth serves to express the human condition, why is it necessary to express that condition? Certainly Jonas cannot be maintaining, as perhaps Bultmann does, that myth alone reveals the human condition, for Jonas employs twentieth-century philosophy to decipher the meaning of myth. Certainly Jonas is not touting Gnostic mythology as part of a whole religion that he, like Bultmann, is espousing. Where, then, Bultmann fails to make the New Testament palatable to atheistic moderns, Jonas fails to make Gnostic myths necessary for them.

Like Freud and Jung, Jonas labels myth "projection": "To the Gnostic, this fact [about the world] is the subject of revealed knowledge, and it determines gnostic eschatology: *we* may see in it the projection of his basic experience, which thus created for itself its own revelatory truth."[23] "I am convinced that what in the myth, e.g. in the Poimandres and in certain Ophitic systems, is described as an objective, spatial journey of the soul, could eventually transform into the structural model for an innerpersonal process; and I believe that later mysticism in effect represents an internalization of this schema."[24] Yet Jonas is not, strictly, psychologizing myth. He is saying that what especially early Gnosticism presents as a description of the external world comes to be recognized by later Gnostics as the projection onto the world not of the human psyche but of the human experience of the world.[25] The subject matter of myth for Jonas, as for Bultmann, is no more human nature itself than the world itself. It remains the place of humans in the world.[26]

C. G. Jung

C. G. Jung and Joseph Campbell offer the fullest reprieve to the death sentence that Tylor pronounces on myth.[27] For the two transform both the function and the subject matter of myth. Like Eliade, they make the function of myth more—indeed, other—than explanatory. Like Bultmann and Jonas, they make the subject of myth other than the physical world. Because I have discussed Campbell's theory at length elsewhere, I will focus here on Jung.[28]

For Jung, myth functions to reveal the existence of the unconscious: "Myths are original revelations of the preconscious [i.e., collective] psyche, involuntary statements about unconscious psychic happenings. . . . Modern psychology treats the products of unconscious fantasy-activity as self-portraits of what is going on in the unconscious, or as statements of the unconscious psyche about itself."[29] Whoever takes myth literally *thinks* that it is revealing the existence of something external like the godhead and the immaterial world, but in fact it is revealing the workings of the unconscious.

Myth functions not merely to tell one about the unconscious but actually to open one up to it. Because the unconscious for Jung is inherently unconscious, one can never experience it directly but must experience it via myths and other symbolic manifestations.

Like Jonas, Jung is entranced by ancient Gnosticism because he sees in it an uncanny parallel to the present. Where for Jonas the key similarity is the experience of alienation from the *world,* for Jung the key similarity is the experience of alienation from *oneself.* The alienation is projected onto the world, so that one feels severed from the world, but one is really severed from oneself. The world is the manifestation, not the source, of that alienation.

For Jung, late antiquity and the twentieth century are the periods in Western history when human beings have most felt lost, aimless, unfulfilled, incomplete—

with traditional myths and religions no longer working and humans consequently being cut off from their unconscious:

> The psychological interest of the present time is an indication that modern man expects something from the psyche which the outer world has not given him: doubtless something which our religion ought to contain, but no longer does contain, at least for modern man. . . . That there is a general interest in these matters cannot be denied. . . . The world has seen nothing like it since the end of the seventeenth century. We can compare it only to the flowering of Gnostic thought in the first and second centuries after Christ. . . . What is striking about these Gnostic systems is that they are based exclusively on the manifestations of the unconscious. . . . The passionate interest in these movements undoubtedly arises from psychic energy which can no longer be invested in obsolete religious forms.[30]

Jung sees Gnostics as the ancient counterparts to moderns—better, to what should be called "twentieth-century moderns." Non-Gnostics are the counterparts to "nineteenth-century moderns." In Jung's history of the psyche, "nineteenth-century moderns" have properly forged independent egos. They have substantially withdrawn their projections from the external world, which they therefore encounter in itself, unfiltered by the unconscious. That demythicized world is composed of trees, not tree gods. In largely withdrawing their projections from the world, nineteenth-century moderns have rightly differentiated themselves from both the world and the unconscious.

Invariably, however, these moderns have not merely separated themselves from their unconscious, for which Jung applauds them, but rejected it altogether. They have thereby pitted themselves—their egos—against their unconscious. Like moderns generally for Eliade, nineteenth-century moderns for Jung consider themselves wholly rational, unemotional, scientific, and atheistic. Religion, through which earlier humanity had realized its unconscious, gets dismissed by them as a prescientific delusion. Marx, Nietzsche, and Freud epitomize nineteenth-century modernity for Jung.

In contrast to nineteenth-century moderns, twentieth-century moderns are conscious of their nonrational side, whether or not of its unconscious source. Like nineteenth-century moderns, twentieth-century ones reject religion as a prescientific relic; but unlike nineteenth-century moderns, they are dissatisfied with a scrupulously rational life and yearn for the kind of fulfillment that religion once provided. They seek new, nonprojective outlets to replace the dead, projective ones of religion. They do not, like their psychological predecessors, boast of having transcended the need that religion once satisfied.

In identifying contemporary moderns with twentieth-century persons, Jung deems them not average but distinctive. For him, most persons today are psychologically equivalent either to nineteenth-century moderns, and therefore oblivious to any nonrational needs, or to premoderns, and therefore content with traditional means of fulfilling them. In their sensitivity both to the existence of nonrational inclinations and to the demise of past means of satisfying them, twentieth-century moderns constitute a select minority.

Jungian patients are the twentieth-century counterparts to ancient Gnostics, who in turn are the ancient counterparts to Jungian patients: "The spiritual currents of our time have, in fact, a deep affinity with Gnosticism."[31] Like Gnostics, twentieth-century moderns feel alienated from their roots and are seeking to overcome the alienation. Where Gnostics feel severed from the outer world, twentieth-century moderns feel severed from the inner one. They do not, like Gnostics, project their alienation onto the cosmos.

Despite his reference to contemporary "Gnostic systems," Jung, like Jonas, considers Gnosticism an ancient, not a contemporary, phenomenon. Just as Jonas sees existentialism as the present-day *counterpart* to Gnosticism, not the present-day *version* of Gnosticism,[32] so Jung sees analytical psychology. For both, the periods paralleled are unique in human history. States Jonas: "There is one situation, and only one that I know of in the history of Western man, where that [present-day] condition [of alienation] has been realized and lived out with all the vehemence of a cataclysmic event. That is the Gnostic movement."[33] To quote Jung again, "We can compare [the present] only to the flowering of Gnostic thought in the first and second centuries after Christ."[34]

Jung, like Jonas, gives myth a reprieve by translating its subject matter into a contemporary idiom. But Jung offers a far more detailed glossary and grammar than Jonas. He makes sense psychologically of the state of Gnostics not merely upon receipt of the revelation but also both before and after. Jung renders into psychological lingo the course of Gnostic myths from the prefallen state of the world through the fallen one to the restored one.[35]

Understood in Jungian terms, Gnostic myths, which either present or presuppose a cosmogony, describe the development not of the world but of the human psyche. The godhead symbolizes the primordial unconscious. It is the source or agent of everything else. Prior to emanating anything, it lacks nothing. It is whole, self-sufficient, perfect. The godhead thus symbolizes the unconscious before the emergence of the ego out of it.

The emergence of matter alongside the material godhead symbolizes the beginning, but only the beginning, of the emergence of the ego out of the unconscious. Inert matter itself does not symbolize the ego, which requires a reflective entity conscious of itself as a subject distinct from the external world. The ego fully emerges not with the creation of either the Demiurge or Primal Man but only with the creation of individual human beings.

The ego is symbolized not by the spark but by the thinking part of the human body, the unspecified center of human thoughts and actions vis-à-vis the external world. The spark, as the link to the forgotten godhead, symbolizes the unconscious. As long as one remains unaware of the spark, one remains an unrealized self. As long as one's values are material, one is merely an ego.

Insofar as a Jungian interpretation of myth is psychological, it collapses the literal distinction between the outer world and humanity. Both matter and the body symbolize the development of the ego—raw matter symbolizing the beginning of the process and the thinking portion of the body the end. Similarly, both the immaterial godhead and the spark symbolize the unconscious, if also at opposite stages of development.

The ego in Jungian psychology develops not just alongside the unconscious but also out of it. Those Gnostic myths in which matter originates out of the godhead express the dependence of the ego on the unconscious. Those myths in which matter is preexistent and merely comes into contact with the godhead evince dissociation of the unconscious from the ego and thereby foreshadow the problems that dissociation spells.

Non-Gnostics, who for Jung's interpretation should also possess a divine spark, are not only ignorant of their origin and the origin of the world but also smugly content with the false, material nature of both. Their complacency makes them apt counterparts to nineteenth-century moderns. Gnostics have also forgotten the true nature of themselves and the world, but they are nevertheless dissatisfied with the existing nature of both. Their dissatisfaction makes them suitable counterparts to twentieth-century moderns.

If ignorance alone, according to Gnostic tenets, keeps humans tied to the material world, knowledge frees them from it. Because humans are ignorant, that knowledge must come from outside them. Because the powers of the material world are ignorant, too, that knowledge must come from beyond them as well. It can come from only the godhead. The dependence of humanity on the godhead matches the dependence of the ego on the unconscious to reveal itself.

The response of Gnostics to the revelation parallels that of twentieth-century moderns to their own discovery: gratitude. The disclosure of a heretofore unknown self and, for Gnostics, of a heretofore unknown world provides a fulfillment tantamount to salvation. As Jung says of twentieth-century moderns, "I do not believe that I am going too far when I say that [twentieth-century] modern man, in contrast to his nineteenth-century brother, turns to the psyche with very great expectations, and does so without reference to any traditional creed but rather with a view to Gnostic experience."[36]

The response of non-Gnostics to the revelation parallels that of nineteenth-century moderns to their own discovery: fear. The disclosure, which applies to non-Gnostics as well as to Gnostics, shatters the non-Gnostics' vaunted image of both human nature and the world.

Gnostic myths preach total identification with one's newly discovered divinity. Because that identification symbolizes the Gnostic's identification with the unconscious, Jungian psychology would consider it no less lopsided and no less dangerous than the non-Gnostic's identification with the ego—more precisely, with ego consciousness, or consciousness of the external world. Jungian psychology would consider both attitudes unbalanced. It would say that non-Gnostics, like nineteenth-century moderns, suffer from an exaggerated persona: their ego identifies itself wholly with the conscious, public personality. But Jungian psychology should equally say that Gnostics, whether or not twentieth-century moderns, suffer from an exaggerated, or inflated, ego, which, conversely, identifies itself wholly with the rediscovered unconscious. Minimally, the consequence of inflation is excessive pride in the presumed uniqueness of one's unconscious. Maximally, the consequence is outright psychosis, or the dissolution of any consciousness of the external world. The Jungian aim is no more to reject ego consciousness for the unconscious than, like the nineteenth-century aim, to reject the unconscious for ego consciousness. Rather, the aim is to balance the two.

Jung himself idiosyncratically interprets Gnosticism as seeking the equivalent of balance between ego consciousness and the unconscious rather than identification with the unconscious. Unlike Jonas, Jung is so eager to find similarities between ancients and moderns that he misses the differences.[37] But Jung's misinterpretation of Gnosticism does not preclude a more accurate Jungian interpretation of Gnosticism, according to which Gnosticism espouses the equivalent of inflation rather than balance.

By interpreting the Gnostic's permanent return to the godhead as inflationary, Jungian psychology would even be able to make sense of what in Gnostic metaphysics is paradoxical: the creation by an omniscient and omnipotent godhead of a world that the godhead then seeks to destroy. Jungian psychology would make not the creation but the dissolution of the world the mistake. Though it would admittedly thereby be evaluating Gnosticism by its own world-affirming rather than world-rejecting ideal, it would at least be able to make sense of creation. The unconscious, as symbolized by the godhead, would not be erring in creating the ego, as symbolized by the material side of humanity. The unconscious would truly be both omniscient and omnipotent. It is the ego that would be neither: lacking both the knowledge and the will to resist the allure of the unconscious, it would be returning of its own accord to the unconscious, which, to be sure, would be enticing it.

Where Jonas transforms only the subject matter of myth, Jung also transforms the function. Jung would say that Gnostic mythology served not just to reveal the unconscious but actually to put Gnostics in touch with it. Jung even deems the Gnostics budding psychologists: "it is clear beyond a doubt that many of the Gnostics were nothing other than psychologists."[38] Jung thus accords Gnostic mythology, and mythology generally, a role as well as a viewpoint that is acceptable to moderns. Still, Jung does not go so far as Joseph Campbell, who proclaims myth outright indispensable. As valuable for Jung as myth is, religion, art, dream, and the "active imagination" can serve as well, even if he sometimes loosely uses the term "myth" to apply to all of them. For Jung, the functions that myth serves are themselves indispensable, but myth is not itself indispensable to serving them. And in even keener contrast to Campbell, myth for Jung can never substitute for therapy, to which it is only a most helpful adjunct.[39]

Jung ventures beyond Jonas in granting myth a future not only by providing a function as well as a subject matter that is acceptable to moderns but also, like Eliade, by uncovering modern as well as ancient myths. Jung does not claim to find modern *Gnostic* myths, but he does claim to find modern myths of other varieties. Because he psychologizes the subject matter of all myths, he circumvents Eliade's dilemma that myths acceptable to moderns lack the element necessary for their efficacy: gods. For Jung, gods are merely the symbols that ancient myths used to represent archetypes. Modern myths, using other symbols, are equally efficacious.

Whether the theories of myth discussed are correct is not at issue here. At issue is whether those theories commit themselves to a future for myth. Of the four theories that do—Eliade's, Bultmann's, Jonas's, and Jung's—Jung's theory envisions the brightest future for myth.

III • THE MYTH AND RITUAL THEORY

A MONG THE MANY THEORIES of myth and many theories of ritual, the myth and ritual theory is distinctive in connecting myths to rituals. The myth and ritual, or myth-ritualist, theory maintains that myths and rituals operate together. The theory claims not that myths and rituals happen to go hand in hand but that they must. In its most uncompromising form, the theory contends that myths and rituals cannot exist without each other. In a milder form, the theory asserts that myths and rituals originally exist together but may subsequently go their separate ways. In its mildest form, the theory maintains that myths and rituals can arise separately but subsequently coalesce.

ORIGINAL FORMULATION

In a few introductory pages of his *Lectures on the Religion of the Semites* (hereafter *LRS*), the Victorian biblicist and Arabist William Robertson Smith pioneered the myth-ritualist theory.[1] Smith begins by warning against the anachronistic "modern habit . . . to look at religion from the side of belief rather than of practice" (*LRS,* 17). Smith's approach to ancient religion is behaviorist. Instead of first looking for the "creed" that will provide "the key to ritual and practice" (*LRS,* 18), he does the reverse: he first finds the ritual, which will then unlock the creed. Indeed, he cautions against even expecting to find a creed, for "the antique religions had for the most part no creed; they consisted entirely of institutions and practices" (*LRS,* 18). Smith grants that ancients, whom he compares with primitives, doubtless performed rituals for some reason: "No doubt men will not habitually follow certain practices without attaching a meaning to them" (*LRS,* 18). But he claims that the meaning was secondary and could even fluctuate: "as a rule we find that while the practice was rigorously fixed, the meaning attached to it was extremely vague, and the same rite was explained by different people in different ways, without any question of orthodoxy or heterodoxy arising in consequence" (*LRS,* 18).

In classical Greece, for example, "certain things were done at a temple, and people were agreed that it would be impious not to do them. But if you had asked why they were done, you would probably have had several mutually exclusive explanations from different persons, and no one would have thought it a matter of the least religious importance which of these you chose to adopt" (*LRS,* 18). Moreover, the explanations given for a ritual did not stir strong feelings. Rather than formal declarations of belief—creeds—the various explanations were stories, or myths, which simply described "the circumstances under which the rite first came to be established, by the command or by the direct example of the god" (*LRS,* 18). "The rite, in short, was connected not with a dogma [i.e., creed] but with a myth" (*LRS,* 18). "In all the antique religions, mythology takes the place of dogma" (*LRS,* 18).

At the same time ritual was much more important in ancient religion than myth: "this mythology was no essential part of ancient religion, for it had no sacred sanction and no binding force on the worshippers. The myths connected with individual sanctuaries and ceremonies were merely part of the apparatus of the worship; they served to excite the fancy and sustain the interest of the worshipper; but he was often offered a choice of several accounts of the same thing, and provided that he fulfilled the ritual with accuracy, no one cared what he believed about its origin" (*LRS,* 19). Consequently, Smith spurns the attention conventionally accorded not only creed but also myth in ancient religion: "mythology ought not to take the prominent place that is too often assigned to it in the scientific study of ancient faiths" (*LRS,* 19). Smith goes as far as to declare that "ritual and practical usage were, strictly speaking, the sum total of ancient religions" (*LRS,* 21).

According to Smith, "in almost every case the myth was derived from the ritual, and not the ritual from the myth" (*LRS,* 19). Myth arose only once the reason for the ritual had somehow been forgotten: "Now by far the largest part of the myths of antique religions are connected with the ritual of particular shrines, or with religious observances of particular tribes and districts. In all such cases it is probable, in most cases it is certain, that the myth is merely the explanation of a religious usage; and ordinarily it is such an explanation as could not have arisen till the original sense of the usage had more or less fallen into oblivion" (*LRS,* 19). Myth was superfluous as long as the reason for the ritual remained clear. Only once the reason was lost was myth created to explain and perhaps to justify the ritual, which might nevertheless have continued to be practiced anyway.

Smith's brand of myth-ritualism is tame. Rituals antedate myths and thereby do not initally require myths. Conversely, myths can eventually flourish apart from rituals. But Smith remains the pioneering myth-ritualist because he was the first to propose that the earliest myths arose in connection with rituals. While myth-ritualism requires some indispensable connection between myth and ritual, it does not require a link of equality. For Smith, ritual is conspicuously more important than myth, which he calls "secondary" (e.g., *LRS,* 20). He proposes the myth-ritualist theory to explain myth, not ritual. Myth depends on ritual, even if ritual comes to depend on myth. Without ritual, there would be no myth, whether or not without myth there would cease to be ritual.

In claiming that myth is an explanation of ritual, Smith is denying that myth is an explanation of the world—the standard conception of myth, espoused classically by Edward Tylor.[2] For Tylor, myth is an account of events in the physical world. Myth is more important than ritual, which is the *application,* not the *subject,* of myth. Myth constitutes creed, which is merely expressed in the form of a story. For Tylor, myth serves the same function as science. Indeed, myth is the ancient and primitive counterpart to modern science. For both Smith and Tylor, science has neither myths nor rituals.

DEVELOPMENT OF THE THEORY

In the several editions of *The Golden Bough,* the classicist and anthropologist James Frazer developed the myth-ritualist theory far beyond that of his close friend Smith.[3] While Frazer is best known for his tripartite division of all culture into the stages of magic, religion, and science, the bulk of his tome is devoted to an intermediate stage between religion and science—a stage of magic and religion combined. Only in this in-between stage is myth-ritualism to be found, for only here do myths and rituals work together. In the stage of sheer magic there are rituals—the routines involved in carrying out the directions—but no myths, for there are no gods. In the stage of religion there are both myths and rituals, but they are barely connected. Myths describe the character and behavior of gods, where rituals seek to win divine favor. Rituals may presuppose myths, which would suggest what activities would most please the gods, but they are otherwise independent of myths.

By contrast, in the following stage of magic and religion combined, myths and rituals work together. Frazer, rarely consistent, in effect presents two distinct versions of myth-ritualism. In the first version myth describes the life of the god of vegetation, and ritual enacts the myth, or at least that portion of the myth describing the death and rebirth of the god. The ritual operates on the basis of the Law of Similarity, according to which the imitation of an action causes it to happen. The ritual does not manipulate vegetation directly. Rather, it manipulates the god of vegetation. But as the god goes, so goes vegetation. The assumption that vegetation is under the control of a god is the legacy of religion. The assumption that vegetation can be controlled, even if only through the god, is the legacy of magic. The combination of myth and ritual is the combination of religion and magic: "Thus the old magical theory of the seasons was displaced, or rather supplemented, by a religious theory. For although men now attributed the annual cycle of change primarily to corresponding changes in their deities, they still thought that by performing certain magical rites they could aid the god who was the principle of life, in his struggle with the opposing principle of death. They imagined that they could recruit his failing energies and even raise him from the dead."[4] In the ritual a human being plays the role of the god and acts out what he magically causes the god to do. While the actor may be the king, Frazer does not strongly tie this version of myth-ritualism to kingship.

In Frazer's second version of myth-ritualism the king is central. Where in the first version the king, even when the actor in the ritual, merely plays the part of the god of vegetation, in the second version the king is himself divine, which means that the god resides in him. Just as the health of vegetation depends on the health of its god, so now the health of the god depends on the health of the king: as the king goes, so goes the god of vegetation and so, in turn, goes vegetation itself. To ensure a steady supply of food, the community kills its king while he is still in his prime and thereby safely transfers the soul of the god to his successor:

> For [primitives] believe . . . that the king's life or spirit is so sympathetically bound up with the prosperity of the whole country, that if he fell ill or grew senile the cattle would sicken and cease to multiply, the crops would rot in the fields, and men would perish of widespread disease. Hence, in their opinion, the only way of averting these calamities is to put the king to death while he is still hale and hearty, in order that the divine spirit which he has inherited from his predecessors may be transmitted in turn by him to his successor while it is still in full vigour and has not yet been impaired by the weakness of disease and old age.[5]

The king is killed either at the end of a fixed term or at the first sign of infirmity. Certainly the sudden death of a king can never be precluded, but the killing of the king before his likely passing guarantees as nearly as possible the continuous health of the god and so of vegetation. The aim is to fend off winter. The withering of vegetation during the winter of even a year-long reign is ascribed to the weakening of the king.

This second version of myth-ritualism has proved the more influential by far, but it in fact provides only a tenuous link between myth and ritual and in turn between religion and magic. Instead of enacting the myth of the god of vegetation, the ritual simply changes the residence of the god. The king dies not in imitation of the death of the god but as a sacrifice to preserve the health of the god. What part myth plays here, it is not easy to see. Instead of reviving the god by magical imitation, the ritual revives the god by a transplant. It would therefore be better to restrict the term "myth-ritualism" to Frazer's first version of the theory.

In Frazer's true myth-ritualist scenario, myth arises prior to ritual rather than, as for Smith, after it. The myth that gets enacted in the combined stage emerges in the stage of religion and therefore antedates the ritual to which it is applied. In the combined stage, myth, as for Smith, explains the point of ritual, but not only once the meaning of ritual has been forgotten. Rather, myth *gives* ritual its meaning. In the combined stage, ritual would not be undertaken without myth: one would not ritualistically enact the death and rebirth of the god of vegetation without the myth of the death and rebirth of that god.

Myth for Frazer, as for Tylor, serves to explain the world, but for Frazer explanation is only a means to an end: controlling the world. Myth for Frazer, no less than for Tylor, is the ancient and primitive counterpart to modern science, but for Frazer it is the counterpart to applied science and not primarily, as for Tylor, to scientific theory.

For all Frazer's extension of the myth-ritualist theory beyond Smith, he gradually became an ever more vociferous Tylorean and even a critic of the very ritualists he had inspired.[6] In turn, he came to be condemned by some myth-ritualists for exactly his Tylorean stance. Far purer exemplars of the myth-ritualist theory than he are Jane Harrison and S. H. Hooke, the leaders of the initial main groups of myth-ritualists: classicists and biblicists.[7] Their positions are close and constitute the strongest form of myth-ritualism. Fittingly, they disagree most sharply over the status of Frazer: where Harrison lauds him as her mentor, Hooke lambastes him as the arch-Tylorean.

Harrison and Hooke begin by pitting their theory against the intellectualist one of Tylor and others. Referring to the peoples of the ancient Near East, especially those of Egypt and Mesopotamia, Hooke says that they "were not occupied with general questions concerning the world but with certain practical and pressing problems of daily life. There were the main problems of securing the means of subsistence, to keep the sun and moon doing their duty, to ensure the regular flooding of the Nile. . . . In order to meet these needs the early inhabitants of Egypt and Mesopotamia developed a set of customary actions directed towards a definite end."[8] Those actions were rituals. What Hooke says of the ancient Near East, Harrison says of ancient Greece.

In explaining how rituals served to control the otherwise uncontrollable forces of nature, Hooke and Harrison follow Frazer. Ritual works on the basis of the Law of Similarity. The ritual acts out the death and rebirth of the god of vegetation, who, as for Frazer, is the chief god of the pantheon. While the god is dead, the land is infertile; when he is revived, so is the land. The ritual is performed at the end of winter—better, at the point when one wants winter to end. A human being plays the part of the god.

Unlike Frazer, Hooke and Harrison postulate no distinct, prior stages of magic and religion and begin instead with the equivalent of Frazer's stage of magic and religion combined. For them, myth-ritualism is likely the earliest stage of religion. For Hooke and Harrison, no less than for Frazer, myth-ritualism is the ancient and primitive counterpart to modern science. For them, as for Frazer, modern science replaces not only myth-ritualism but myth and ritual per se.

As a myth-ritualist, Hooke, who scorns Frazer as a Tylorean, is ironically even closer to Frazer than Harrison, who applauds him. For Hooke stresses the role of the king, which Harrison downplays. Sometimes for Hooke, as sometimes for Frazer, the king is only the human representative of the god of vegetation. The king imitates the death and rebirth (as well as the victory, marriage, and inauguration) of the god and thereby automatically causes the god and in turn vegetation to do the same. Other times for Hooke, as other times for Frazer, the king is himself divine, in which case the ritual is the actual killing and replacement of him. Yet Hooke still places the ritual at the end—the would-be end—of winter rather than, as for Frazer, at the end of a king's prescribed reign or at the onset of weakness. Hooke thus faces the same inconsistencies as Frazer over the status of the king.

Venturing beyond both Frazer and Hooke, Harrison, inspired by thinkers ranging from Henri Bergson to Émile Durkheim, adds to the ritual of the renewal of vegetation the ritual of initiation into society. Indeed, she argues that the original ritual, while still performed annually, was exclusively initiatory. There was no myth. God was only the projection of the euphoria produced by the ritual—a straight application of Durkheim. Subsequently, god became the god of vegetation, the myth of the death and rebirth of that god arose, and the ritual of initiation became an agricultural ritual as well. Just as the initiates symbolically died and were reborn as full-fledged members of society, so the god of vegetation and in turn crops literally died and were reborn. Eventually, the initiatory side of the combined ritual faded, and only the Frazerian ritual of vegetation remained.

Harrison and Hooke alike deny vigorously that myth is an explanation even of ritual, much less of the world. "The myth," states Harrison, "is not an attempted explanation of either facts or rites."[9] In denying that myth is an explanation of ritual, she and Hooke really mean no more than Frazer the myth-ritualist: that myth flourishes alongside ritual to provide its script rather than, as for Smith, arising only after the meaning of ritual has been forgotten. Myth can still, then, be regarded as an explanation of ritual, but of living ritual. Myth is recited as the ritual is enacted, just as for Frazer. Myth is therefore like the sound in a film or the narration of a pantomime. Says Hooke: "In general the spoken part of a ritual consists of a description of what is being done. . . . This is the sense in which the term 'myth' is used in our discussion."[10] Says Harrison: "The primary meaning of myth . . . is the spoken correlative of the acted rite, the thing done."[11]

Where for Smith myth arises later than ritual, and where for Frazer ritual arises later than the myth used with it, for Harrison and Hooke myth and ritual arise simultaneously. "It has been much disputed," notes Harrison, "whether the myth arises out of the rite or the rite out of the myth. . . . As a matter of fact the two operations arose together and are practically inseparable."[12] Elsewhere, however, Harrison places ritual prior to myth.

Harrison and Hooke carry myth-ritualism further than Frazer in conferring on myth the same kind of power contained in ritual. Where for Frazer the power of myth is merely dramatic, for Harrison and Hooke it is outright magical. "The spoken word," says Hooke, "had the efficacy of an act."[13] "A myth," says Harrison, "becomes practically a story of magical intent and potency."[14] We have here word magic—and perhaps a glint of the notion of speech acts.

APPLICATION OF THE THEORY TO THE ANCIENT WORLD

With Harrison and Hooke the development of the theory of myth-ritualism peaked. The next stage was the application of the theory. The initial application was still to the ancient world. Most famously, the classicists Gilbert Murray, F. M. Cornford, and A. B. Cook applied Harrison's theory to such ancient Greek phenomena as tragedy, comedy, the Olympic games, science, and philosophy.[15] These seemingly secular, even antireligious phenomena were interpreted as latent expressions of the myth of the death and rebirth of the god of vegetation.

Among biblicists, Ivan Engnell, Aubrey Johnson, and Sigmund Mowinckel accepted Hooke's formulation of the myth-ritualist theory but differed over the extent to which ancient Israel in particular adhered to the myth-ritualist pattern.[16] Engnell saw an even stronger adherence than Hooke; Johnson and especially Mowinckel, a weaker one. Hooke was never the mentor of the biblicists, the way Harrison was for the classicists, but he was still the key figure among them. He was their myth-ritualist stalwart.

APPLICATION OF THE THEORY WORLDWIDE

More broadly, the anthropologist A. M. Hocart and the historian of religion E. O. James applied the myth-ritualist theory to cultures around the world.[17] Hocart uses a simplified version of myth-ritualism—the lowest common denominator of Frazer, Hooke, and Harrison. James's more complicated version combines Frazer's two versions of myth-ritualism. The extension of myth-ritualism by Hocart and James, while worldwide, was less radical than that of Harrison's followers because the application was to manifestly religious phenomena—that is, to overt myths and rituals.

Invoking Frazer, the anthropologist Bronislaw Malinowski applied his own, qualified version of the theory to the myths of native peoples worldwide.[18] Malinowski argues that myth gives rituals a hoary origin and thereby sanctions them, but he argues that myth sanctions many other cultural phenomena as well. Society depends on myth to encourage adherence to rules and customs of all kinds, not merely to rituals. The historian of religion Mircea Eliade applied a similar form of the theory to the myths of all cultures.[19] Myth for him, too, sanctions phenomena of all kinds, not merely rituals, by giving them a primeval origin. Yet Eliade goes beyond Malinowski in stressing the importance of the ritualistic enactment of myth in the fulfillment of the ultimate function of myth: when enacted, myth serves as a time machine, carrying one back to the time of the myth and thereby bringing one closer to god.

APPLICATION OF THE THEORY TO LITERATURE

The most notable application of the myth-ritualist theory outside of religion has been to literature. Harrison herself boldly derived all art, not just literature, from ritual. She speculates that eventually people ceased believing that the imitation of an action caused that action to occur. Yet rather than abandoning ritual, they now practiced it as an end in itself. Ritual for its own sake became art, her clearest example of which is drama. More modestly than she, Murray and Cornford rooted specifically Greek epic, tragedy, and comedy in myth-ritualism. Murray then extended the theory to Shakespeare.[20]

Other standard-bearers of the theory—derived from Frazer, Harrison, or Hooke—have included Jessie Weston on the Grail legend, E. M. Butler on the Faust legend, C. L. Barber on Shakespearean comedy, Herbert Weisinger on Shakespearean tragedy and on tragedy per se, Francis Fergusson on tragedy, Lord Raglan on hero myths and on literature as a whole, C. M. Bowra on primitive song, and Stanley Edgar Hyman and Northrop Frye on literature generally.[21] As literary critics, these myth-ritualists have understandably been concerned less with myth itself than with the mythic origin of literature. Works of literature are interpreted as the outgrowth of myths once tied to rituals. For those literary critics indebted to Frazer, as the majority are, literature harks back to myths that were originally the scripts of the key primitive ritual of regularly killing and replacing the king in order to ensure crops for the community. "The king must die" becomes the familiar summary line.

For literary myth-ritualists, myth becomes literature when it is severed from ritual. Myth tied to ritual is religious literature; myth cut off from ritual is secular literature, or just literature. When tied to ritual, myth can serve any of the active functions ascribed to it by the myth-ritualists. Myth bereft of ritual is demoted to mere commentary. To paraphrase Marx and Engels, myth linked to ritual can change the world, whereas myth severed from ritual can only interpret it.

Independently of Frazer and others, René Girard has proposed his own linkage of myth, ritual, and literature.[22] For him, literature is the legacy of myth, which recounts, albeit in distorted form, the ritualistic sacrifice of an innocent victim, who can range from the most helpless member of society to the king. The central connection for him between myth and the killing of a figure celebrated as a savior is reminiscent of the myth-ritualism of Frazer. While Girard seeks to show how literature reflects myth, he goes beyond other literary myth-ritualists in proposing his own theory of myth and ritual. Instead of functioning to explain the killing, as other myth-ritualists would assume, myth for Girard functions to hide it—and thereby to preserve the stability of society. Girard roots sacrifice not, like Frazer, in hunger but in aggression.

REVISIONS OF THE THEORY

Working on their own, the biblicist Theodor Gaster and the anthropologist Adolf Jensen independently proposed versions of myth-ritualism that make myth more important than ritual.[23] However tenuous their contention that their fellow myth-ritualists downplay myth, they do offer a new twist to the relationship between myth and ritual.

The anthropologist Clyde Kluckhohn went much further.[24] He tempered the myth-ritualist dogma that myths and rituals are inseparable. He argued that, operating separately or together, myth and ritual serve the psychological function of alleviating anxiety: anxiety arising from the physical world, from society, and from oneself. Myth provides prescribed ways of understanding; ritual, prescribed ways of behaving. The alleviation of anxiety abets society as much as individuals—an echo of Malinowski. When, for Kluckhohn, myths and rituals do operate together, they operate in the same general manner as for Harrison and Hooke: the myth explains what the ritual enacts.

While allowing, like Kluckhohn, for the independence of myth and ritual, the classicist Walter Burkert maintains that when the two do come together, they reinforce each other.[25] Myth bolsters ritual by giving mere human behavior a divine origin: do this because the gods did or do it. Conversely, ritual bolsters myth by turning a mere story into prescribed behavior of the most dutiful kind: do this on pain of anxiety, if not punishment. Where for Smith myth serves ritual, for Burkert ritual equally serves myth. Like Girard, Burkert roots myth in sacrifice and roots sacrifice in aggression, but he does not limit sacrifice to human sacrifice, and he roots sacrifice itself in hunting—the original expression of aggression. Moreover, myth for Burkert functions not to hide the fact of sacrifice but to preserve it and its role in enabling human beings to cope with the guilt they feel over their aggression and the anxiety they feel over their mortality. Finally, Burkert connects myths not only to rituals of sacrifice but also, like Harrison, to rituals of initiation. Myth here serves the same socializing function as ritual.

By far the most radical and influential contemporary variety of myth-ritualism has been structuralism, pioneered by the anthropologist Claude Lévi-Strauss.[26] While Lévi-Strauss focuses overwhelmingly on myth, he does consider ritual as well. According to Lévi-Strauss, all human beings think in the form of classifications and project them onto the world. Humans think specifically in the form of pairs of oppositions, which Lévi-Strauss calls "binary oppositions." Not only myths but all other human activities as well display humanity's pairing impulse.

Myth is distinctive in not only expressing oppositions, which are equivalent to contradictions, but also resolving them: "the purpose of myth is to provide a logical model capable of overcoming a contradiction."[27] Myth resolves a contradiction dialectically, by providing either a mediating middle term or an analogous, but more easily resolved, contradiction.

Not only do whole myths have the same dialectical relationship to one another that the parts of each have internally, but so do myths and rituals. Rather than mirroring each other, as for other myth-ritualists, myth and ritual are the reverse of each other. Lévi-Strauss thus presents a new, structuralist slant to the relationship between myth and ritual. As he says in contrasting his brand of myth-ritualism to prior ones, "The current [i.e., nonstructuralist] theory, according to which a [chronological] term-to-term correspondence exists between two orders (whether the rite acts out the myth, or the myth explicates the rite), is reducible to the particular case of a more general [structuralist] relation. The study of individual cases makes myths and rites appear as different transformations of identical elements."[28] Myths and rituals remain umbilically linked, but as opposing rather than parallel members of a pair.

As influential as the myth-ritualist theory has been among not only theorists of myth or ritual but also specialists in the myths and rituals of individual cultures,[29] most theorists of myth and most theorists of ritual have rejected the theory in any of its forms.[30] They maintain that myths and rituals exist largely independently of each other. Most theorists of myth continue to focus on myth alone, and most theorists of ritual continue to focus on ritual alone. Even those theorists of myth or of ritual who accept some linkage between the two usually limit the tie to a fraction of myths and rituals.

Whatever the actual nexus between myths and rituals turns out to be, the myth-ritualist theory remains valuable. It suggests aspects of myth that might otherwise get overlooked—notably, the relationship between belief and practice, between narrative and action. The theory also suggests parallels between myth and other cultural phenomena like science and literature that might otherwise get missed.[31]

IV · THE GRAIL LEGEND AS FRAZERIAN MYTH AND RITUAL

O F ALL THE ELEMENTS of the Arthurian legend, none has proved more entrancing than the quest for the Grail. Chrétien de Troyes first bestowed special significance on the word "grail" in his *Le Conte del Graal* (1174–77). There Perceval, who is seated next to the wounded Fisher King, witnesses a procession of objects that include a bleeding lance and above all a bejeweled dish, or "grail" (*graal*). Had Perceval, who had been instructed to ask no questions, inquired about the Grail, the King, who was maimed in the thigh, would have been healed. So in turn would the land, which has suffered along with the King: as the King has fared, so has the land. The Grail has supernatural power—a single wafer placed in it had kept alive the King's father—but it is not connected with Christianity. Indeed, it is referred to as *a* grail, not *the* Grail.

It was Robert de Boron who, in *Joseph d'Arimathie* (c. 1190), first Christianized the grail. The now "Holy" Grail became the cup that Jesus used at the Last Supper and that Joseph of Arimathea used to gather Jesus' blood as he washed the body before burial. Similarly, the bleeding lance became the spear with which Jesus was struck while on the cross. Joseph, we learn, was instructed to set a table—a parallel to that of the Last Supper—where the Mass was celebrated and the Grail used as the chalice. The nourishment now provided by the Grail was spiritual as well as physical.

From the anonymous five-part Vulgate Cycle (c. 1210–1235) we discover that the Grail was brought to Britain by Joseph's descendants and is now ensconced in a hidden castle, guarded by the Grail keeper. The keeper, at once king and priest, has himself been mysteriously wounded in the thigh by a spear. Again, as the keeper goes, so goes the land, which is now called the Waste Land.

The Grail saga culminates in Sir Thomas Malory's *Le Morte d'Arthur* (1469 or 1470). King Arthur of Britain now reigns in Camelot over a round table of knights. The Grail, however, is missing. When, at Pentecost, it suddenly appears, floating in the sunlight, the knights pledge themselves to retrieve it. Of the many who try, only Bors, Perceval, and Galahad succeed. To varying degrees they are then initiated into its mysteries. The maimed king guarding the Grail—it is not Arthur—is healed, and so, thereby, is the land. The three successful knights proceed to the heavenly city of the East, where the ultimate mystery is disclosed and where the Grail again serves as the chalice in the Mass. Galahad, who receives the fullest revelation, dies in an ecstatic reverie. Perceval succeeds the Grail king, who, once healed of his wound, dies a natural death. Bors returns to Camelot. The Grail itself is taken up into heaven.

The origin of the Grail has confounded scholars for centuries. Most modern authorities fall into either the Celtic or the Christian camp.[1] The dominant view today, one epitomized by the work of Robert Loomis, makes the legend originally Celtic and only subsequently Christian.

In her 1920 classic work, *From Ritual to Romance* (hereafter *FRR*), Jessie Weston (1850–1928) proposed a third, radically distinct view: that the Grail legend goes back to a primitive vegetation cult and only later was shaped by Celtic and Christian lore.

FRAZER'S MYTH-RITUALISM

Like Northrop Frye, Jessie Weston is concerned with the development of literature out of myth. Like Frye as well, she accepts the theory of James Frazer, who ties myth to ritual. Where Frye asserts that all literature stems from myth—"It is part of the critic's business to show how all literary genres are derived from the quest-myth"[2]—Weston restricts her claim to romance. Neither Weston nor Frye *equates* myth with literature. They contend that literature *comes from* myth, not that it *is* myth. Their interest is genetic. Hence Weston says that "the aim of these studies is, as indicated in the title, to determine the *origin* of the Grail" (*FRR,* 5). For both Weston and Frye, the keenest difference between literature and myth is that literature has been detached from ritual.

While Frye *accepts* Frazer's theory of myth, Weston *touts* it: "I avow myself an impenitent believer in Sir J. G. Frazer's main theory" (*FRR,* 10). Like early Freudians and Jungians, she has dual, perhaps inconsistent, ends. On the one hand she assumes Frazer's theory and interprets the Grail legend accordingly. On the other hand she invokes her interpretation as support for Frazer's theory. Thus on the one hand she writes, "Some years ago, when fresh from the study of Sir J. G. Frazer's epoch-making work, *The Golden Bough,* I was struck by the resemblance existing between certain features of the Grail story, and characteristic details of the Nature Cults described. The more closely I analysed the tale, the more striking became the resemblance, and I finally asked myself whether it were not possible that in this mysterious legend . . . we might not have the confused record of a ritual, once popular, later surviving under conditions of strict secrecy?" (*FRR,*

3–4). On the other hand she writes, "I would draw attention to the manner in which the evidence set forth in the chapters on the Mystery cults, and especially that on *The Naassene Document,* a text of extraordinary value from more than one point of view, supports and complements the researches of Sir J. G. Frazer" (*FRR,* 6).

Weston was by no means the first person to apply Frazer's theory of myth and ritual to literature. Her most notable predecessors were the group of classicists known as the Cambridge Ritualists: Jane Harrison, F. M. Cornford, A. B. Cook, and Oxford's Gilbert Murray. It was above all Murray and Cornford who investigated the myth-ritualist origin of Greek epic, tragedy, and comedy. Weston was a contemporary of the Cambridge Ritualists but came to Frazer late in life: *From Ritual to Romance,* her concluding Frazerian work, was published when she was seventy.[3] She was therefore more truly the successor of the Ritualists, whom she thus cites as authorities. Another Frazerian predecessor cited by her is E. K. Chambers, whose specialty was medieval drama. Weston's many Frazerian successors include E. M. Butler on the Faust legend, C. L. Barber and Herbert Weisinger on Shakespeare, Francis Fergusson on tragedy, Lord Raglan on hero myths and on literature generally, C. M. Bowra on primitive song, and Stanley Edgar Hyman as well as Frye on literature as a whole. To be sure, some of these literary myth-ritualists take their inspiration directly from the Cambridge Ritualists and only indirectly from Frazer, but for all of them literature echoes myths that were originally the scripts of primitive rituals.

Frazer is likely best remembered for his division of the development of culture into the stages of magic, religion, and science. In both magic and science, events in the physical world are caused by the behavior of impersonal, mechanical forces. Magic and science differ over what those forces are and by what laws they operate. In religion, which oddly comes between magic and science rather than either before or after them, events in the physical world are caused by the decisions of gods. Both magic and science offer the prospect of direct and certain control over nature—once one discovers the forces and the laws that regulate nature. Religion, by contrast, provides only indirect and uncertain control: one must persuade the gods to do one's bidding, and no matter how much one supplicates, obeys, flatters, or bribes them, they may still demur.

For Frazer, the chief subject of myths is gods. Because magic involves no gods, it involves no myths. There *is* ritual: the routine of carrying out magical directions, which in the most familiar case of magic involves collecting the ingredients for a voodoo doll, constructing the doll, pricking the doll, and reciting a formula over the doll. But without an accompanying myth, there can scarcely be myth-ritualism.

Religion, by contrast, contains both myths and rituals. Myths provide biographies of the gods and thereby help believers figure out which rituals will curry the gods' favor. Yet even in this stage there is no myth-ritualism, for myth is not the script of ritual.

How, then, is Frazer, the inspiration for Weston and so many other myth-ritualists, himself a myth-ritualist? The answer is that for all Frazer's rigid differentiation of culture into three distinct stages, the bulk of *The Golden Bough,* especially in the second and third editions, ironically deals with the unnamed stage, or semi-stage, that comes between religion and science and that constitutes a fusion of supposed opposites: magic and religion. The religious element of this combined stage is the belief in gods who directly affect nature. The magical element is the belief in the power to control gods, who are thereby reduced to the status of genielike forces:

> Thus the old magical theory of the seasons was displaced, or rather supplemented, by a religious theory. For although men now attributed the annual cycle of change primarily to corresponding changes in their deities, they still thought that by performing certain magical rites they could aid the god who was the principle of life, in his struggle with the opposing principle of death. They imagined that they could recruit his failing energies and even raise him from the dead.[4]

Ritual here is the means by which the gods are controlled. Myth now is the script of ritual. The two are of equal importance.[5]

The heart of myth-ritualism for Frazer is the ritualistic enactment of the myth of the death and rebirth of the god of vegetation. Human survival depends on vegetation, which must continually be revived:

> the annual death and revival of vegetation is a conception which readily presents itself to men in every stage of savagery and civilisation; and the vastness of the scale on which this ever-recurring decay and regeneration takes place, together with man's intimate dependence on it for subsistence, combine to render it the most impressive annual occurrence in nature, at least within the temperate zones. . . . Hence it is natural that in the magical dramas designed to dispel winter and bring back spring the emphasis should be laid on vegetation.[6]

Frazer transforms myth after myth into the biography of a vegetation god. Adonis, for example, ceases to be a human who dies young and instead becomes a god who dies and is resurrected perennially. Frazer blithely ignores Adonis's demise at the "hands" of a boar and focuses instead on Adonis's annual descent to Hades to be with Persephone. The course of his life thereby corresponds to that of vegetation, of which he is consequently the god. The fate of crops depends not on any decision of his, as in the stage of religion, but on his condition. While he is above ground and therefore alive, so are the crops; while he is below ground and therefore dead, the crops are as well.

The annual ritual, performed while the crops are dead, enacts Adonis's life: "the ceremony of the death and resurrection of Adonis must also have been a dramatic representation of the decay and revival of plant life."[7] The myth provides the script of the play. Imitation of the rebirth of Adonis serves magically to effect it: by the first of Frazer's two laws of magic, to imitate what one wants to happen is to produce it.[8]

To understand Weston's reliance on Frazer, one must consider the relationship for him not only between god and vegetation but also between king and god. On this issue Frazer is inconsistent. Sometimes for him the king is merely human and merely plays the role of the god of vegetation in the ritual. Other times for Frazer the god resides in the king, who is therefore himself divine. Here the health of the god depends on the health of the king, just as the health of vegetation depends on the health of its god. The ritual here performed is not the king's imitation of the death and rebirth of the vegetation god but the actual killing of the king and the transfer of the soul of the god to the body of the next king:

For [primitives] believe . . . that the king's life or spirit is so sympathetically bound up with the prosperity of the whole country, that if he fell ill or grew senile the cattle would sicken and cease to multiply, the crops would rot in the fields, and men would perish of widespread disease. Hence, in their opinion, the only way of averting these calamities is to put the king to death while he is still hale and hearty, in order that the spirit which he has inherited from his predecessors may be transmitted in turn by him to his successor while it is still in full vigour and has not yet been impaired by the weakness of disease and old age.[9]

The king is killed either at the end of a fixed term as short as a year or at the first sign of serious illness. If, by contrast, "the man-god dies what we call a natural death, it means, according to the savage, that his soul has either voluntarily departed from his body and refuses to return, or more commonly that it has been extracted, or at least detained in its wanderings, by a demon or sorcerer. In any of these cases the soul of the man-god is lost to his worshippers, and with it their prosperity is gone and their very existence endangered."[10]

Because the king, according to Frazer, is actually killed and replaced rather than, by imitation, killed and resurrected, it is hard to see the magical element in this, the chief ritual of the combined magical-religious stage. Yet magic there is. First, the god is being manipulated rather than beseeched. He is being kept healthy by being kept in the body of a healthy king.

More important, the king is magically identical with the god and the god with vegetation. The king is to the god as a voodoo doll is to the person of whom it is a likeness: just as the doll affects the person precisely because it is identical with the person rather than merely symbolic of the person, so the king affects the god because the king really is the god rather than a mere symbol or even the harborer of the god. The god affects vegetation for the same magical reason. Because the reigning king *is* the god, the king does not imitate the god. Perhaps, then, the relationship between king and god, and in turn between god and vegetation, is closer to that between a strand of hair and the person whose strand it is. To have a part of something in one's possession is, by Frazer's second law of magic, to have the whole.

In myth-ritualism the ritual is the enactment of the myth. When for Frazer the king plays the role of the god, the ritual enacts the life of the god described in myth. But when for Frazer the king *is* the god, yet when at the same time the king *rather than* the god dies, and dies not in imitation of the life of the god but as a sacrifice to maintain the health of the god, it is admittedly not easy to see what role myth plays in the ritual.[11]

WESTON AS A FRAZERIAN

How is Jessie Weston a Frazerian? To begin with, she operates comparatively. The preliminary evidence that the Grail legend originates in what she calls the "Nature Cult" is the pervasiveness of the cult among primitive, ancient, and contemporary peasant peoples. Paralleling the purportedly distinctive beliefs and customs of "civilized" peoples with those of earlier ones is quintessentially Frazerian. Hence Weston opens her study of the Grail legend with kindred tales and practices from the Rig-Veda. While her immediate aim is to try to pinpoint the historical roots of the Grail legend, her broader, Frazerian aim is to denude the Grail phenomenon of its uniqueness. The Grail becomes one more instance of the Nature Cult.

More significant, Weston places the Grail in Frazer's combined, magical-religious stage of cultural development. What she says of the Rig-Veda, she proceeds to say of the Grail:

> In the previous chapter we considered certain aspects of the attitude assumed by our Aryan forefathers towards the great processes of Nature in their ordered sequence of Birth, Growth, and Decay. We saw that while on one hand they, by prayer and supplication, threw themselves upon the mercy of the divinity, who, in their belief, was responsible for the granting, or withholding, of the water, . . . they, on the other hand, believed that, by their own actions, they could stimulate and assist the Divine activity. (FRR, 34)

Throwing oneself upon the mercy of a god is religion. Aiding a god combines magic with religion, and it is on this process that Weston concentrates. Insofar as humans ritualistically revive a weakened god, Weston is following Frazer's first version of the relationship between king and god. Here the king is merely human and merely plays the part of the vegetation god, who has become weak on his own.

In myth-ritualist fashion the state of nature in the Nature Cult thus reflects not, as in religion, a decision by a god but the condition of the god: "At this stage the progress of the seasons, the birth of vegetation in spring, or its revival after the autumn rains, . . . symbolically represented the corresponding stages in the life of this anthropomorphically conceived Being" (*FRR,* 35). This god, "upon whose life and reproductive activities the very existence of Nature and its corresponding energies was held to depend, . . . was himself subject to the vicissitudes of declining powers and death, like an ordinary mortal" (*FRR,* 41).

In the Grail legend the fertility of the land depends on "the life, and unimpaired vitality," of the figure who is "at once god and king" (*FRR,* 62). Versions of the Grail story in which the misfortune of the land is blamed not on the king but on the quester after the Grail are for Weston derivative. Insofar at the king and the god are one, Weston is following Frazer's second version of the relationship between king and god. Here the god is weak because the king in whom he resides is weak. Yet antithetically to Frazer, Weston's quester seeks to restore and serve the ailing king, not to kill and replace him. Where for Frazer the welfare of the community requires the killing of a weak king, in the Grail legend the welfare of the community requires his rejuvenation.

Weston skirts two technical issues in Frazer's theory: the exact relationship of the king to the land, and the exact relationship of the ritual to the king. She never explains why the land fares as the king fares. If, as she says, the king is also a god, then presumably the nexus between king and god is the same as the one in Frazer's second version of their relationship: that of magical identity. Similarly, Weston neglects to explain how the quester's ritual manages to revive the king. Presumably, the ritual works magically, as in the revival of the god by the king in Frazer's first version of their relationship, but by which of Frazer's laws of magic she does not say. Still, her preoccupation with the magical linkage of ritual to king to god to vegetation is consummately Frazerian.

Among the specific Grail symbols for which Weston finds ancient parallels, the most salient are the Lance, the Cup, the dish (which is sometimes identical with the Cup), and the Sword. Of the four, the most important are the Lance and the Cup, which *is* the Grail. For Weston, the Lance and the Cup are conspicuous symbols of male and female genitals. Her Frazerian argument is comparativist: "That Lance and Cup are, *outside* the Grail story, 'Life' [i.e., reproductive] symbols, and have been such from time immemorial, is a fact; why, then, should they not retain that character *inside* the framework of that story?" (*FRR,* 76).

Following Frazer, for whom the ritual of human fertility magically effects the fertility of vegetation, Weston ties the reproduction of crops to human reproduction. The Grail king's wound is sexual, and following Frazer's second version of the relationship between king and god, the king's infertility is the cause of the infertility of the land. Not coincidentally, the figures with whom Weston draws the closest parallels to the Grail king are Adonis and Attis—the first gored to death in the groin, the second driven to self-castration. Thus in the Grail legend "the central figure is either a dead knight on a bier . . . or a wounded king on a litter; when wounded[,] the injury corresponds with that suffered by Adonis and Attis" (*FRR*, 48).

Weston, again following Frazer, is especially eager to refute a Christian interpretation of her subject. Usually, she maintains that a Christian interpretation simply does not work. For example, the attempt to make the Lance the lance that pierced Christ on the cross ignores the association of the Lance with the Cup—an association that Christianity cannot explain. Similarly, the association of the Fisher King with the fish metaphor in the New Testament fails to explain the fallen condition of the Fisher King.

Conversely, Weston maintains that a crosscultural interpretation does work. The Lance is a common phallic symbol. The fish "is a Life symbol of immemorial antiquity, and . . . the title of Fisher has, from the earliest ages, been associated with Deities who were held to be specially connected with the origin and preservation of Life" (*FRR*, 125). Hence the Fisher King is deemed responsible for maintaining the land and his people.

Even when, according to Weston, a Christian interpretation works, it is derivative. It simply repackages the perennial philosophy:

> That Christianity might have borrowed from previously existing cults certain outward signs and symbols, might have accommodated itself to already existing Fasts and Feasts, may be, perforce has had to be, more or less grudgingly admitted; that such a *rapprochement* should have gone further, that . . . Christianity should have been held for no new thing but a fulfilment of the promise enshrined in the Mysteries from the beginning of the world, will to many be a strange and startling thought. Yet so it was, and I firmly believe that it is only in the recognition of this one-time claim of essential kinship between Christianity and the Pagan Mysteries that we shall find the key to the Secret of the Grail. (*FRR*, 149)

On the basis of the parallels that she finds between the hoary Nature Cult and the Grail legend, Weston concludes that the legend is but a "literary version" of the cult rather than the product of sheer imagination. It would, she says, be "simply inconceivable" that "a story which was originally the outcome of pure literary invention should in the course of re-modelling have been accidentally brought into close and detailed correspondence with a deeply rooted sequence of popular faith and practice" (*FRR*, 62).

THE GNOSTIC ORIGIN OF THE GRAIL LEGEND

Weston is not content to attribute the Grail legend to a generic Nature Cult. She seeks a specific source. Neither Christianity nor Celtic religion fits. Only Gnosticism does.

The Gnostic origin of the Grail legend involves what Weston terms the "esoteric" side of the legend. Despite her insistence on the quest for the Grail as a quest for fertility, she simultaneously argues that the quest is for mystical oneness with god. Fertility, the goal of the exoteric cult, benefits the community; esoteric communion benefits the select individual. Weston credits Frazer with deciphering the public side of the Nature Cult but assumes—rightly—that he is oblivious to any private one:

> Sir James Frazer, and those who followed him, have dealt with the public side of the cult, with its importance as a recognized vehicle for obtaining material advantages; it was the social, rather than the individual, aspect which appealed to them. Now we find that . . . these cults were considered not only most potent factors for assuring the material prosperity of land and folk, but were also held to be the most appropriate vehicle for imparting the highest religious teaching. The Vegetation deities, Adonis-Attis, and more especially the Phrygian god, were the chosen guides to the knowledge of, and union with, the supreme Spiritual Source of Life, of which they were the communicating medium. (*FRR*, 157–58)

The ritual and the god remain the same in both the esoteric and the exoteric cult. The goal is what changes.

For Weston, the historical link between the two sides of the Nature Cult was the Christian Gnostic group known as the Naassenes. The fullest source of information on the Naassenes is Hippolytus, who presents an extract from a Naassene sermon, or document, that is an exegesis of a hymn to Attis. In the hymn Attis is equated syncretistically with other gods, including Adonis, and so becomes identical with the highest god.[12]

Because the Naassenes practiced a spiritualized form of cult and worshiped both Adonis and Attis as equivalent to the Gnostic god, Weston takes the group to have fused the physical with the spiritual. For Weston, the trajectory was from vegetation cult to mystery cult to Naassene cult to Mithraic cult, a kindred cult brought to Celtic Britain, where, centuries later, the Grail legend arose and later became Christianized.

Weston's book brims with historical speculations. A connection between the dualistic, syncretistic mystery cults and Gnostic groups like the Naassenes is not inconceivable.[13] Considerably more tenuous is the fundamental tie that Weston draws between fertility cults and Gnosticism. As she recognizes but somehow downplays, the purported esoteric side of fertility cults is, taken to Gnostic lengths, incompatible with the exoteric one. The exoteric aim of fertility cults is irremediably physical: to ensure food and children. Any esoteric, Gnostic aim would be relentlessly antiphysical: to escape from the body and from the world which thrives on food and sex. In Gnosticism reproduction is the most egregious offense, not the most cherished end. While there were libertine Gnostics, they indulged themselves to demonstrate their imperviousness to temptation. They were flouting, not flaunting, the body. Matter remained evil. Surely no such irony motivated Weston's esoteric practitioners.[14]

Weston does say that the original aim of fertility cults was physical and only subsequently became spiritual: "This ritual, in its earlier stages comparatively simple and objective in form, under the process of an insistence upon the inner and spiritual significance, took upon itself a more complex and esoteric character, the rite became a Mystery, and with this change the *role* of the principal actors became of heightened significance" (*FRR,* 109–10). But for her the esoteric end came to supplement, not supplant, the exoteric one. As already quoted in part, "in the intermediate *pre-* and *post-*Christian era these cults were considered not only most potent factors for assuring the material prosperity of land and folk, but were also held to be the most appropriate vehicle for importing the highest religious teaching" (*FRR,* 157–58). While the material end was the sole one sought by the masses, the immaterial one was sought, in addition rather than instead, by the elite.

THE RECEPTION OF WESTON'S THESIS

Weston's overall thesis has endured the same fate as the myth-ritualist theory of which it is an application. Initially lauded by professionals for its capacity to make sense of the Grail material, it has since been rejected as unsubstantiated. The changing assessment of Roger Sherman Loomis, the most famous proponent of a Celtic origin, is representative. In his first book on the Grail, *Celtic Myth and Arthurian Romance* (1927), he accepted Weston's central argument altogether: "And luckily the evidence is so palpable that one need not be either an initiate or a specialist in primitive religion to feel its force. One may not find so convincing Miss Weston's views on the transmission and later history of the material, but her main thesis, as developed in her books, is amply supported."[15] In his last major work on the Grail, *The Grail* (1963), Loomis describes his outright recantation of his acceptance of Weston's thesis: "In 1927 I first ventured to publish my speculations about the Grail legend in a book entitled *Celtic Myth and Arthurian Romance*. Though I still hold to many of the opinions there set forth, I came to realize within a few years that other opinions were mistaken, and a retraction of certain chapters was inserted in the copies which remained. I retracted in particular my adherence to Dr. Jessie Weston's ingenious hypothesis concerning the Grail and Lance, for lack of valid and clearly pertinent evidence."[16] Still, Weston's work, like Frazer's, has remained popular among nonspecialists and will surely continue to do so.

V • FAIRY TALES SÍ, MYTHS NO: BRUNO BETTELHEIM'S ANTITHESIS

AS A FREUDIAN FOLKLORIST, Alan Dundes has continually bemoaned the typical indifference of Freudians to folklore and the common hostility of folklorists to Freud:

The survey of the psychological study of folklore in the United States from 1880 to 1980 turns out to be a rather bleak one. Psychologists, for the most part, have not concerned themselves with folklore. Some psychiatrists, specifically Jungians and Freudians, have written at some length about folklore, but their efforts have had little if any influence upon mainstream folklore theory and method. Folklorists, both literary and anthropological, have generally tended to eschew any form of psychological analysis.[1]

Dundes stresses how hard it is "to convey just how adamantly opposed to psychoanalytic interpretation the majority of conventional [folklore] scholars are. . . . [P]sychoanalysts have only a marginal interest in folklore."[2] Of the study of the Grimm tales in particular, he says:

The anti-psychological bias is so strong among folklorists that they don't even mention the numerous psychoanalytic essays devoted to Grimm tales in print. . . . The situation is roughly as follows: folklorists and psychoanalysts have for nearly a century analyzed the Grimm tales in almost total ignorance of one another. Folklorists blindly committed to anti-symbolic, anti-psychological readings of folktales make little or no effort to discover what, if anything, psychoanalysts have to say about the tales they are studying. Psychoanalysts, limited to their twentieth-century patients' free associations to the nineteenth-century Grimm versions of folktales, are blithely unaware of the existence of hundreds of versions of the same tale types so assiduously assembled by folklorists in archives or presented in painstaking detail in historic-geographic monographs.[3]

DUNDES ON BETTELHEIM

Dundes is consequently eager to praise those few scholars who do undertake psychoanalytic studies of folklore. Among contemporary efforts, the most acclaimed has been Bruno Bettelheim's 1976 study of the Grimm tales, *The Uses of Enchantment* (hereafter *UOE*),[4] which Dundes praises as one of "the few bright spots in the history of the psychological study of folklore in the United States."[5] Dundes praises Bettelheim for his positive view of the psychoanalytic function of fairy tales. Where early Freudians tended to view fairy tales as manifestations, if not exacerbations, of neuroses, Bettelheim views them as vehicles of maturation.[6] Where early Freudians were wary of the effect of fairy tales on children, Bettelheim recommends them as ideal aids in growing up. Dundes also praises Bettelheim for distinguishing between the oral and the written nature of fairy tales, for advocating only originally oral tales for children, and for opposing illustrated and bowdlerized versions of tales. As a Freudian, Dundes agrees with Bettelheim that tales work their magic unconsciously, though he finds oddly non-Freudian Bettelheim's aversion to making children conscious of the Freudian meaning.

There are various grounds on which others have criticized Bettelheim but on which Dundes does not. For example, Bettelheim, though by no means Dundes himself, assumes that true fairy tales have happy endings, that the meaning of the tales is universal rather than bound by time and place, that the tales are told from a neutral rather than a distinctively male viewpoint, and that the tales always deal with family relations.

Yet Dundes is ultimately most critical of Bettelheim, on both folkloristic and other grounds. Dundes shows that Bettelheim sometimes confuses myths with folktales. He also shows that Bettelheim wrongly assumes the universality of tale types.

Dundes's main criticism is that Bettelheim at once ignores most of his psychoanalytic predecessors and outright plagiarizes others.[7] Dundes initially lodged these charges in passing. He has since devoted a whole essay to them. He is prepared to excuse Bettelheim's obliviousness to folkloristic studies of fairy tales, but he is dismayed at Bettelheim's apparent unfamiliarity with the pioneering psychoanalytic studies of, above all, Franz Ricklin and Géza Róheim.[8] Dundes notes that "Bettelheim's neglect of Róheim is especially egregious as Róheim wrote whole essays on many of the tales Bettelheim chose to analyze."[9] Far less excusable than Bettelheim's oversight is his use sub rosa of the work of Róheim, Otto Rank, Julius Heuscher, and Dundes himself. Bettelheim's plagiarism, states Dundes, "is not just a matter of occasional borrowings of random passages, but a wholesale borrowing of key ideas."[10]

For me, even more disconcerting than Bettelheim's failure to consider his Freudian forebears in his analysis of fairy tales is his failure to consider his Freudian *contemporaries* in his more passing analysis of *myths*. There is no issue here of plagiarism, for in discussing myths Bettelheim disregards rather than appropriates con-temporary Freudian views. The views he espouses are akin to classical Freudian ones. It is the disjunction between Bettelheim's up-to-date approach to fairy tales and his old-fashioned approach to myths that is striking.

BETTELHEIM'S OPPOSITION OF FAIRY TALES TO MYTHS

In the first place Bettelheim is distinctive among Freudians in pitting myths against fairy tales. Most Freudians, early and contemporary alike, see myths and fairy tales as akin.[11] Freud himself regards the two as kindred fulfillments of re-pressed wishes.[12] By contrast, Bettelheim sees them as antithetical:

> Put simply, the dominant feeling a myth conveys is: this is absolutely unique; it could not have happened to any other person, or in any other setting; such events are grandi-ose, awe-inspiring, and could not possibly happen to an ordinary mortal like you or me. . . . By contrast, although the events which occur in fairy tales are often unusual and most improbable, they are always presented as ordinary, something that could hap-pen to you or me or the person next door when out on a walk in the woods. . . . Myths project an ideal personality acting on the basis of superego demands, while fairy tales depict an ego integration which allows for appropriate satisfaction of id desires. This difference accounts for the contrast between the pervasive pessimism of myths and the essential optimism of fairy tales. (*UOE,* 37, 41)

BETTELHEIM'S PREFERENCE FOR FAIRY TALES OVER MYTHS

In the second place Bettelheim is distinctive among Freudians in conspicuously favoring fairy tales over myths. Those classical or contemporary Freudians who do contrast myths to fairy tales ordinarily favor myths over fairy tales. Even Ró-heim, whom Dundes credits with originating many of the contrasts between myths and fairy tales that Bettelheim adopts without acknowledgment, character-izes myths as providing "a more adult" and folktales as providing "a more in-fantile" "form of the same conflict."[13] Folktales for Róheim express the sheer fulfillment of wishes: "the child obtains a fulfilment in imagination of those unconscious wishes which it cannot yet obtain in reality."[14] By contrast, myths depict the subsequent punishment for this fulfillment.[15] For Róheim, folktales are sheer fantasies, whereas myths "link up phantasy and reality."[16] Hence Oedipal folktales end in parricide; Oedipal myths, in submission to the resurrected father.[17] In "fairy tales and popular legends dealing with the co-operation between mortals and immortals, the supernatural beings are always deceived; human cunning wins the day."[18] In myths, "the heroes sin against the gods and must atone for this with an eternal punishment or an eternal task."[19] Where in the tale of Jack and the

Beanstalk Jack outsmarts the ogre, becomes rich, and lives happily ever after, in the myth of Prometheus the hero "becomes the representative of renunciation; and his achievement, the great cultural act of the discovery of fire, is performed with energy, or better libido, that has been diverted from its original aim."[20]

Much like the early Freudian Róheim, contemporary Freudian Jacob Arlow sees fairy tales as the fulfillment of wishes and myths as a means of renunciation.[21] Arlow, too, contrasts Jack to Prometheus—and adds the case of Moses. Where Jack brashly steals what he wants from the fatherlike giant above, Prometheus fears Olympian Zeus and indeed is punished by Zeus for stealing fire. In contrast to both rebels, Moses in the Exodus myth ascends Mount Sinai as the servant, not the antagonist, of the heavenly God:

> The fairy-tale version of this problem belonged to the wish-fulfilling tendency of childhood in which contribution of the superego is minimal and unformed and the fear of retaliation is disposed of omnipotently. . . . What is epitomized in this variation [i.e., the myth of Prometheus] is the stage beyond the untroubled wish fulfillment of the simple fairy tale, the overwhelming impact of the fear of retaliation. . . . What was originally [i.e., in Prometheus] a crime of defiance and aggression against the gods is, in this later version [i.e., the myth of Moses], represented as carrying out the wishes of God Himself.[22]

Even though Arlow calls fairy tales "truncated myths,"[23] and even though he places the Prometheus story in between a straight fairy tale and a full-fledged myth, the contrast that he draws between the "fairy-tale version" and the mythic version of the ascent motif obviously favors myths over fairy tales.[24]

It is, ironically, by the same criteria as Róheim's and Arlow's that Bettelheim gives the nod to fairy tales over myths. To be sure, Bettelheim does not go so far as to pronounce myths sheer wish fulfillments. On the contrary, echoing Arlow, he says that "Myths typically involve superego demands in conflict with id-motivated action" (*UOE*, 37). But for Bettelheim, in contrast to Róheim as well as to Arlow, so uncompromising is the mythic superego that the maturation it preaches is unattainable: "Mythical heroes offer excellent images for the development of the superego, but the demands they embody are so rigorous as to discourage the child in his fledgling strivings to achieve personality integration" (*UOE*, 39).

Even though for Bettelheim fairy tales no less than myths preach maturation, they do so in gentler ways and thereby succeed where myths fail: "In the myth there is only insurmountable difficulty and defeat; in the fairy tale there is equal peril, but it is successfully overcome. Not death and destruction, but higher integration . . . is the hero's reward at the end of the fairy tale" (*UOE*, 199). Bettelheim's view of myths as hindering rather than spurring psychological growth is close to the classical Freudian view of fairy tales and myths alike.

Dundes suggests that Bettelheim takes from Róheim the point that folktales end happily and myths tragically.[25] Yet Bettelheim and Róheim still evaluate myths and fairy tales antithetically. Bettelheim uses Róheim's distinction to tout folktales over myths; Róheim uses it to tout myths over folktales. For Róheim, folktales end happily because, contrary to Bettelheim, they foster illusions about reality and thereby keep one fixated at childhood. Myths end tragically because they face up to reality and thereby promote maturation—not, as for Bettelheim, despair.

BETTELHEIM'S DISREGARD OF CONTEMPORARY FREUDIANS ON MYTH

In the third and final place Bettelheim does not merely prefer fairy tales to myths, as he is surely entitled to do, but inexplicably disregards contemporary Freudian approaches to myths in so doing. Bettelheim is brilliantly innovative in his approach to fairy tales but incongruously regressive in his approach to myths. He analyzes myths the way most early Freudians do.[26] Róheim, whose analysis foreshadows contemporary ones, is here an exception among early Freudians. Bettelheim castigates myths because he finds in them no more than classical Freudians do. He celebrates fairy tales because he finds in them what Arlow and other contemporary Freudians find instead in myths! Unlike Arlow, Bettelheim allows for no middle ground between fairy tales and myths. A story is either one or the other.

For Bettelheim, as for all other Freudians, both myths and fairy tales deal with the problems of growing up—the problems of mastering instincts, breaking with parents, and establishing oneself in society. Both genres deal with "overcoming narcissistic disappointments, oedipal dilemmas, sibling rivalries; becoming able to relinquish childhood dependencies; gaining a feeling of selfhood and of self-worth, and a sense of moral obligation" (*UOE*, 6). But "there is a crucial difference in the way these [problems] are communicated" (*UOE*, 37). Myths present these problems as unresolvable and thereby keep one tied to childhood. Fairy tales offer realistic solutions to them and thereby help one to grow up.

In myths, according to Bettelheim, childhood desires either are fulfilled rather than curbed, just as in dreams,[27] or else are consequently punished rather than overcome. Where early Freudians focus on fulfillment, Bettelheim focuses on punishment. Róheim is again an exception among early Freudians.[28] Where most early Freudians stress Oedipus's managing to kill his father and to marry his mother,[29] Bettelheim emphasizes Oedipus's subsequent blinding and exile (see *UOE*, 38–39). (Freudians tend to categorize the Oedipus tale as a myth.) Hence for Bettelheim, "in fairy tales the hero's story shows how these potentially destructive infantile [Oedipal] relations can be, and are, integrated in developmental processes. In the myth, oedipal difficulties are [simply] acted out and in consequence all ends in total destruction" (*UOE*, 198).

According to Bettelheim, the figures in myths are so superior to ordinary mortals that even when their problems are resolved, only heroes or even only gods seem capable of resolving them: "A mere mortal is too frail to meet the challenges of the gods. Paris, who does the bidding of Zeus as conveyed to him by Hermes, and obeys the demand of the three goddesses in choosing which shall have the apple, is destroyed for having followed these commands, as are untold other mortals in the wake of this fateful choice" (*UOE*, 37). By contrast, the figures in fairy tales are ordinary mortals, whose ability to resolve problems encourages others to attempt the same: "Whatever strange events the fairy-tale hero experiences, they do not make him superhuman, as is true for the mythical hero. This real humanity suggests to the child that, whatever the content of the fairy tale, it is but fanciful elaborations and exaggerations of the tasks he has to meet, and of his hopes and fears" (*UOE*, 40).

Strikingly, the praise that Bettelheim bestows on fairy tales vis-à-vis myths mimics the praise that Arlow and other contemporary Freudians confer on myths vis-à-vis fairy tales. Spurred by the development of ego psychology, Arlow, Sidney Tarachow, Mark Kanzer, Max Stern, and Warner Muensterberger view myths much more positively than Freud, Rank, Ricklin, and Karl Abraham did—Róheim again being an exception. For contemporary Freudians, myths help solve the problems of growing up rather than perpetuate them, are progressive rather than regressive, and abet adjustment to the adult world rather than childish flight from it. Myths serve less to vent bottled-up drives than to sublimate them. What Bettelheim says of fairy tales almost parrots what Arlow said of myths fifteen years earlier:

Psychoanalysis has a greater contribution to make to the study of mythology than [merely] demonstrating, in myths, wishes often encountered in the unconscious thinking of patients. The myth is a particular kind of communal experience. It is a special form of shared fantasy, and it serves to bring the individual into relationship with members of his cultural group on the basis of certain common needs. Accordingly, the myth can be studied from the point of view of its function in psychic integration—how it plays a role in warding off feelings of guilt and anxiety, how it constitutes a form of adaptation to reality and to the group in which the individual lives, and how it influences the crystallization of the individual identity and the formation of the superego.[30]

For contemporary Freudians, mythic figures are both worthy and capable of emulation by ordinary persons rather than, as for Bettelheim, either unworthy or incapable.[31] For present-day Freudians, myths are different from dreams rather than, as for Bettelheim, like them: "Where the dream represents the demands of the instincts, the myth tends to perpetuate and represent the demands of society on the mental apparatus for symbolization and acceptance."[32] Arlow laments that lay critics of psychoanalysis continue to "assume that [for psychoanalysts] myths and dreams are indistinguishable."[33]

The issue is not whether Bettelheim's dismissal of myths as ineffective is right or wrong. Indeed, Dundes himself would doubtless prefer aspects of Bettelheim's analysis of myths to Arlow's. The issue is that Bettelheim ignores the contemporary Freudian approach to myth as fully as he ignores specific classical Freudian analyses of fairy tales. He writes in a void.

At the same time Bettelheim's analysis of even fairy tales is in several respects crudely outdated. First, he interprets fairy tales, and also myths, allegorically: one entity stands for the ego, another for the id, a third for the superego. By contrast, contemporary Freudians stress the multiple meanings of the elements in fairy tales and myths alike—a reflection of the contemporary stress on the multiple functions of cultural phenomena.

Second, Bettelheim interprets fairy tales, and again myths as well, moralistically: fairy tales preach messages that must be heeded, lest woeful consequences ensue. By contrast, contemporary Freudians emphasize the flexibility and open-endedness of fairy tales and myths alike: fairy tales and myths offer options, which the reader or hearer is free to choose and even to alter. The rigidity and self-righteousness that Bettelheim finds in both fairy tales and myths may reveal less about his subject than about him.

VI • JUNG ON MYTHOLOGY

AT LEAST THREE MAJOR questions can be asked of myth: what is its subject matter, what is its origin, and what is its function? Theories of myth differ not only on the answers they give to these questions but also on the questions they seek to answer. Some theories concentrate on the subject matter of myth, others on the origin, still others on the function. C. G. Jung's is one of the few theories that answer fully all three questions. A single statement summarizes his answer: "Myths are original revelations of the preconscious psyche, involuntary statements about unconscious psychic happenings, and anything but allegories of physical processes."[1] The subject matter is not literal but symbolic: not the external world but the human mind. Myth originates and functions to satisfy the psychological need for contact with the unconscious.

THE SUBJECT MATTER OF MYTH

James Frazer's *The Golden Bough* provides the classic expression of the view that the subject matter of myth is physical processes. For Frazer, the chief myths of all religions describe the death and rebirth of vegetation, a process symbolized by the myth of the death and rebirth of the god of vegetation. Thus "the story that Adonis spent half, or according to others a third, of the year in the lower world and the rest of it in the upper world, is explained most simply and naturally by supposing that he represented vegetation, especially the corn, which lies buried in the earth half the year and reappears above ground the other half."[2]

Jung likewise interprets the myth of the death and rebirth of a god as symbolic, but symbolic of a process taking place in the mind, not in the world. That process is the return of the ego to the unconscious—a kind of temporary death of the ego—and its reemergence, or rebirth, from the unconscious: "I need only mention the whole mythological complex of the dying and resurgent god and its primitive precursors all the way down to the re-charging of fetishes and churingas with magical force. It expresses a transformation of attitude by means of which a new potential, a new manifestation of life, a new fruitfulness, is created."[3]

Jung does not deny that the psychological process of the death and rebirth of the ego *parallels* the physical process of the death and rebirth of vegetation. He denies that the physical process *accounts for* the psychological one, let alone for the mythic one. For Frazer, the leap from vegetation to god is the product of logic and imagination: "primitives" observe the course of vegetation and hypothesize the existence of a god to account for it—even if for Frazer himself the god is a mere symbol of vegetation. For Jung, the leap is too great for the human imagination to make. Humans generally, not merely primitives, lack the creativity required to concoct consciously the notion of the sacred out of the profane. They can only transform the profane into a sacred that already exists for them.[4] Humans must already have the idea of god within their minds and can only be projecting that idea onto vegetation and the other natural phenomena that they observe:

> This latter analogy [between god and natural phenomenon] explains the well-attested connection between the renewal of the god and seasonal and vegetational phenomena. One is naturally inclined to assume that seasonal, vegetational, lunar, and solar myths underlie these analogies. But that is to forget that a myth, like everything psychic, cannot be solely conditioned by external events. Anything psychic brings its own internal conditions with it, so that one might assert with equal right that the myth is purely psychological and uses meteorological or astronomical events merely as a means of expression. The whimsicality and absurdity of many primitive myths often makes the latter explanation seem far more appropriate than any other.[5]

Even early Jung, who was prepared to give more weight to experience than later Jung, distinguishes between the experience of the sun itself and the experience of the sun as a god. Experience of the sun provides the *occasion* for the manifestation of the sun archetype but does not *cause* that archetype:

> I have often been asked where the archetypes or primordial images come from. It seems to me that their origin can only be explained by assuming them to be deposits of the constantly repeated experiences of humanity. One of the commonest and at the same time most impressive experiences is the apparent movement of the sun every day. We certainly cannot discover anything of the kind in the unconscious, so far as the known physical process is concerned. What we do find, on the other hand, is the myth of the sun-hero in all its countless variations. It is this myth, and not the physical process, that forms the sun archetype. . . . The archetype is a kind of readiness to produce over and over again the same or similar mythical ideas.[6]

It is not only allegories of physical processes that Jung rejects as the real subject matter of myth. He also rejects literal interpretations of myth that still make the subject matter outer rather than inner. For example, the pioneering Victorian anthropologist Edward Tylor insists that the subject matter of myth is gods of nature rather than, as for Frazer, the natural phenomena they control and even inhabit. For Tylor, myths are actual explanations of natural phenomena and not merely, as for Frazer, colorful descriptions of them. Gods are the purported agents behind natural processes and not simply allegories of those processes. As Tylor says in exasperation at those who would interpret myths allegorically, "When the Apache Indian pointed to the sky and asked the white man, 'Do you not believe that God, the Sun, . . . sees what we do and punishes us when it is evil?' it is impossible to say that this savage was talking in rhetorical simile."[7]

Jung conflates Tylor's theory with Frazer's, stating, for example, that "people are very loath to give up the idea that the myth is some kind of explanatory allegory of astronomical, meteorological, or vegetative processes."[8] The phrase "explanatory allegory" conflates Tylor's theory—myth as explanation—with Frazer's—myth as allegory. Jung asks rhetorically "why the sun and its apparent motions do not appear direct and undisguised as a content of the myths."[9] Tylor's answer would be that myths describe sun gods and not merely the sun because myths are about sun gods and not merely about the sun. Yet even if Jung were to distinguish Tylor's view from Frazer's, he would still invoke his fundamental claim that human beings cannot consciously invent gods. Humans can only project onto the world gods already in their minds. For Jung, myth is no more about gods than about the physical world. It is about the human mind. Myth must be read symbolically, as for Frazer, and the symbolized subject is a process, as also for Frazer, but the process is an inner rather than an outer one.

Jung interprets as projections not only nature myths but all other kinds of myths as well. He says that "in fact, the whole of mythology could be taken as a sort of projection of the collective unconscious. . . . Just as the constellations were projected into the heavens, similar figures were projected into legends and fairytales or upon historical persons."[10] Hero myths, of which Jungians are especially enamored, are projections onto mere human beings of a divine or quasi-divine status: "the hero myth is an unconscious drama seen only in projection, like the happenings in Plato's parable of the cave. The hero himself appears as a being of more than human stature."[11] Moderns, while often professed atheists, still create myths by projecting onto their fellow human beings exaggerated qualities that turn them into superhuman figures: "[T]he archetypes usually appear in projection; and, because projections are unconscious, they appear on persons in the immediate environment, mostly in the form of abnormal over- or under-evaluations which provoke misunderstandings, quarrels, fanaticisms, and follies of every description.

Thus we say, 'He makes a god of so-and-so,' or, 'So-and-so is Mr. X's *bête noire.*' In this way, too, there grow up modern myth-formations, i.e., fantastic rumours, suspicions, prejudices."[12]

Once Jung differentiates a psychological interpretation of myth from a nonpsychological one, he must differentiate his particular psychological interpretation from Freud's. Jung grants the Freudian claim that there exist "fantasies (including dreams) of a personal character, which go back unquestionably to personal experiences, things forgotten or repressed, and can thus be completely explained by individual anamnesis [i.e., recollection]."[13] But he is far more concerned to vaunt his own claim that, in addition to these manifestations of the personal, Freudian unconscious, there exist "fantasies (including dreams) of an impersonal character, which cannot be reduced to experiences in the individual's past, and thus cannot be explained as something individually acquired."[14] These fantasies must emanate from a different unconscious, which, rather than the creation of an individual, must be inherited. Jung insists that myths are always the product of this distinctively Jungian, collective unconscious: "These fantasy-images [of an impersonal character] undoubtedly have their closest analogues in mythological types. . . . The products of this second category resemble the types of structures to be met with in myth and fairytale so much that we must regard them as related."[15]

On the one hand Jung employs the collective unconscious to interpret myths. On the other hand he employs myths to interpret the collective unconscious: "In order to interpret the products of the unconscious, I also found it necessary to give a quite different reading to dreams and fantasies. I did not reduce them to personal factors, as Freud does, but—and this seemed indicated by their very nature—I compared them with the symbols from mythology and the history of religion, in order to discover the meaning they were trying to express."[16] Myths here steer one away from a Freudian diagnosis.

Going further, Jung uses myths to *establish* the collective unconscious. The first step in the proof is the demonstration of the universality of motifs, and myths provide evidence of that universality. As he says, "The material brought forward—folkloristic, mythological, or historical—serves in the first place to demonstrate the uniformity of psychic events in time and space."[17] The next step in the proof is the refutation of Freud's account of the universality of motifs. Jung cites the recurrence of mythic motifs that supposedly defy a Freudian explanation. For example, he continually appeals to the appearance in myths of the idea of birth from two mothers to refute Freud's analysis of Leonardo da Vinci's famous depiction of Jesus' being hovered over by Anne as well as Mary as a projection of Leonardo's own childhood experience:

Freud interprets this remarkable picture in terms of the fact that Leonardo himself had two mothers. This causality is personal. We shall . . . simply point out that interwoven with the apparently personal psychology there is an impersonal motif well known to us from other fields. This is the motif of the *dual mother,* an archetype to be found in many variants in the field of mythology and comparative religion and forming the basis of numerous "représentations collectives." I might mention, for instance, the motif of the *dual descent,* that is, descent from human and divine parents, as in the case of Heracles, who received immortality through being unwittingly adopted by Hera. . . . Now it is absolutely out of the question that all the individuals who believe in a dual descent have in reality always had two mothers, or conversely that those few who shared Leonardo's fate have infected the rest of humanity with their complex. Rather, one cannot avoid the assumption that the universal occurrence of the dual-birth motif together with the fantasy of the two mothers answers an omnipresent human need which is reflected in these motifs.[18]

It is a testimony to the confidence of both Jungians and Freudians in their psychologies that mythology since the time of the masters has come to be taken by both groups less as evidence of the unconscious and more as an expression of it.

Jung maintains that because the collective unconscious is inherently unconscious, "in the last analysis, therefore, it is impossible to say what [its contents] refer to. Every interpretation necessarily remains an 'as-if.' The ultimate core of meaning may be circumscribed, but not described."[19] It is not merely Freud but other theorists as well who thus wrongly assume the subject matter, or referent, of myth to be specifiable. If one heeds Jung, "there is no longer any question whether a myth refers to the sun or the moon, the father or the mother, sexuality or fire or water; all it does is to circumscribe and give an approximate description of an *unconscious core of meaning.*"[20]

Jung is by no means abandoning the attempt to interpret myth. He is simply cautioning against would-be definitive interpretations of myth. More precisely, he is cautioning against would-be definitive *Jungian* interpretations of myth. He is prepared to rule out all non-Jungian interpretations, but he is not prepared to rule in any one Jungian interpretation. Insofar as the contents of the collective unconscious are archetypes, the definitive meaning of myths is the expression of archetypes. But because archetypes are innately unconscious, they can express themselves only obliquely, through symbols. Furthermore, not only does every myth contain multiple archetypes, but every archetype harbors inexhaustible meanings. No symbol can convey even obliquely the array of meanings of the archetype it expresses. As Jung says of the difficulty a poet faces in trying to express an archetypal experience:

[T]he primordial experience is the source of his creativeness, but it is so dark and amorphous that it requires the related mythological imagery to give it form. In itself it is wordless and imageless, for it is a vision seen "as in a glass, darkly." It is nothing but a tremendous intuition striving for expression. . . . Since the expression can never match the richness of the vision and can never exhaust its possibilities, the poet must have at his disposal a huge store of material if he is to communicate even a fraction of what he has glimpsed, and must make use of difficult and contradictory images in order to express the strange paradoxes of his vision.[21]

For some theorists, myths are difficult to interpret because their meaning is symbolic rather than literal. For Jung, the greatest difficulty is not that myths are encrypted symbolically but that the symbols used to convey their meaning do so both indirectly and, worse, inadequately. The issue is epistemological, and Jung continually invokes Immanuel Kant to differentiate what we can know from what we cannot. Kant's distinction between the unknowable, noumenal reality and the knowable, phenomenal one becomes for Jung not only the distinction between metaphysics and psychology but also the distinction within psychology between the unconscious and consciousness. It becomes as well the distinction between archetypes and symbols.

For Jung, interpreting myths poses a double difficulty. The initial but less weighty difficulty is the need to recognize the motifs in myths as symbols. Jung is impatient with those who read myths literally, for they thereby mistake the symbols for the symbolized. Once motifs are recognized as symbols, the weightier difficulty is deciphering their meaning. Symbols are the only medium for conveying archetypes, but they are an imperfect medium. Nothing can bridge the divide between the unconscious and consciousness. Indeed, Jung dismisses Freud's view of the unconscious precisely because Freud seemingly bridges the divide by deriving the unconscious from consciousness. For Jung, myths, as a symbolic manifestation of archetypes, can never be deciphered exhaustively. It is not merely that one can never be sure of the correctness of the interpretation—a problem that would hold even if myths referred entirely to conscious processes. It is that no myth can convey fully the meaning invested in it by the archetypes it conveys. The point is not simply that a myth can harbor a plurality of meanings—again, a problem that would hold even if myths referred wholly to conscious processes. The point is that any myth is limited in what it can convey. In stressing that myth falls short of conveying the meanings invested in it, Jung is by no means disparaging it. On the contrary, he declares myth the best medium for conveying the unconscious: "Myth is the primordial language natural to these psychic processes, and no intellectual formulation comes anywhere near the richness and expressiveness of mythical imagery."[22]

For Jung, interpreting myths poses a third difficulty as well. Myths for him do not merely convey meanings. They convey meanings to adherents. Myths are intended by the unconscious to reveal its contents to those whose myths they are. To reach their intended audience, myths must be translatable into a language the audience knows. Just as archetypes must be translated, however insufficiently, into myths, so myths must be translated, however insufficiently, into the language of those whose myths they are. Just as archetypes are dependent on myths to convey their meaning, so myths are dependent on interpretations to convey *their* meaning. Even if the meaning of a myth is the expression of the archetypes it harbors, the myth must still be interpreted by whoever is to benefit from it. As Jung says, "And whatever explanation or interpretation does to it [i.e., the myth], we do to our own souls as well, with corresponding results for our own well-being. The archetype—let us never forget this—is a psychic organ present in all of us. A bad explanation means a correspondingly bad attitude to this organ, which may thus be injured. But the ultimate sufferer is the bad interpreter himself."[23]

Tracking the relationship of archetypes to myths to interpretations is like tracking the translation of a message from one language into a second language which lacks many of the equivalents of the first, and then into a third language which lacks many of the equivalents of the second. Yet the second language must be translated into the third if the indispensable message of the first language is not to be lost. To be cut off from that original message is to be cut off from one's own unconscious—a psychological disaster:

> In reality we can never legitimately cut loose from our archetypal foundations unless we are prepared to pay the price of a neurosis, any more than we can rid ourselves of our body and its organs without committing suicide. If we cannot deny the archetypes or otherwise neutralize them, we are confronted, at every new stage in the differentiation of consciousness to which civilization attains, with the task of finding a new *interpretation* appropriate to this stage, in order to connect the life of the past that still exists in us with the life of the present, which threatens to slip away from it.[24]

Insofar as a new interpretation of a myth conveys some aspect of the myth (and in turn of an archetype) not previously conveyed, we "dream the myth onwards."[25]

By nature, all theorists of myth, not just Jung, are interested in the similarities rather than the differences among myths. To encompass all cases of myth, theorists not only identify overt similarities but also uncover similarities beneath apparent differences. Jung, however, goes further. He repeatedly declares myths to be not merely similar but outright identical—an identity that he attributes to their identical origin: "It is the same as with myths and symbols, which can arise autochthonously in every corner of the earth and yet are identical, because they are fashioned out of the same worldwide human unconscious, whose contents are infinitely less variable than are races and individuals."[26] By the identity of myths worldwide, Jung must mean the identity of the archetypes they manifest. He cannot mean that myths themselves are identical. He may be downplaying the differences as insignificant, but he cannot be denying them.

Yet for all his insistence on the universal identity of the archetypal contents of myths, Jung is also attentive to the differences. When he analyzes specific myths, the identification of archetypes becomes only the first, not the last, step in the process. One must analyze the specific symbols used to convey those archetypes, the meaning of those archetypes in the specific myth in which they appear, and the meaning of that myth in the life of the specific adherent to the myth. A myth is not merely a myth in its own right. It is a myth for someone. The meaning of a myth is more than its general meaning for all humanity. One must understand the person or the society to understand the myth: "So it is with the individual images [in a myth]: they need a context, and the context is not only a myth but an individual anamnesis."[27] Hence for Jung the analysis of myth is best undertaken as part of therapy. The frequent characterization of Jung as oblivious to the particulars of a myth and its adherents is inaccurate and unfair. Undeniably, for many Jungians, including Erich Neumann and the Jungian-oriented Joseph Campbell, the meaning of a myth is exclusively the universal one. But for Jung himself and for Jungian analysts practicing today, the meaning is the particular one as well as the universal one.[28]

THE ORIGIN OF MYTH

As a theorist of myth, Jung is concerned with accounting for the similarities among myths. There are two possible explanations: diffusion and independent invention. Diffusion means that myths originate in one society and spread elsewhere. Independent invention means that every society invents myths on its own. The prime argument of diffusionists is that the similarities among myths are too precise to have arisen independently. The prime argument of independent "inventionists" is that the similarities are too widespread geographically to be the product of diffusion. Additionally, "inventionists" argue that diffusion, even when granted, fails to explain either the origin of a myth in the society in which it arises or the acceptance of the myth by the societies to which it spreads.

Jung is staunchly committed to independent invention as the origin of myth. He makes the standard argument that there is no evidence and indeed no possibility of contact among all of the societies with similar myths: "Every endeavour has been made to explain the concordance of myth-motifs and -symbols as due to migration and tradition; Goblet d'Almellas' *Migration of Symbols* is an excellent example of this. But this explanation, which naturally has some value, is contradicted by the fact that a mythologem [i.e., archetype] can arise anywhere, at any time, without there being the slightest possibility of any such transmission."[29]

Jung makes the same argument in the case of individuals. His most famous example, that of the "Solar Phallus Man," is of an institutionalized patient who believed that the sun had a phallus and that the movement of the sun's phallus was the cause of wind. Jung then came upon a comparable fantasy in a book describing the vision of a member of the ancient cult of Mithras. Assuming that the patient could not have known of the book, Jung forever after cited the similarity as concrete evidence of independent invention:

> The patient was a small business employee with no more than a secondary school education. He grew up in Zurich, and by no stretch of imagination can I conceive how he could have got hold of the idea of the solar phallus, of the vision moving to and fro, and of the origin of the wind. I myself, who would have been in a much better position, intellectually, to know about this singular concatenation of ideas, was entirely ignorant of it and only discovered the parallel in a book of Dieterich's which appeared in 1910, four years after my original observation (1906).[30]

More important, Jung further uses this example as evidence of the distinctively Jungian version of independent invention: through heredity rather than through experience. Independent invention as experience means that every society creates myths for itself. Independent invention as heredity means that every society as well as individual inherits myths. Of the Solar Phallus Man, Jung thus says, "This observation [of independent invention] was not an isolated case: it was manifestly not [to be sure] a question of inherited ideas, but of an inborn disposition to produce parallel thought-formations, or rather of identical psychic structures common to all men, which I later called the archetypes of the collective unconscious."[31]

For Tylor, Frazer, and Freud, the similarities among myths stem from independent invention through experience. For Tylor, everyone is born with a need to explain the world, but the explanations themselves are not innate. Where moderns invent science to explain baffling experiences, primitives invent myths. Because all primitives for Tylor experience the same perplexing phenomena, and because all primitives sensibly postulate gods to account for them, myths are bound to be similar. But each primitive society invents gods and in turn myths on its own, in response to the similar experiences of its members.

Likewise for Frazer, everyone is born with a need to eat, but the explanations of the source of food are not innate. Where moderns invent science to explain the source of food, primitives invent myths. Because all primitives experience hunger, and because all primitives postulate gods to account for the source of food, myths are bound to be similar. But each primitive society invents gods and in turn myths on its own, in response to the similar experiences of its members. Frazer provides the quintessential statement of independent invention through experience: "the resemblance which may be traced in this respect between the religions of the East and West is no more than what we commonly, though incorrectly, call a fortuitous coincidence, the effect of similar causes acting alike on the

similar constitution of the human mind in different countries and under different skies."[32]

For Freud, everyone is born with an incestuous drive that surfaces at age three
to five. Everyone experiences that drive individually. From one's forebears one
inherits only the drive itself, not their experiences of it. Because everyone in
society also experiences frustration in trying to satisfy that drive, myths are invented as one indirect, disguised, compensatory outlet for the blocked drive.
Again, similar experiences are bound to give rise to similar myths. In his classic
application of Freud's theory, Otto Rank maintains that all hero myths, if not all
myths, even have a similar plot, yet it is still one invented by each society on
its own.[33]

In contrast to Tylor, Frazer, and Freud alike, Jung contends that everyone is
born not merely with a need of some kind that the invention of myth fulfills but
with myths themselves. More precisely, we are all born with the raw material of
myths, but material already elevated to the mythic level.

For Tylor, the myth makers of each society start with the impersonal forces of
the physical world and proceed to hypothesize gods to account for those forces
and to invent myths to describe the actions of gods. For Frazer, the same is true.
For Freud, myth makers start with a child and the child's parents and proceed to
transform the child into a hero, the child's parents into royalty or nobility, and
the conflicts between children and parents into hero myths.

For Jung, myth makers start with the archetypes themselves—for example, the
archetype of the hero. The archetype does not symbolize something else in turn
but is itself the symbolized. In every society myth makers invent specific stories
that express those archetypes, but the myth makers are inventing only venues for
the manifestation of already mythic material. The figure Odysseus, for example,
gets either invented or appropriated to serve as a Greek expression of heroism.
But heroism is not itself invented, the way it is for Tylor, Frazer, and Freud. For
Jung, heroism, like divinity, constitutes so superhuman a status that humans could
not consciously have invented the idea. They must therefore have inherited it.
What are invented are the myths expressing heroism. The myth of Odysseus is
passed on from generation to generation by acculturation, but the hero archetype
that it expresses is passed on by heredity.

For Tylor, Frazer, and Freud, experience, even if it is of innate needs, provides
the impetus for the creation of myths. For Freud, for example, the experience of
one's parents' reaction to one's incestuous drives spurs the creation of myth. For
Jung, by contrast, experience provides only the occasion for the expression of
already mythic material. Myths do not transform parents into gods or heroes but
only articulate the experience of parents *as* gods or heroes—that is to say, as
archetypal figures. Archetypes *shape* experience rather than *derive* from it. For
example, the archetype of the Great Mother does not, as Freud would assume,

result from the magnification of one's own mother but, on the contrary, expresses itself through her and thereby shapes one's experience of her. The archetype forms the core of one's "mother complex." Jung's insistence on the existence of innate fantasies that are projected onto the mother rather than derived from her is much like the emphasis of the Kleinian school of psychoanalysis.[34]

THE FUNCTION OF MYTH

For Jung, myth serves many functions, not all of them psychological. But the prime function of myth is psychological: to reveal the unconscious. As already quoted, "Myths are original revelations of the preconscious psyche, involuntary statements about unconscious psychic happenings."[35] Myth does not inadvertently reveal the unconscious. Its creation is guided by the unconscious, which intentionally reveals itself. What is "involuntary" is on the part of consciousness, the recipient of the revelation. For Jung, the unconscious seeks to communicate its presence to consciousness as clearly as possible. It does not, as for Freud, speak in code to elude detection. It simply speaks its own language: "My idea is that the dream does not conceal; we simply do not understand its language. For instance, if I quote to you a Latin or a Greek passage some of you will not understand it, but that is not because the text dissimulates or conceals; it is because you do not know Greek or Latin."[36]

The analyst is bilingual and thus able to translate the language of the unconscious into the language of consciousness—to the extent, that is, that the language of the unconscious is translatable. The lay person takes the language of the unconscious either as mere gibberish or as the language of consciousness. In the case of dreams, the lay inclination is to dismiss the content as gibberish. But in the case of myths, which are the product of conscious as well as unconscious elaboration, the lay inclination is to take the content at face value. By contrast, a Jungian analyst takes the content symbolically, recognizing mythic speech as a foreign language rather than the native language.

Myth for Jung functions not merely to announce the existence of the unconscious but actually to enable humans to experience it. Myth provides not only information about the unconscious but also entrée to it: "The protean mythologem and the shimmering symbol express the processes of the psyche far more trenchantly and, in the end, far more clearly than the clearest concept; for the symbol not only conveys a visualization of the process but—and this is perhaps just as important—it also brings a re-experiencing of it, of that twilight which we can learn to understand only through inoffensive empathy, but which too much clarity only dispels."[37] The telling of myths "causes these processes to come alive again and be recollected, thereby re-establishing the connection between conscious and unconscious."[38]

For all his scorn for those psychologically benighted theorists who take the subject matter of myth to be the external world, Jung himself often waxes romantic about the external function of myth. Myth for him links the inner world to the outer one by personifying the impersonal outer world:

> Primitive man is not much interested in objective explanations of the obvious, but he has an imperative need—or, rather, his unconscious psyche has an irresistible urge—to assimilate all outer sense experiences to inner, psychic events. It is not enough for the primitive to see the sun rise and set; this external observation must at the same time be a psychic happening: the sun in its course must represent the fate of a god or hero who, in the last analysis, dwells nowhere except in the soul of man.[39]

Personifying the external world gives it meaningfulness and relevance. A personified world operates responsively, in accordance with the purposes of gods and the pleas of humans, rather than mechanically. To cite Jung's favorite example, "The Pueblo Indians believe that they are the sons of Father Sun, and this belief endows their life with a perspective (and a goal) that goes far beyond their limited existence. . . . Their plight is infinitely more satisfactory than that of a man in our own civilization who knows that he is (and will remain) nothing more than an underdog with no inner meaning to his life."[40] The function of myth here is not explanatory but existential. Myth makes humans feel at home in the world, even if it does so by explaining events in the world.

Undeniably, most modern myths for Jung are nonprojective. They presuppose the withdrawal of projections from the outer world, which is now experienced as impersonal and therefore meaningless: "We have stripped all things of their mystery and numinosity; nothing is holy any longer."[41] Put another way, modern myths for Jung are secular. They cannot do what religious myths used to do: "giving [man] the security and inner strength not to be crushed by the monstrousness of the universe."[42] Myths for moderns do not function to connect the inner world with the outer world, which is now the domain of science. Instead, modern myths function to connect—better, to reconnect—moderns to the inner world. Modern myths still provide meaningfulness, but that meaningfulness now lies entirely within humans rather than also within the world. While Jung bemoans the effect of "de-deification" on the modern experience of the world, he recognizes the necessity of the process for the development of consciousness.

Yet the characterization of the external world as in fact meaningless really holds for only the earlier Jung. Once Jung, in collaboration with the physicist Wolfgang Pauli, develops the concept of synchronicity, the world for him regains its meaningfulness even without its personality. Indeed, that meaningfulness is now inherent in the world rather than imposed on it through projection: "Synchronistic experiences serve our turn here. They point to a latent meaning which is independent of [our] consciousness."[43] Meaningfulness for later Jung stems not from the existence of god, or personality, in the world but from the symmetry between human beings and the world. Rather than alien and indifferent to humans, the world proves to be akin to them—not because gods respond to human wishes or because human wishes directly affect the world but because human thoughts correspond to the nature of the world. As Jung says of his favorite example of synchronicity, that of a resistant patient who was describing a dream about a golden scarab when a scarab beetle appeared, "at the moment my patient was telling me her dream a real 'scarab' tried to get into the room, as if it had understood that it must play its mythological role as a symbol of rebirth."[44] Here the world seemingly responds to the patient's dream, but more exactly the world merely, if fortuitously, matches the patient's dream. It is the patient's conscious attitude that is "out of sync" with the world.

Synchronicity is not itself myth. Synchronicity is the experience of the world as meaningful. Myth would be an account of that experience. Synchronicity is an acausal nexus between the inner, human world and the outer, natural one. Myth is a causal account of events in the outer world, and the cause is divine. Since, however, the payoff of myth for Jung is not an account of the world but the feeling of at-homeness in it, synchronicity offers an existential benefit comparable with that offered by myth. With the concept of synchronicity, Jung restores to the world a meaningfulness that the withdrawal of projections still demanded by Jung removes.[45]

For Jung, myth serves other functions as well. Parallels in myths to elements in a patient's dream serve heuristically to suggest archetypal interpretations of that dream: "For this reason it is particularly important for me to know as much as possible about primitive psychology, mythology, archaeology, and comparative religion, because these fields offer me invaluable analogies with which I can enrich the associations of my patients."[46]

Occasionally, Jung attributes to myth a social function: providing a guide for behavior. The lives of characters in myth become models to be emulated: "For instance, the way in which a man should behave is given by an archetype. That is why primitives tell the stories they do. . . . Our ancestors have done so and so, and so shall you. Or such and such a hero has done so and so, and this is your model. Again, in the teachings of the Catholic Church there are several thousand saints. They show us what to do, they serve as models. They have their legends and that is Christian mythology."[47]

There are theorists of myth for whom the prime function of myth is the inculcation of correct behavior. In the classic statement by the anthropologist Bronislaw Malinowski, "The myth comes into play when rite, ceremony, or a social or moral rule demands justification, warrant of antiquity, reality, and sanctity."[48] Jung's occasional social functionalism runs less counter than askew to his focus on the individual rather than the social utility of myth.

MYTHS AND DREAMS

Every theorist assumes some analogue to myth. For Tylor, the analogue is science. Myth for him is the primitive counterpart to modern scientific theory, and it is by analogy to modern scientific theory that he elucidates myth. For Frazer, the analogue is also science, though less scientific theory than applied science. Myth for him is the primitive counterpart to modern technology, and it is by analogy to modern technology that he explicates myth.

For both Freud and Jung, dream provides the analogue. Like dreams, myths arise from the unconscious, serve to restore connection to the unconscious, and must be interpreted symbolically. Says Jung, "The conclusion that the myth-makers thought in much the same way as we still think in dreams is almost self-evident."[49]

Yet Jung and Freud alike also recognize the differences between myths and dreams. Dreams are not usually projected onto the world, whereas myths are: myths purport to be about the world, not merely about oneself. Ordinarily, dreams are dreamed by individuals, whereas myths are believed by a group. Dreams are created anew by each dreamer; myths are passed on from one generation to the next. Myths no less than dreams are manifestations of the unconscious, but myths are consciously created, even if their creators are guided by the unconscious.

To be sure, Jung regularly declares that "the primitive mentality does not *invent* myths, it *experiences* them."[50] He even states that

> We can see almost daily in our patients how mythical fantasies arise: they are not thought up, but present themselves as images or chains of ideas that force their way out of the unconscious, and when they are recounted they often have the character of connected episodes resembling mythical dramas. That is how myths arise, and that is the reason why the fantasies from the unconscious have so much in common with primitive myths. [M]yth is nothing but a projection from the unconscious and not a conscious invention at all.[51]

Doubtless Jung is overstating his point. Surely he means merely that primitives, living so close to primordial unconsciousness, subject their myths to less conscious reworking than moderns do in, say, writing a novel or a screenplay. He cannot mean that primitive myths, let alone modern ones, involve no conscious reworking by their tellers.

Indeed, Jung considers myths a less pristine manifestation of the unconscious than dreams: the "manifestation" of an archetype, "as we encounter it in dreams and visions, is much more individual, less understandable, and more naïve than in myths, for example."[52] A myth as heard or read is coherent, whereas a dream as dreamed or remembered is not: "The medium in which [myths and dreams] are embedded is, in the former case [i.e., myths], an ordered and for the most part immediately understandable context, but in the latter case [i.e., dreams] a generally unintelligible, irrational, not to say delirious sequence of images which nonetheless does not lack a certain hidden coherence."[53] Consequently, the interpretation of myths requires more reconstruction than the interpretation of dreams.

There is a final difference for Jung between myths and dreams. Where many dreams for Jung come from the personal unconscious, all myths emanate from the collective unconscious. Jung even identifies archetypal dreams by their mythological content:

> The collective unconscious influences our dreams only occasionally, and whenever this happens, it produces strange and marvellous dreams remarkable for their beauty, or their demoniacal horror, or for their enigmatic wisdom—"big dreams," as certain primitives call them. . . . In many dreams and in certain psychoses we frequently come across archetypal material, i.e., ideas and associations whose exact equivalents can be found in mythology. From these parallels I have drawn the conclusion that there is a layer of the unconscious which functions in exactly the same way as the archaic psyche that produced the myths.[54]

In this respect, myths are closer to the unconscious than dreams.[55]

MYTH AS A WAY OF THINKING

While some theorists of myth are concerned with only the function or even only the origin of myth, most are concerned with the content of myth. Some theorists stress the similarities between the content of myth and the content of science. For Tylor and Frazer, for example, myth and science are explanations of the same physical events. Other theorists stress the distinctiveness of the content of myth. For the theologian Rudolf Bultmann and the philosopher Hans Jonas, for example, myth describes not the external world but the human experience of that world.[56]

A few theorists go beyond the distinctiveness of the content of myth to the distinctiveness of mythic thinking. Where for Tylor and Frazer myth involves the same processes of observation, inference, and generalization as science, for the philosopher and armchair anthropologist Lucien Lévy-Bruhl mythic thinking is the opposite of scientific thinking. It involves the projection of mystical qualities onto the world and is oblivious to contradictions.[57] For the anthropologist Claude Lévi-Strauss, by contrast, mythic thinking is as rigorous as modern scientific thinking and is preoccupied with identifying logical contradictions. Mythic thinking here, too, involves projection, but what is projected onto the world are contradictions which myth then seeks to overcome.[58]

For both Freud and Jung, mythic thinking is dream thinking, but on the nature of dream thinking they differ. For Freud, myths, like dreams, represent a compromise between primary process thinking, which operates according to the pleasure principle, and secondary process thinking, which operates according to the reality principle. Male hero myths, for example, conventionally express Oedipal wishes, but in disguised form. Manifestly, the hero is a victim, a victim of fate and of his parents; latently, the hero is the culprit. Manifestly, the hero seeks power; latently, the hero seeks sex. Manifestly, the hero is the named historical or legendary figure; latently, the hero is the myth maker or any reader grabbed by the myth. The expression of Oedipal wishes in disguised form is a compromise between the pleasure principle, which seeks to vent the wishes outright, and the reality principle, which opposes the satisfaction of them altogether. While the wishes contained in myths evince the primary process thinking of the pleasure principle, the disguise that transforms the latent wishes into the manifest myth represents censorship rather than primary process thinking. What Freud calls "dream work"—the elaborate process by which the latent meaning is converted into the manifest one—is not, then, an expression of primary process thinking but, on the contrary, the conversion of primary process thinking into secondary process thinking.[59]

For Jung, as for Freud, there are two kinds of thinking: "fantasy" thinking, which is like primary process thinking, and "directed," or "logical," thinking, which is like secondary process thinking. Where directed thinking is deliberate, organized, and purposeful, fantasy thinking is spontaneous, associative, and directionless: "What happens when we do not think directedly? Well, our thinking then lacks all leading ideas and the sense of direction emanating from them. We no longer compel our thoughts along a definite track, but let them float, sink or rise according to their specific gravity." Fantasy thinking "leads away from reality into fantasies of the past or future."[60] By contrast, directed thinking turns outward to the world. While Jung would certainly not say that fantasy thinking operates by the pleasure principle, he does say that directed thinking operates by the reality principle: "To that extent, directed or logical thinking is reality-thinking, a thinking that is adapted to reality, by means of which we imitate the successiveness of objectively real things, so that the images inside our mind follow one another in the same strictly causal sequence as the events taking place outside it. We also call this 'thinking with directed attention.'"[61]

For Jung, as for Freud, mythic thinking is fantasy thinking. But where for Freud myths, like most dreams, represent a compromise between primary and secondary process thinking because they represent a compromise between the pleasure principle and the reality principle, for Jung myths and dreams are the outright expression of fantasy thinking—the rough equivalent of primary process thinking. When, as noted, Jung declares that "myth is nothing but a projection from the unconscious and not a conscious invention at all," he is insisting that myth is an untampered manifestation of fantasy thinking.[62] Rather than a defense against the naked expression of the unconscious, as for Freud, myth for Jung *is* the naked expression of the unconscious. Myths and dreams must still be interpreted, but because they are like hieroglyphics rather than because they are like a secret code. They await, even beckon, interpretation rather than stymie it. For Freud, the manifest level of a myth or a dream hides, if also reveals, the latent level, and the process of interpretation is the use of the manifest level to uncover the latent one masked by it. For Jung, the latent level *is* manifest—for those who have ears to hear. Consequently, myths and dreams for Jung evince a distinctive way of thinking, whereas myths and dreams for Freud evince a distinctive way of masking a distinctive way of thinking.

Freud and Jung agree that myths go beyond dreams to project fantasy thinking onto the world. Myths transform the outer world into an extension of the inner one. Mythic thinking is thus not merely a way of thinking but a way of thinking about the world—and in turn a way of experiencing the world: "We move in a world of fantasies which, untroubled by the outward course of things, well up from an inner source to produce an ever-changing succession of plastic or phantasmal forms. . . . Everything was conceived anthropomorphically or theriomorphically, in the likeness of man or beast. . . . Thus there arose a picture of the universe which was completely removed from reality, but which corresponded exactly to man's subjective fantasies."[63] More than a story, myth becomes a worldview.

Insofar as Jung parallels myths with fantasies, myths would hardly be limited to "primitives." Yet insofar as Jung contrasts fantasy thinking to directed thinking, myths would seem to be largely primitive. For primitives are ruled entirely by fantasy thinking. Although scarcely absent among moderns, fantasy thinking has been supplemented and considerably supplanted by directed thinking, which is to be found above all in modern science. At the least, then, one would expect moderns to have far fewer myths than primitives. Certainly Jung accepts the conventional assumption of his day, summed up in Ernst Haeckel's Law of Recapitulation, that the biological development of the individual (ontogeny) duplicates that of the species (phylogeny): "The supposition that there may also be in psychology a correspondence between ontogenesis and phylogenesis therefore seems justified."[64] The child is therefore the counterpart to the primitive, and vice versa.

The adult is the counterpart to the modern and vice versa. Just as the child is governed wholly by fantasy thinking and only the adult guided substantially by directed thinking, so the primitive is governed wholly by fantasy thinking and only the modern guided significantly by directed thinking. Myths would therefore seem to be a predominantly primitive phenomenon. As Jung says, "These considerations tempt us to draw a parallel between the mythological thinking of ancient man and the similar thinking found in children, primitives, and in dreams."[65] Yet Jung argues forcefully that moderns as well as primitives have and even must have myths, though perhaps not to the same degree.

KINDS OF MYTHS

Jung's key essay on myth is "The Psychology of the Child Archetype," where he uses myths of the child to set forth his overall theory of myth. Typically presenting his theory by distinguishing it from Freud's, Jung contends that the figure of the child in mythology symbolizes not, as for Freud, the actual child but the archetypal child. Further, Jung contends that the figure of the child points not merely back to childhood, as for Freud, but also on to adulthood. Because myths for Freud serve to fulfill the lingering childhood wishes of neurotic adults, they perpetuate a childhood state. Because myths for Jung serve to spur normal adults to recognize their unconscious and to integrate it with ego consciousness, they advance rather than retard psychological growth. As he says of myths of the child, "One of the essential features of the child motif is its futurity. The child is potential future. . . . It is therefore not surprising that so many of the mythological saviours are child gods. This agrees exactly with our experience of the psychology of the individual, which shows that the 'child' paves the way for a future change of personality. In the individuation process, it anticipates the figure that comes from the synthesis of conscious and unconscious elements in the personality."[66]

The child somehow symbolizes a specific archetype on the one hand and, even more, the whole personality in its development from primordial unconscious to ego consciousness to self on the other. Thus the mythic child is less human than divine. While remaining literally a child, the mythic child symbolizes the lifelong process of psychological maturation. Child myths depict children as both youngsters and future adults. The child is truly father to the man.

By definition, theories of myth purport to cover all kinds of myths. In practice, few do. At the least, every theory is best suited to a particular kind of myth. The subject matter determines the suitability. For example, Frazer's theory, which assumes the symbolic subject matter of the chief myths to be the course of vegetation, best fits myths that literally describe the death and rebirth of gods. Tylor's wider-ranging theory, according to which the subject matter of myth is the cause of any event in the physical world, still fits only myths that literally describe the decisions of gods to bring about events in the physical world. The theory of the historian of religions Mircea Eliade, for whom the subject matter of myth is the legacy of the past actions of gods or heroes, fits only myths about the past, and really only myths about the introduction in the hoary past of cultural and natural phenomena that still exist today—for example, marriage and thunder.[67]

Freudian and Jungian theories best fit hero myths, for the subject matter of myth for both is striving and accomplishment. For both, heroism can evince itself at varying stages of psychological development. For Freudians, the hero can, like Oedipus, be the stereotypical rebel against the tyrannical father. Here the hero symbolizes the adult still neurotically tied to the Oedipal stage of development.[68] But the Freudian hero can also, like Moses vis-à-vis God, be the heir of the father, identifying himself with the father and thereby forging psychological maturity.[69] Alternatively, myths for Freudians can go back to pre-Oedipal states. The Freudian hero can even be the creator god himself, thereby accomplishing the same feat as the female: giving birth.[70]

Hero myths for Jungians begin not even with creation but with the state prior to creation, and they carry the process of psychological development all the way forward from the prenatal state to the state beyond the development of ego consciousness, which is the classic Freudian end. In Jungian terms, myths deal with the second, distinctively Jungian half of life as well as with the first, Freudian half. The key psychological feat for Freudians is the establishment of independence from one's parents. Jungians, too, seek to liberate their patients from their parents, but for them the key feat of the first half of life is the establishment of a measure of independence from the unconscious. The feat of the second half is, almost paradoxically, the restoration of contact with the unconscious. In Freudian myths the hero, who can be divine or human, is the son who either defeats his father or, better, reconciles himself with his father. In Jungian myths the hero, who can similarly be divine or human, is ego consciousness, which in the first half of life must defeat the unconscious out of which it has emerged and which in the second half of life must return to the unconscious and reconcile itself with it. The classic Jungian hero, no less than the classic Freudian one, is male, but his conventional nemesis is the mother rather than the father. The subject matter of hero myths for Jungians is realms of the mind rather than members of the family, but relations between those realms are mythically depicted in familial terms: ego consciousness is the son and the unconscious the Great Mother, herself most often depicted as a dragon. Like Freudians, Jungians subsume creation myths under hero myths by making creation itself a heroic act, which symbolizes the birth not of the external world but of ego consciousness: "Now we know that cosmogonic myths are, at bottom, symbols for the coming of consciousness."[71]

Myths of the child, of the hero, and of creation are group myths, as myths for Jung have traditionally been. But the decline of religion has obliged moderns to seek their own, private myths. Jung had the creativity to forge—or to find—his own myth, and he announces at the outset of his autobiography, *Memories, Dreams, Reflections,* that he will proceed to "tell my personal myth,"[72] which refers either to the course of his whole life or, more narrowly, to his speculations about life after death. Far from an inferior alternative to a group myth, a personal myth for Jung is the ideal, for it alone is geared to the uniqueness of one's psyche. A personal myth seeks to nurture those particular aspects of one's personality that have been neglected. At times, Jung even defines myth as personal: "Myth is more individual and expresses life more precisely than does science. Science works with concepts of averages which are far too general to do justice to the subjective variety of an individual life."[73] Jung's emphasis here on the individuality of myths "balances"—to use the prized Jungian epithet—his emphasis elsewhere on the similarity, even identity, of myths worldwide.

MYTHS AND PRIMITIVES

For Jung, myths serve primarily to open adults up to their unconscious, from which, in the course of growing up, they have ineluctably become severed. Myths "compensate or correct, in a meaningful manner, the inevitable one-sidednesses and extravagances of the conscious mind."[74] But for Jung it is only the ego consciousness of moderns that is sufficiently developed to be severed from the unconscious. As he says, "Since the differentiated consciousness of civilized man has been granted an effective instrument for the practical realization of its contents through the dynamics of his will, there is all the more danger, the more he trains his will, of his getting lost in one-sidedness and deviating further and further from the laws and roots of his being."[75] It is therefore hard to see how myths "compensate" primitives, who for Jung hover so close to unconsciousness that their ego consciousness has barely begun to develop: "Primitive mentality differs from the civilized chiefly in that the conscious mind is far less developed in scope and intensity. Functions such as thinking, willing, etc. are not yet differentiated; they are pre-conscious, and in the case of thinking, for instance, this shows itself in the circumstances that the primitive does not think *consciously,* but that thoughts appear. . . . Moreover, he is incapable of any conscious effort of will."[76] The primitive mind for Jung is no less one-sided than the modern one, but it is one-sidedly unconscious rather than, like the modern one, one-sidedly conscious.

Nevertheless, Jung considers myths to be as indispensable for primitives as for moderns. Indeed, he is referring to primitives, if not to them alone, when, as quoted, he states that "myths are original revelations of the preconscious psyche, involuntary statements about unconscious psychic happenings, and anything but allegories of physical processes."[77] Primitives may live far closer to the unconscious than moderns do, but the primitive unconscious is still unconscious and still seeks to reveal itself to primitives. Just as primitives as well as moderns have dreams, so primitives as well as moderns have myths. Surely Jung's linkage of mythic thinking to fantasy thinking to children's thinking to primitive thinking dictates that primitives will have at least as many myths as moderns, and may well rely on them even more.

Jung assumes that primitives interpret their myths literally, as referring to the outer world. But primitive myths still function to reveal to primitives their own inner world. Their myths merely do so circuitously, via projection onto the outer world: "All the mythologized processes of nature, such as summer and winter, the phases of the moon, the rainy seasons, and so forth, are in no sense allegories of these objective [i.e., external] occurrences; rather they are symbolic expressions of the inner, unconscious drama of the psyche which becomes accessible to man's consciousness by way of projection—that is, mirrored in the events of nature."[78]

Despite Jung's own association of mythic with childish with primitive, he castigates Freudians for making the same associations: "The first attempts at myth-making can, of course, be observed in children, whose games of make-believe often contain historical echoes. But one must certainly put a large question-mark after the [Freudian] assertion that myths spring from the 'infantile' psychic life of the race. . . . [T]he myth-making and myth-inhabiting man was a grown reality and not a four-year-old child. Myth is certainly not an infantile phantasm, but one of the most important requisites of primitive life."[79] Since Jung's own linkage of myths to children to primitives does not denigrate myths, the supposed Freudian denigration must stem from more than the linkage.

MYTHS AND MODERNS

Moderns for Jung have largely withdrawn their forebears' projections from the external world, which they therefore both experience and explain naturally rather than supernaturally. In "de-deifying" the world, moderns have demythicized it: "Only in the following centuries, with the growth of natural science, was the projection withdrawn from matter and entirely abolished together with the psyche. . . . Nobody, it is true, any longer endows matter with mythological properties."[80] Moderns still project, but their projections are chiefly onto other human beings: "Projection is now confined to personal and social relationships."[81]

Yet Jung hardly denies the continued existence of myths. Myths in modernity can take several forms. Minimally, there is the invocation of traditional myths by artists: "Dante decks out his experience in all the imagery of heaven, purgatory, and hell; Goethe brings in the Blocksberg and the Greek underworld; Wagner needs the whole corpus of Nordic myth, including the Parsifal saga; Nietzsche resorts to the hieratic style of the bard and legendary seer; Blake presses into his service the phantasmagoric world of India, the Old Testament, and the Apocalypse."[82] Artists often update traditional myths by recasting them in modern garb: "Mythological motifs frequently appear, but clothed in modern dress; for instance, instead of the eagle of Zeus, or the great roc, there is an airplane; the fight with the dragon is a railway smash; the dragon-slaying hero is an operatic tenor; the Earth Mother is a stout lady selling vegetables; the Pluto who abducts Persephone is a reckless chauffeur, and so on."[83]

More significant for Jung has been the outright revival of traditional myth, of which his grandest example is the revival of the worship of Wotan in twentieth-century Germany: "But what is more than curious—indeed, piquant to a degree—is that an ancient god of storm and frenzy, the long quiescent Wotan, should awake, like an extinct volcano, to new activity, in a civilized country that had long been supposed to have outgrown the Middle Ages."[84] In parts of Germany Wotan was taken as no mere literary metaphor but a real god, worshiped with the slaughtering of sheep. Here myth is lived out, not merely interpreted. While Wotan was not considered a weather god, he was considered the divine force behind Germany's destiny.

Still more significant for Jung has been the creation of new, distinctively secular myths, of which his best example is the belief in flying saucers. Because flying saucers are a technologically advanced phenomenon, they fit the modern scientific self-image and make for an ideal kind of modern myth: "It is characteristic of our time that the archetype . . . should now take the form of an object, a technological construction, in order to avoid the odiousness of mythological personification. Anything that looks technological goes down without difficulty with modern man."[85] Even though the belief in flying saucers is not tied to a story, the belief still qualifies as a myth, for it is a belief in something superhuman in the external world, and it is a widely shared belief.

What interests Jung about the belief in flying saucers is what interests him about myths generally: the psychology of their adherents. At the same time Jung appreciates that the myth of flying saucers, like earlier myths, serves not only psychological needs but also existential ones. The myth personifies the external world and thereby makes it akin to the human one. About the possible reality of flying saucers, Jung remains typically open-minded.[86] The reality of them would not dissolve the psychology of them, for they already belong to what he calls "the reality of the psyche." The outer reality of them would constitute synchronicity.

For some theorists, such as Tylor and Frazer, myth is an exclusively primitive phenomenon. Whenever found among moderns, it is either a mere "survival" or an atavism. For other theorists, such as Rudolf Bultmann, myth can be made acceptable to moderns. For still other theorists, notably Eliade and Campbell, myth is panhuman. While less insistent on this point than Eliade or Campbell, Jung certainly considers myth to be a continuing phenomenon, even if not quite a panhuman one: "Has mankind ever really got away from myths? . . . One could almost say that if all the world's traditions were cut off at a single blow, the whole of mythology and the whole history of religion would start all over again with the next generation. Only a very few individuals succeed in throwing off mythology in epochs of exceptional intellectual exuberance—the masses never."[87]

EARLIER PSYCHOLOGICAL INTERPRETATIONS OF MYTH

For Jung, the recognition of the psychological nature of myth comes gradually. The stages are not simply primitive and modern. While Jung takes for granted that primitives are oblivious to the psychological meaning of their myths, he points to a "philosophical interpretation of myths . . . already grown up among the Stoics, which today we should not hesitate to describe as psychological."[88] Jung sees the continuation of that tradition in the Church Fathers and down into the medieval and Renaissance periods. The tradition that he traces from Gnosticism to alchemy to modern science involves ever more psychological self-consciousness, though he fluctuates in the degree of self-consciousness he finds. At his most charitable, he is prepared to say that

> Since all cognition is akin to recognition, it should not come as a surprise to find that what I have described as a gradual process of development had already been anticipated, and more or less prefigured, at the beginning of our era. . . . The alchemists . . . in their own way knew more about the nature of the individuation process than we moderns do. . . . The same knowledge, formulated differently to suit the age they lived in, was possessed by the Gnostics. The idea of an unconscious was not unknown to them.[89]

More typically, Jung traces a sharp progression in self-consciousness from the Gnostics to, especially, the later alchemists: "The older alchemists were still so unconscious of the psychological implications of the opus that they understood their own symbols as mere allegories—or semiotically—as secret names for chemical combinations, thus stripping mythology, of which they made such copious use, of its true meaning and using only its terminology. Later this was to change, and already in the fourteenth century it began to dawn on them that the lapis was more than a chemical compound."[90]

MYTH AND RELIGION

There are theorists of myth who subsume myth under religion. For Tylor and Frazer, for example, all myths are religious myths. For them, a secular myth would be a contradiction in terms. Other theorists allow for secular as well as religious myths. For Eliade, for example, myths prior to modernity are religious myths; modern myths are secular ones. Jung is here like Eliade.

For Jung, myth and religion have traditionally worked in tandem. Religion has preserved myth, and myth has sustained religion. The heart of religion for Jung is neither belief nor practice but experience, and myth provides the best entrée to the experience of God, which means to the unconscious. Jung thus praises early Christianity for both adopting and adapting various pre-Christian myths: "The fact that the myth [of the phoenix] was assimilated into Christianity by interpretation is proof, first of all, of the myth's vitality; but it also proves the vitality of Christianity, which was able to interpret and assimilate so many myths." A religion that fails to reinterpret its myths is dead. The "spiritual vitality" of a religion "depends on the continuity of myth, and this can be preserved only if each age translates the myth into its own language and makes it an essential content of its view of the world."[91]

Unlike early Christianity, modern Christianity, according to Jung, has failed to update its myths. That failure is an aspect of its overall failure to reinvigorate itself. Sometimes Jung says that modern Christianity has gone astray by severing belief from experience and trying in vain to rely on sheer belief. Jung's objection here is twofold: that belief without experience is empty, and that the belief is often incompatible with modern scientific and historical knowledge. Other times Jung says that modern Christianity has gone awry in seeking to meet the challenge of modernity by turning belief into faith severed from knowledge. Jung's objection here is that even faith requires experience to sustain itself. As Jung sums up his criticisms of both options:

> The Churches stand for traditional and collective convictions which in the case of many of their adherents are no longer based on their own inner experience but on *unreflecting belief,* which is notoriously apt to disappear as soon as one begins thinking about it. The content of belief then comes into collision with knowledge, and it often turns out that the irrationality of the former is no match for the ratiocinations of the latter. Belief is no adequate substitute for inner experience, and where this is absent even a strong faith which came miraculously as a gift of grace may depart equally miraculously.[92]

While these particular criticisms do not involve myth, still other times Jung says that modern Christianity has erred in its attempt to update itself by *eliminating* myth—as if myth were a gangrenous limb that must be amputated to save the patient. Jung is here referring to Bultmann's "demythologization" of the New Testament. Jung's first objection is that the supposed incompatibility of myth with modern knowledge stems from a false, literal interpretation of myth: "Theology [wrongly] rejects any tendency to take the assertions of its earliest records as written myths and, accordingly, to understand them symbolically."[93] Jung's second objection is that myth is indispensable to experience and thereby to religion: "Indeed, it is the theologians themselves who have recently made the attempt—

no doubt as a concession to "knowledge"—to "demythologize" the object of their faith while drawing the line [between myth and religion] quite arbitrarily at the crucial points. But to the critical intellect it is only too obvious that myth is an integral component of all religions and therefore cannot be excluded from the assertions of faith without injuring them."[94] Here Christianity has sought to overcome the opposition between faith and modern knowledge by discarding belief at odds with knowledge. But in eliminating myth, it has eliminated experience as well.

At yet other times Jung says that modern Christianity has rightly turned to myth to resurrect itself but has still failed to reinterpret myth symbolically and thereby make it palatable to moderns: "[R]eligions have long turned to myths for help. . . . But you cannot, artificially and with an effort of will, believe the statements of myth if you have not previously been gripped by them. If you are honest, you will doubt the truth of the myth because our present-day consciousness has no means of understanding it. Historical and scientific criteria do not lend themselves to a recognition of mythological truth; it can be grasped only by the intuitions of faith or by psychology."[95]

Ironically, Bultmann, despite the misleading term "demythologization," strives to do the same as Jung: not to eliminate myth from the New Testament but, on the contrary, to reinterpret myth symbolically in order to make it acceptable to moderns. And Bultmann, also like Jung, contends that the true meaning of the New Testament has always been symbolic, though for Bultmann myth read symbolically describes the human condition rather than, as for Jung, the human mind.

By Christian mythology, Jung means the life of Christ. Read literally, the Gospels are incompatible with both history and science. But if, says Jung, "the statement that Christ rose from the dead is to be understood not literally but symbolically, then it is capable of various interpretations that do not conflict with knowledge and do not impair the meaning of the statement."[96] Read psychologically, the life of Christ becomes a symbol of the archetypal journey of the hero from primordial unconsciousness (birth) to ego consciousness (adulthood) to return to the unconscious (crucifixion) to reemergence from it to form the self (resurrection). Understood symbolically, Christ serves as a model for Christians seeking to cultivate their relation to the self. Without denying the historicity of Christ, Jung maintains that Christ can be inspirational even as a mythical hero. Indeed, for Jung the prime appeal of Christ's life has always been mythical, which for Jung means psychological:

> Christ lived a concrete, personal, and unique life which, in all essential features, had at the same time an archetypal character. This character can be recognized from the numerous connections of the biographical details with worldwide myth-motifs. . . . The life of Christ is no exception in that not a few of the great figures of history have

realized, more or less clearly, the archetype of the hero's life with its characteristic changes of fortune. . . . Since the life of Christ is archetypal to a high degree, it represents to just that degree the life of the archetype. But since the archetype is the unconscious precondition of every human life, its life, when revealed, also reveals the hidden, unconscious ground-life of every individual.[97]

Jung argues, further, that the Gospels themselves present a combined mythical and historical figure: "In the gospels themselves factual reports, legends, and myths are woven into a whole. This is precisely what constitutes the meaning of the gospels, and they would immediately lose their character of wholeness if one tried to separate the individual from the archetypal with a critical scalpel."[98] Just like Bultmann, to whom he is in fact so close, Jung thus claims to be explicating the symbolic meaning intended by the Gospels all along. For both Jung and Bultmann, the obstacles that modernity poses to a literal rendition of Christ's life offer an opportunity to make clear for the first time the meaning intended from the outset. A virtue is truly made out of a necessity.

Jung never faults Christian mythology itself for its outdatedness, only its interpreters: "Our myth has become mute, and gives no answers. The fault lies not in it as it is set down in the Scriptures, but solely in us, who have not developed it further, who, rather, have suppressed any such attempts."[99] Jung does lambaste mainstream Christianity for its one-sidedness—above all, for its failure to give sufficient credence to evil: "The old question posed by the Gnostics, 'Whence comes evil?' has been given no answer by the Christian world."[100] But this limitation is a separate issue. Even if one-sided, Christian mythology can still be interpreted anew by each generation. In fact, Jung hopes that modern Christians will not only psychologize their mythology but also broaden it to include evil, as epitomized by nuclear war.

Yet for all Jung's efforts to make Christianity acceptable to moderns by psychologizing it, he recognizes that religion has simply ceased to be an option for many moderns, surely including to some degree Jung himself.[101] Nonreligious moderns must either adopt secular myths such as that of flying saucers or else forge their own, personal myths, as Jung was able to do. Or they must find a substitute for myth such as art or dreams.

TERMS

Jung uses various terms which must be distinguished: instinct, archetype, image, symbol, sign, allegory, "mythological motif," "mythologem," and myth. Instincts and archetypes are related but distinct. An instinct is a reflex action. An archetype is the emotional and intellectual significance of that action: "What we properly call instincts are physiological urges, and are perceived by the senses. But at the same time, they also manifest themselves in fantasies and often reveal their presence only by symbolic images. These manifestations are what I call the archetypes. . . . The unconscious . . . seems to be guided chiefly by instinctive trends, represented by corresponding thought forms—that is, by the archetypes."[102] Shutting one's eyes upon looking at the sun is clearly instinctual. Even feeling terrified or fascinated by the sight is still instinctual. By contrast, experiencing the sun as a god is archetypal. An archetypal experience is not any emotional event but only an overwhelming one, the extraordinariness of which stems exactly from the power of the archetype encountered through projection. Many, though certainly not all, phenomena experienced archetypally are experienced as gods. The key evidence of the modern withdrawal of projections from the external world is the experience of the world as natural rather than divine.

Despite Jung's somewhat misleading synonym "primordial images," archetypes are not themselves pictures but rather the inclination to form them in typical ways. Symbols are the actual pictures formed. Symbols are the means by which archetypes, themselves unconscious, communicate to consciousness. Each archetype requires an infinite number of symbols—as many symbols as there are dimensions of the archetype. Archetypes are transmitted by heredity; symbols, by acculturation. Archetypes are the same universally; symbols vary from culture to culture:

> Again and again I encounter the mistaken notion that an archetype is determined in regard to its content, in other words that it is a kind of unconscious idea. . . . It is necessary to point out once more that archetypes are not determined as regards their content, but only as regards their form and then only to a very limited degree. . . . Its form . . . might perhaps be compared to the axial system of a crystal, which, as it were, preforms the crystalline structure in the mother liquid, although it has no material existence of its own. This first appears according to the specific way in which the ions and molecules aggregate. The archetype in itself is empty and purely formal, nothing but a *facultas praeformandi,* a possibility of representation which is given *a priori.* The [symbolic] representations themselves are not inherited, only the forms.[103]

For example, a specific savior like Buddha would be a symbol. The archetype manifested through the Buddha would be the category *saviors.* Through the Buddha, Buddhists would encounter those aspects of the savior archetype captured by the symbol. Other saviors like Jesus would capture other aspects of the savior archetype. Any symbol, however rich, is capable of capturing only a limited number of aspects of its archetype. Which symbol is employed by the archetype depends on which aspects of the archetype the subject, whether individual or group, needs to cultivate.

An archetype for Jung is not the symbol of something else but the symbolized itself. The archetype of the child, for example, refers not to any actual children but to itself. The archetype is irreducible. An actual child can symbolize the child archetype but not vice versa:

> It may not be superfluous to point out that lay prejudice is always inclined to identify the child motif [i.e., archetype] with the concrete experience "child," as though the real child were the cause and pre-condition of the existence of the child motif. In psychological reality, however, the empirical idea "child" is only the means (and not the only one) by which to express a psychic fact that cannot be formulated more exactly. Hence by the same token the mythological idea of the child is emphatically not a copy of the empirical child but a *symbol* clearly recognizable as such: it is a wonder-child, a divine child, begotten, born, and brought up in quite extraordinary circumstances, and not—this is the point—a human child.[104]

Identifying archetypes is not easy. First, the number of archetypes is unlimited: "There are as many archetypes as there are typical situations in life."[105] Second, archetypes can take the most disparate of forms: natural objects like the moon and fire, artifacts like rings and weapons, human beings like mothers and children, superhuman figures like gods and witches, legendary figures like heroes and monsters, abstractions like circles and squares, ideas like the anima and the self, and events like birth and death. Third, the same entity can be both a symbol and an archetype. For example, Zeus may be a clear-cut symbol, but sky gods can be both an archetype and a set of symbols in turn of the god archetype, which itself can be both an archetype and a set of symbols of the self archetype.

Jung vigorously distinguishes symbols from mere "signs" or "allegories"—terms he uses interchangeably. A sign or allegory has only a single meaning. A symbol has multiple meanings. The meaning of a sign or allegory is denotative. The meaning of a symbol is connotative. The meaning of a sign or allegory is conscious. The deepest meaning of a symbol is unconscious. A sign or allegory is consciously chosen to convey its meaning. A symbol may arise spontaneously, as in dreams, and even a conscious choice is directed by the unconscious. A sign or allegory conveys fully the signified or allegorized, so that to know the meaning of a sign or allegory is to know the complete meaning of the signified or allegorized. A symbol conveys only a portion of what it symbolizes, so that to know the meaning of a symbol is to gain only a glimpse of the symbolized.

Jung never makes clear what accounts for the limitations of symbols. Seemingly, the finiteness of any symbol, however rich, restricts the number of aspects of an archetype it can convey. For example, Homer's Helen can convey only the erotic and seductive aspects of the anima archetype; the Virgin Mary, only the motherly, compassionate ones. Alternatively, the limits may lie in the ability of human beings to decipher the array of meanings of any symbol. Perhaps for Jung both limitations hold.

Presumably, the Freudian unconscious expresses itself through signs and allegories because its contents were originally conscious and are therefore in principle wholly retrievable. But when Jung says that "an allegory is a paraphrase of a conscious content, whereas a symbol is the best possible expression for an unconscious content whose nature can only be guessed, because it is still unknown," he is seemingly excluding Freudian meanings as allegories and is confining allegories to the signified of, say, nature mythology.[106] As he states, "Symbols are not signs or allegories for something known; they seek rather to express something that is little known or completely unknown."[107] But by "unknown" Jung doubtless means forever, not just presently, unknown. Therefore only the Jungian unconscious expresses itself through symbols because only its contents are inherently unconscious and so cannot be directly accessed by conscious effort.

Jung also calls archetypes "mythological motifs" and "mythologems." But sometimes he applies these terms to the symbols expressing archetypes. Still other times he applies the terms neither to archetypes nor to symbols but to parts of myths—for example, to the virgin birth portion of the myth of Jesus. The terms never refer to whole myths. As he says, "These products [i.e., mythologems] are never (or at least very seldom) myths with a definite form, but rather mythological components."[108]

Myths are more than archetypes. They are stories which, read symbolically, contain archetypes. Archetypes are "mythological components which, because of their typical nature, we can call 'motifs,' 'primordial images,' types or—as I have named them—*archetypes*."[109] An archetype is a motif found not merely within one myth but within many myths. A motif found in only one myth would not qualify as an archetype. Any myth ordinarily contains multiple archetypes, though one archetype is often dominant. The plot of myth is not only the manifestation of one or more archetypes but also the development of them and their interaction. On the literal level the subject of a myth is a particular like Zeus. On the symbolic level the subject is the archetype symbolized by Zeus—for example, sky gods. The activities of Zeus symbolize the development of the archetype of the sky god and its relationship to other archetypes, as symbolized by Hera, Prometheus, and other gods.

DEVELOPMENTS IN JUNGIAN THEORY

The most influential Jungian theorists of myth after the master himself have been Erich Neumann (1905–1960), Marie-Louise von Franz (1915–1998), and James Hillman (1926–). One might consider adding Joseph Campbell (1904–1987), the greatest popularizer of myth of this century, but Campbell is too eclectic to qualify as a full-fledged Jungian. Neumann systematizes the developmental, or evolutionary, aspect of Jungian theory. Jung himself certainly correlates myths with stages of psychological development, but Neumann works out the stages, beginning with the "uroboric" state of sheer unconsciousness and proceeding to the incipient emergence of the ego out of the unconscious, the development of an independent ego consciousness, and the eventual return of the ego to the unconscious to create the self. Like Jung, Neumann characterizes the course of psychological development as one of continuing heroism. Neumann concentrates on heroism in the first half of life, both in *The Origins and History of Consciousness* (1949, trans. 1954) and even more in *The Great Mother* (1955), which indeed focuses on primordial unconsciousness itself as the matrix of all subsequent development. Neumann's emphasis on heroism in the first half of life complements Campbell's devotion to heroism in the second half in *The Hero with a Thousand Faces* (1949, 2d ed. 1968).

Von Franz is best known for her many books on fairy tales—among them *An Introduction to the Psychology [or Interpretation] of Fairy Tales* (1970, rev. 1996), *A Psychological Interpretation of "The Golden Ass" of Apuleius* (1970, rev. 1980), *Problems of the Feminine in Fairytales* (1972), *Shadow and Evil in Fairy Tales* (1974, rev. 1995), *Individuation in Fairy Tales* (1977, rev. 1990), and *The Psychological Meaning of Redemption in Fairytales* (1980). But she is also the author of the fullest Jungian book on creation myths, *Patterns of Creativity Mirrored in Creation Myths* (1972, rev. 1995). For von Franz, creation myths symbolize the same process of the emergence and development of the ego out of the primordial unconscious as hero myths of the first half of life do for Neumann. But for her, creation myths are far more abstract and impersonal than hero myths since their literal subject matter is the birth of the whole world rather than of a single figure within it. No less than Neumann does von Franz deem the act of creation heroic, but she focuses on myths of creation of the cosmos itself. Rather than classifying stages in the process of creation like Neumann, she classifies means of creation—for example, creation by two creators instead of one. Like Neumann, von Franz stresses the difficulty of creation, which likewise represents the ego's difficulty in breaking free of the unconscious. For her, myths that present creation as a long and arduous effort better fit the development of the psyche than those that depict it as a quick, effortless act.

By far the most radical innovation in the Jungian theory of myth has been the development of "archetypal" psychology, which in fact considers itself post-Jungian. The chief figure in this movement is Hillman, whose main theoretical works include *The Myth of Analysis* (1972), *Loose Ends* (1975), *Re-Visioning Psychology* (1975), *The Dream and the Underworld* (1979), *Puer Papers* (ed. 1979), *Archetypal Psychology* (1983), and (with Karl Kerényi) *Oedipus Variations* (1991). Another important figure in the movement is David Miller, perhaps best known for *The New Polytheism* (1979). Archetypal psychology faults classical Jungian psychology on multiple grounds. By emphasizing the compensatory, therapeutic message of mythology, classical Jungian psychology purportedly reduces mythology to psychology and gods to concepts. In espousing a unified self (or "Self") as the ideal psychological authority, Jungian psychology supposedly projects onto psychology a Western, specifically monotheistic, more specifically Christian, even more specifically Protestant, outlook. The Western emphasis on progress is purportedly reflected in the primacy Jungian psychology accords both hero myths and the ego, even in the ego's encounter with the unconscious: the encounter is intended to abet development. Finally, Jungian psychology is berated for placing archetypes in an unknowable realm distinct from the knowable realm of symbols.

As a corrective, Hillman and his followers advocate that psychology be viewed as irreducibly mythological. Myth is still to be interpreted psychologically, but psychology is itself to be interpreted mythologically. One grasps the psychological meaning of the myth of Saturn by imagining oneself to be the figure Saturn, not by translating Saturn's plight into clinical terms like depression. Moreover, the depressed Saturn represents a legitimate aspect of one's personality. Each god deserves its due. The psychological ideal should be pluralistic rather than monolithic—in mythological terms, polytheistic rather than monotheistic. Hillman takes his mythic cues from the Greeks rather than from the Bible, however simplistic his equation of Greece with polytheism and of the Bible with monotheism may be. Insisting that archetypes are to be found *in* symbols rather than outside them, Hillman espouses a relation to the gods in themselves and not to something beyond them. The ego becomes but one more archetype with its attendant kind of god, and it is the "soul" rather than the ego that experiences the archetypes through myths. Myth serves to open one up to the soul's own depths. The payoff is aesthetic rather than moral: one gains a sense of wonder and contemplation, not a guide to living. The most apposite myths for the archetypal school are those of the playful puer and of the receptive anima rather than, as for classical Jungians, those of the striving hero and of the fully integrated wise old man.

VII • ADONIS: A GREEK ETERNAL CHILD

THE MYTH OF ADONIS, the main sources for which are Apollo-dorus and Ovid, describes the miraculous birth of a preternaturally beau-tiful human out of a tree, the fighting over him by goddesses, and his annual sojourn in Hades with one of those goddesses.[1] The myth seems as far removed from the everyday world as a myth can be. The events it narrates are supernatural, and they take place in either the woods or the underworld, not in any society. Yet I suggest that, despite appearances, the myth in fact concerns neither the physical nor the supernatural world but the social one. The characters are really humans, not gods, and they live *in* society, not outside it. The myth, I suggest, is a political myth: it dramatizes the prerequisites for membership in the polis. But it does so negatively, by presenting the life of one least equipped for the responsibility entailed by citizenship. One learns what to do by seeing a model of what not to do. Adonis is illsuited for life in the polis because he is illsuited for its cornerstone: the family. His life involves the severest violations of family life: incest, murder, license, possessiveness, celibacy, and childlessness.

FRAZER'S ADONIS

Of all the interpretations of the myth of Adonis, the most popular remains that of James Frazer in *The Golden Bough* (hereafter *GB*).[2] Frazer assumes that the myth of Adonis is not about gods or even about human beings but about forces of nature, which the gods personify. Adonis is only a symbol of vegetation. In that case his life can scarcely constitute a model, positive or negative, for others. His behavior is mechanical rather than deliberate. The myth cannot teach a lesson, negative or positive, unless Adonis has behaved improperly or properly, which he can have done only if he has chosen his behavior, in which case he must have a mind and so be a personality, divine or human. Furthermore, Frazer views myth as the primitive counterpart to modern science. In that case myth only explains, not evaluates, events. Even if, then, Frazer deemed human beings rather than the physical world the true subject of myth, myth would still yield no norms. It would merely explain, not assess, human behavior. One would still have to venture outside myth to secure political values. In short, for Frazer the myth of Adonis is hopelessly apolitical.

Frazer places Adonis in all three of his prescientific stages of culture: those of magic, religion, and magic and religion combined. Though to differing degrees, in all three stages Adonis for Frazer is a mere personification of vegetation and not a personality. Vegetation does not symbolize Adonis; Adonis symbolizes vegetation. Frazer locates the potted gardens of Adonis, a feature of the cult, in his first, magical stage. Since in this stage humans believe that impersonal forces rather than personalities cause events in the physical world, Adonis here cannot be a personality. Greeks would be planting seeds in earth-filled pots not to persuade a divine personality to grant growth but, by the magical Law of Imitation, to force the impersonal earth itself to grow: "For ignorant people suppose that by mimicking the effect which they desire to produce they actually help to produce it" (*GB*, 396). Mimicking the growth of crops would ensure their actual growth.

In Frazer's second, religious stage, Adonis is an outright personality. He is the god of vegetation. Indeed, Frazer distinguishes religion from magic on precisely the grounds that now divine personalities rather than impersonal forces cause events in the physical world. As the god of vegetation, Adonis could, most simply, be asked for crops. Or the request could be reinforced by ritualistic and ethical obedience. Frazer himself says that rites of mourning were performed for Adonis—not, as in the next stage, to undo his death but to seek his forgiveness for it (see *GB*, 393–94). For Adonis has died not, as in the next stage, because he has descended to the underworld but because in cutting, stamping, and grinding the corn—the specific part of vegetation he symbolizes—humans have killed him. Rather than "the natural decay of vegetation in general under the summer heat or the winter cold," the death of Adonis is "the violent destruction of the corn by man" (*GB*, 393–94). Yet Adonis is somehow still sufficiently alive to be capable of punishing humans, something which the rituals of forgiveness are intended to avert. Since, however, Adonis dies because vegetation itself does, the god is here really only a metaphor for the element that he supposedly controls. As vegetation goes, so goes Adonis.

In Frazer's third prescientific stage, which combines the first with the second, Adonis's death means his descent to the underworld for his stay with Persephone. If in stage two as vegetation goes, so goes Adonis, now as Adonis goes, so seemingly goes vegetation. Frazer assumes that whether or not Adonis wills his descent, he is too weak to ascend by himself. By acting out his rebirth, humans facilitate it. On the one hand the enactment employs the magical Law of Imitation. On the other hand it does not, as in the first stage, compel but only bolsters Adonis, who, despite his present state of death, is somehow still hearty enough to revive himself, just not fully. He needs a catalyst, which the enactment provides. In this stage gods still control the physical world, but their effect on it is automatic rather than deliberate. To enact the rebirth of Adonis is to spur his rebirth and, through it, the rebirth of vegetation (see *GB,* 377).

Yet even if Adonis chooses to descend to the underworld—how much choice he has is not clear—he is not choosing infertility, which is simply the automatic consequence of his sojourn below. Likewise even if he chooses to return, he is not thereby choosing fertility, which similarly simply follows automatically from his resurfacing. Again, Frazer is minimizing the role of decision and therefore of personality. Indeed, Adonis proves to be not the cause of the fate of vegetation but only a metaphor for that fate, so that in fact in stage three as well as in stage two, as vegetation goes, so goes Adonis. For Frazer, the myth that Adonis spent a portion of the year in the underworld "is explained most simply and naturally by supposing that he represented vegetation, especially the corn," which lies buried half the year and reemerges for the other half (*GB,* 392).

In a much larger sense, Frazer, in all three of his prescientific stages, reduces Adonis to the mere personification of vegetation. For even where Frazer does deem Adonis an independent personality, the only aspect of his life which he considers is that which parallels the natural course of vegetation: Adonis's death and rebirth. Yet Adonis's birth is anything but natural. For both Apollodorus and Ovid, his birth results from his mother's incestuous yearning for her father. Adonis's split schedule may become routine, but it is not therefore natural. For Apollodorus, it stems from love and jealousy on the part of Aphrodite and Persephone. Nor is Adonis's eventual death natural. He is killed and in various versions is even murdered—by either a spurned lover, Artemis, or a bested rival, Ares. To be sure, Frazer need not take the myth literally and therefore supernaturally. But he must *translate* the supernatural terms into natural ones, not ignore them.

Frazer ignores above all something not supernatural but human: Adonis's final death. And so he must. For Adonis's life to symbolize the course of vegetation, Adonis must continually die and be reborn. But in fact he does not. He eventually dies "permanently." Not only Ovid's version, which does not involve a trek to the underworld and therefore a cycle of death and rebirth, but even Apollodorus's, which does, ends in Adonis's permanent demise. By whatever means Adonis has overcome death annually, he cannot do so now. He is gone forever, which is why, in Ovid's version, Aphrodite is so disconsolate. How, then, can his mortal life symbolize eternal rebirth? How, then, can he be a god, who may die but does not stay dead, rather than a human being, who does?

Because Frazer reduces Adonis to vegetation, Adonis cannot serve as a model for others, who can hardly be implored to act like or unlike vegetation. The myth for him has no political import.

DETIENNE'S ADONIS

Marcel Detienne devotes a whole book to the myth of Adonis: *The Gardens of Adonis* (hereafter *GOA*).[3] Detienne begins by faulting Frazer and his followers on multiple grounds: for associating Adonis with rebirth rather than with death, for making the function of the myth proto-scientific rather than social, for analyzing the myth as universal rather than as distinctively Greek, and for focusing on the plot rather than the structure of the myth.[4] Where for Frazer, Adonis is an impersonal force rather than a god, for Detienne he is a human being rather than a god. Where for Frazer, Adonis symbolizes vegetation, for Detienne one form of vegetation symbolizes, or parallels, Adonis. Where for Frazer, Adonis, like vegetation, annually dies and revives, for Detienne, Adonis, like the vegetation associated with him, grows up quickly and then just as quickly dies, once and for all.

As a structuralist, Detienne differs with Frazer over not just the meaning and function but also the "operation" of the myth. Though Detienne later rejects the structuralist approach to myth of Claude Lévi-Strauss,[5] his interpretation of the Adonis myth is scrupulously Lévi-Straussian. The meaning of myth therefore lies not, as for Frazer, at the narrative level but at the structural one. It lies not in the plot itself—the birth, adolescence, death, and rebirth of Adonis—but in the dialectical relationship among the elements of the plot—characters, places, times, and events.

For Detienne, following Lévi-Strauss, this dialectical relationship exists on a host of levels: dietary, botanical, astronomical, seasonal, religious, social, and by species. At each level a middle ground lies between extremes. The levels parallel, not symbolize, one another. The relationship among the elements at, say, the dietary level is isomorphic with that at the botanical. Still, the dietary level—with cereals and cooked meat lying between spices at one extreme and lettuce and raw meat at the other—most tightly links the others.

Detienne first associates spices with the gods, cereals and cooked meat with humans, and lettuce and raw meat with animals. Spices get burned during sacrifices to the gods. The smell ascends to the gods, who inhale it as the equivalent of food. Because the meat is cooked rather than burned, it goes to humans, who also cultivate cereals. Just as burned meat goes to the gods in the form of fumes, so raw meat goes to animals, with which Detienne also somehow links lettuce. Spices are further associated with the gods because of their relationship to the sun and so, as the place atop earth, to Olympus. Spices not only are burned by the sun but also grow where and when the sun is nearest: in the hottest places and on the hottest days of summer. By contrast, lettuce is cold and is therefore connected with the coldest places and times: the world below earth—the seas and the underworld—and winter. To eat meat raw is to eat it "cold."

Cereals and cooked meat lie between spices on the one hand and lettuce and raw meat on the other. Just as, for humans, meat must be cooked rather than either burned or eaten raw, so cereals, to grow, need some sun but not too much: "In the middle range, situated at a fair distance from the fire of the sun, are the edible plants, . . . the cereals and the fruits" (*GOA,* 14). Cereals are therefore grown neither above ground nor below it but in it. Where spices are gathered during the summer and lettuce somehow during the winter, crops are harvested in the fall in between.

Spices are tied to the gods for other reasons. Less cultivated than gathered, they require no work and thereby fit the lives of the gods. Conversely, animals, eating only what they find, do not work for their supper either. But the gods eat what they want. Animals eat only what they find. The gods, then, do not have to work to eat better than humans. Animals, by not working, eat worse than humans. Humans again fall in between. They must work to eat; but when they work, they have enough, if barely enough, to eat. In Hesiod's Golden Age, humans were like the gods precisely because they had plenty without working. In the future they will be like animals, refusing to work and so presumably going hungry.

Spices are associated not only with gods but also with promiscuity. Rather than making promiscuity a divine prerogative, Detienne deems Zeus and Hera the perfect couple, even in the face of Zeus's escapades. He also deems Demeter the epitome of motherly and so familial concern: "Where the Demeter-Persephone couple lays emphasis upon the fruit of marriage and the relations between the mother and her legitimate child, the Zeus-Hera couple stresses the ritual conse-cration that sanctions the unity of husband and wife" (*GOA,* 89). Not gods but spices, with their fragrant, hence seductive, aroma, are connected to promiscuity: "In the form of ointments, perfumes and other cosmetic products they [spices] also have an erotic function" (*GOA,* 60). Not coincidentally, spices pervaded the Adonia festival, which was notorious for its promiscuity (see *GOA,* 64–66). Conversely, Detienne links not animals but lettuce and raw meat to sterility and celibacy. For the foul smell of at least rotten, if not raw, meat—Detienne some-how equates the two—repels rather than attracts and thereby fends off sex. Not coincidentally, the women of Lemnos were spurned by men because of their stench (see *GOA,* 94).

Between promiscuity on the one hand and sterility or celibacy on the other stands marriage, with which, notes Detienne, the Thesmophoria festival was con-nected. Though barred to men, the festival really celebrated marriage (see *GOA,* 80). If its celebrants were all female, they were also all married. Falling between the fragrance of the Adonia and the stench of Lemnos, the mildly foul smell of the festival served to fend off men during only the festival (see *GOA,* 80–81).

Detienne connects all of these levels with the life of Adonis and with the ritual-istic gardens dedicated to him. At every level, argues Detienne, Adonis falls in either extreme rather than in the middle. In fact, Adonis jumps from one extreme to the other, bypassing the middle. Adonis's fate represents that of any human who dares to act like a god: he is reduced to the equivalent of an animal. Daring to be promiscuous, he proves impotent.

For Detienne, as a structuralist, the extremes on each level do not *symbolize* the life of Adonis. They *parallel* it. At each level the extremes are to the middle as Adonis is to normal humans. The extremes are analogous to the life of Adonis. Where for Frazer the myth uses symbols of humans to describe impersonal forces of nature, for Detienne it uses impersonal forces of nature as analogues to humans to evaluate human behavior.

The gardens of Adonis, planted during the Adonia festival, involve little work. The plants shoot up immediately. Tending them parallels the toilless lives of the gods. In fact, the gardens are like the spices of the gods. They are merely gathered, not cultivated, and grow in the hottest places and times. They are carried to the roofs of houses at the height of summer. Where regular crops take eight months to grow, the gardens take only eight days. Where regular crops demand the strength of men, the gardens are tended by women. Unlike the spices, however, the gardens die as quickly as they sprout; and unlike regular crops, they die without yielding food (see *GOA*, 10). Having begun above the earth, they end up below it—cast into the sea. In short, the gardens are a futile "get rich quick" scheme to get food without work. Gods need not work, but humans must. When they seek "fast food" instead of regular fare, they get no food at all (see *GOA*, 103–4).

Adonis himself is related to spices through his mother, Myrrha, who becomes a myrrh tree. Adonis's gestation takes place in the tree, and his birth requires his breaking out of it. In Ovid's version wood nymphs even bathe the infant in the myrrh formed from his mother's tears. More important, Adonis is tied to spices through promiscuity. Unable to control her desire, Adonis's mother commits incest with her father. Unable to control their desire, Aphrodite and Persephone fight for custody of the infant Adonis. Adonis himself, for Detienne, is less an innocent victim of divine seduction than a seducer of divinities: "No sooner is he born from the myrrh tree whose form his mother has taken than Adonis arouses, first in Aphrodite and then in Persephone, the possessive and exclusive desire that a mistress feels for her lover" (*GOA*, 63–64).

Adonis is a precocious seducer. Like the gardens, he grows up quickly. But like the gardens as well, he dies quickly. While young, he is killed by a boar. Just as the gardens die too early to yield any food, so Adonis dies too young to marry and have children. Having begun promiscuous, he ends up sterile. Conversely, his mother, who began sterile or at least abstinent—she had spurned all males—becomes promiscuous at the least. Jumping from one extreme to the other, mother and son alike reject and, more, threaten the middle ground of marriage (see *GOA*, 81–82).

Adonis's sterility takes the form of not only childlessness but also effeminacy. His death from the boar shows his unfitness for the masculine hunt. Instead of the hunter, he becomes the hunted: "The perfect antithesis of a warrior hero such as Herakles," Adonis "is nothing more than a victim as weak as he is pitiable" (*GOA*, 67). Adonis's effeminacy signifies insufficient distance between male and female. His mother's initial rejection of all males signifies the opposite. The ideal lies, again, in between: males and females should be related but distinct.

Just as Detienne links Adonis's promiscuity with spices, so he links Adonis's sterility and death with lettuce, in which, in several versions of the myth, Adonis tries vainly to hide from the boar. Just as myrrh "has the power to arouse the desires of an old man," so lettuce "can extinguish the ardour of young lovers." Lettuce "brings impotence, which is equivalent to death" (*GOA*, 68).

Detienne argues that Adonis is, in Mary Douglas's terms, anomalous.[6] He literally does not know his place. He does not know that he is neither god nor animal but human and that what is distinctively human is marriage. In dying before marrying, he fails to fulfill his human nature.

If the *meaning* of the myth for Detienne is the presentation of an almost endless series of levels, the *function* of the myth is social. It advocates marriage as the middle ground between promiscuity on the one hand and sterility or celibacy on the other. At the same time Detienne does not consider the role of marriage in the polis. For him, the myth advocates marriage as an end in itself. I will be arguing that the myth advocates marriage as a bulwark of the polis.

JUNG'S ADONIS

Detienne's interpretation of the myth of Adonis is a double improvement on Frazer's. First, his interpretation of Adonis as not an impersonal force but a personality, divine or human, enables him to stress Adonis's motives. Adonis becomes not just something that automatically lives and dies but someone who wills the course of his life. One can therefore hold him accountable for his behavior and can praise or condemn it as a model for others. Second, Detienne's interpretation of Adonis as not a god but a human enables him to stress Adonis's mortality.

Detienne's analysis of the myth is nevertheless skewed. For he deems Adonis an active culprit rather than a passive victim. According to Detienne, the myth berates Adonis for daring to transcend his human bounds, but Adonis in fact acts out of blindness, not boldness. Far from striving to venture too far, he has no idea of how far he has gone or can go. Far from yearning to be more than human, he is oblivious to what being human means. As a personality, he remains responsible for his actions, which can therefore still be condemned, but his motivation is the opposite of what Detienne depicts. In noting Adonis's effeminacy, Detienne half-recognizes his true nature, but he then interprets effeminacy as an attempt to transcend the ordinary human bounds of male and female rather than as the failure to recognize those bounds in the first place. Adonis fails to marry not because he dares to go beyond the confines of marriage but because he has no conception of marriage.

The theory of myth that, I believe, best illuminates the character of Adonis is that of C. G. Jung. Unlike Frazer and Detienne, Jung himself mentions Adonis only in passing,[7] but he does mention him as an instance of the archetype of the eternal child, or *puer aeternus*. That archetype as well Jung discusses only in passing,[8] though he does devote many pages to an allied archetype, the Great Mother.[9] Marie-Louise von Franz, one of Jung's closest disciples, has written a book on the puer archetype, but she concentrates on cases other than that of Adonis.[10]

From a Jungian point of view, the myth of Adonis functions not merely to present the archetype of the puer but also to assess it. The myth serves as a warning to those who identify themselves with the archetype. To live as a puer, the way Adonis does, is to live as a psychological infant and, ultimately, as a fetus. The life of a puer in myth invariably ends in premature death, which psychologically means the death of the ego and a return to the womblike unconscious.

As an archetype, the puer constitutes a side of one's personality, which, as a side, must be accepted. A puer personality is one who simply goes too far: he makes the puer the whole of his personality. Unable to resist its spell, he surrenders himself to it, thereby abandoning his ego and reverting to sheer unconsciousness.

The reason a puer personality cannot resist the puer archetype is that he remains under the spell of the archetype of the Great Mother, who initially is identical with the unconscious as a whole. Unable to free himself from her, he never forges a strong, independent ego, without which he cannot in turn resist any smothering female he meets. His surrender to the puer archetype means his surrender to the Great Mother, to whom he yearns only to return. A puer "only lives on and through the mother and can strike no roots, so that he finds himself in a state of permanent incest." Jung even calls him a mere "dream of the mother," who eventually draws him back into herself.[11]

The development of the ego depends considerably on society. The institutions of marriage and work serve to anchor one to the external world, with which the ego deals, and thereby to keep the ego from falling back into the unconscious. The ego is strong exactly insofar as one is in touch with the external world. At the same time participation in a society, including the polis, requires the development of a sturdy ego. In contrast to slavery, citizenship requires decision making, which only connectedness to the external world, and so only a strong ego, can provide. Adonis is a puer personality because he has no society to nurture him. Never free of smothering mother figures, he is never free to live in society and to develop psychologically. Exactly because he is retarded psychologically, he is retarded politically. Participation in the polis is beyond him.

Biologically, a puer can range in age from late adolescence to middle or even old age. Psychologically, however, he is an infant. Where for Freud a person in the grip of an Oedipus complex is psychologically fixated at three to five years of age, for Jung a puer is fixated at birth. Where an Oedipus complex presupposes an independent ego "egotistically" seeking to possess the mother for itself, a puer involves a tenuous ego seeking to surrender itself to the mother. A puer seeks not domination but absorption—and thereby reversion to the state prior even to birth.

For Freud, attachment to the mother at any stage means attachment to one's actual mother or mother substitute. It means attachment to the person herself. For Jung, attachment to the mother means attachment to the mother archetype, of which one's actual mother or mother substitute is only a manifestation. Where for Freud a boy should free himself of his yearning, infantile or Oedipal, for his own mother, for Jung a boy should free himself of his inclination to identify himself with the mother archetype. For Freud, the failure to free oneself means eternal attachment to one's own mother. For Jung, it means the restriction of one's personality to the mother archetype within. Where for Freud the struggle for freedom is between one person and another—son and mother—for Jung it is between one part of a person and another—ego and unconscious, which, again, the mother archetype first symbolizes. For Jung, "the mother corresponds to the collective unconscious, and the son to [ego] consciousness."[12]

Because an archetype expresses itself only through symbols, never directly, the aspects of the mother archetype that a child knows are only those filtered through his actual mother or mother substitute. A mother who refuses to let her child go limits him to only the smothering, negative side of the mother archetype. A mother who, however reluctantly, finally lets her child go opens him to the nurturing, positive side of the archetype. Initially, any child is reluctant to leave. A smothering mother, by revealing only the smothering side of the mother archetype, tempts him to stay. A nurturing mother, by revealing the nurturing side of the archetype as well, prods him to resist the temptation. In all its aspects, the mother archetype, as an archetype, is inherited. One's experience of mother figures determines only which aspects of the archetype are elicited. A child who never experiences a nourishing mother figure never develops that dimension of the archetype latent in him.

Approached properly, the puer archetype provides an ego that has managed to sever itself from the unconscious reentry into it. Taken rightly, the puer dimension of a person evinces itself in moments of playfulness, imagination, and spontaneity—moments that complement the rationality and sobriety of the ego. Taken to excess, the puer personality amounts to nothing but these moments. Taken rightly, the puer is childlike. Taken to excess, it is childish.

Although the puer personality arises in infancy, it manifests itself most dramatically at adolescence. A puer personality is even called an eternal adolescent. A puer is impulsive, dreamy, irresponsible, and self-centered. He dreams of accomplishing great deeds but never does them. He makes great plans, but they never materialize. He may work hard, but only sporadically and only when interested. A puer avoids commitments and refuses to be tied down. He craves excitement and seeks risks. Scornful of the mundane, everyday world, he waxes spiritual and otherworldly. Sexually, he is promiscuous. He dreams of a perfect mate but, never finding her, scorns anyone else. He refuses to become attached. He may be a Don Juan. He may turn to homosexuality, at least according to older Jungian views. The difference between a puer personality and a normal adolescent is that a puer remains an adolescent for life. In fact, it is normally at adolescence that the son finally breaks away from the mother. Rites of passage serve precisely to force a break. Still, the puer personality is infantile. It arises in infancy, not adolescence, and at adolescence merely expresses its infantilism in adolescent form.

There is no inconsistency between the promiscuity of adolescence and the reluctance to leave the mother at birth. A puer is promiscuous because he cannot choose a mate, and he cannot choose a mate because he remains attached to the mother. Without the institution of marriage to spur him to mate, he remains a puer forever. To say that a puer is attached to the mother is to say that he knows the world only through the projection of her onto it. He thereby really knows her rather than the world. He is promiscuous not because he dares to defy the convention of marriage but because he is unaware of it. Every female he encounters is either a manifestation of the Great Mother, in which case she is to be outright embraced, or an unworthy inferior to her, in which case she is to be rejected.

A puer may be either conscious or unconscious of his character. To be sure, even a conscious puer experiences alluring females as epiphanies of the Great Mother, but at least he recognizes that other males experience women differently—as possible mates. He simply takes for granted that mystical union alone is right for him. He is both aware and proud of his unconventionality. Examples of conscious pueri are Casanova and Aleister Crowley.[13]

An unconscious puer, by contrast, assumes that everyone else is like him. He assumes that all other males seek unity with women, for no other relationship exists. He considers himself wholly conventional. A literary example of an unconscious puer is Goethe's character Werther, who dismisses the values of both aristocratic and bourgeois society as artificial and who blames society for coming between him and an otherwise responsive Lotte, with whom, moreover, he seeks not intercourse but maternal absorption. A more spectacular, contemporary example is Elvis Presley, a consummate mamma's boy who lived his last twenty years as a recluse in a womblike, infantile world in which all of his wishes were immediately satisfied yet who deemed himself entirely normal, in fact "all-American."[14]

A puer can thus be either an actual person or a symbol. Indeed, some famous historical pueri eventually become symbols themselves. While a historical puer is biologically an adult, a symbolic one may never grow up. These symbolic pueri exemplify exactly the eternally young life that actual puer personalities strive to emulate. Other symbolic pueri are Peter Pan and the Little Prince. Just as a puer may be conscious or unconscious, so he may outwardly be adjusted or maladjusted. Outwardly, he may be settled in a marriage and a job, but he still finds no satisfaction in them. Or he may be unsettled even outwardly, as in the cases of Don Juan and the eternal student.

The opposite of the puer archetype is that of the hero.[15] The hero is the opposite precisely because he succeeds where a puer fails. Strictly, there are two stages of heroism. In the first half of life an ego is heroic in managing to liberate itself from the unconscious and establish itself in society. A hero manages to secure a fulfilling mate and job. A puer fails to do either. In the second half of life a now independent ego is heroic in managing to break with society and return to the unconscious without thereby falling back into it. Where a hero in the first half of life establishes himself in the conventions of society, a hero in the second half defies those conventions. But a hero is consciously defiant. A puer is only unconsciously so. Where a hero risks everything for whatever he has committed himself to, a puer has committed himself to nothing and so risks nothing. Because a puer never establishes an independent ego, he never faces the possible loss of it. Where a real hero is like Daedalus, a puer is like Icarus. Because a puer is a failed hero in the first half of life, he is necessarily a failed hero in the second half as well. Indeed, there is no second half for him.

Adonis is a quintessential puer because he never marries, never works, and dies young. He simply never grows up. His puer personality spans the period from infancy to adolescence. He must first break out of a tree in order to be born. His mother, transformed into the tree, is reluctant to let him out. Like any other mother, she may be overjoyed at his conception, but unlike normal mothers, she wants to hoard him. In Ovid's version, Adonis himself has to find an exit.

Adonis's mother has herself proved unable to break out of her father, the only male who ever arouses her. Even if her incestuous desire results from a curse, the curse is punishment for her indifference to other men, for which a prior attachment to her father is likely the latent cause. In any event her desire is not really for intercourse with her actual father but for absorption in the father archetype. For she, too, has never severed herself from the unconscious and therefore has never grown up. Not coincidentally, she is incapable of raising Adonis, whom others, whatever their motives, must raise instead. She is a puella.[16]

No sooner does Adonis emerge from the tree than, in Apollodorus's version, Aphrodite thrusts him back—not, to be sure, into the tree but into a chest. She thereby undoes the birth that had proved so arduous. She tells no one, for she wants Adonis all to herself. When Persephone, to whom Aphrodite has entrusted the chest without revealing its contents, opens it, she likewise falls in love with Adonis and refuses to return him. Each goddess, just like his mother, wants to possess him exclusively. Though Zeus's decision leaves Adonis free for a third of the year, Adonis readily cedes his third to Aphrodite. Never, then, is he outside the custody of these archetypal mother figures.

Rather than the seducer, as for Detienne, Adonis is really the seduced. He may scurry from goddess to goddess, but only because he is attached to each. He does not come and go on his own. He cannot imagine an independent life. Adonis is unable to resist the blandishments of the goddesses not because his will is weak but because his ego is. Indeed, for Jung the ego controls the will. Adonis is unable to resist the goddesses not because they arouse him sexually but because he does not even recognize them as goddesses. He sees them not as irresistibly beautiful females but as his mother, with whom he wants not intercourse but absorption. Between him and the goddesses there exists the primordial state of mystical oneness that Lucien Lévy-Bruhl, whom Jung often cites, calls *participation mystique*. Psychologically, Adonis is at exactly that stage of humanity to which Lévy-Bruhl and, following him, Jung apply the term "primitive."[17]

Adonis is the most extreme kind of puer—an unconscious as well as outward one. Since he never marries, never has children, never works, and dies young, he is conspicuously an outward puer. Since he has no idea of the difference between his life and anyone else's, he is clearly an unconscious puer as well. He lives in a fog.

Seemingly, a Jungian interpretation of the myth faces the same contradiction as a Frazerian one: that Adonis annually breaks free of the mother yet eventually dies permanently. Like Frazer, a Jungian might dismiss Adonis's final death as an aberration and stress his perennial liberation from the mother. In that case Adonis would be a hero rather than a puer. Indeed, Jung himself identifies Adonis with Frazer's annually reborn corn god: "The corn-god of antiquity was Adonis, whose death and resurrection were celebrated annually. He was the son-lover of the mother, for the corn is the son and fructifier of the earth's womb."[18]

Yet a Jungian interpretation need not ignore Adonis's final demise, which is reconcilable with his recurrent revival. For the annual cycle of death and rebirth can symbolize not Adonis's annual liberation from the mother but the opposite: his annual return to the mother, even if that return ends in release. Where a normal child needs to be born only once to liberate himself from the mother, Adonis, as a puer, continually returns to the mother and so must be born again and again. His final death is simply his permanent rather than temporary return to her. It is the culmination of his past returns rather than a break with them. Previously, he had been strong enough to resist the mother temporarily. Now he can no longer do so.

Put another way, Adonis's cycle of death and rebirth constitutes neurosis: his weak ego compulsively returns to the mother. His final death represents psychosis: in returning forever to the mother, his ego dissolves altogether.[19]

ADONIS AS A GREEK PUER

If Adonis is an instance of the puer archetype, he is a distinctively Greek instance. To begin with, the analogy between humans and plants is remarkably, though not uniquely, Greek. Frazer may reduce human and divine life to a metaphor for plant life, but, as Detienne elaborates, the Greeks themselves deem plant life a metaphor for human life. They symbolize the puer archetype botanically: the gardens are symbolic of Adonis.

Furthermore, the Greeks link the puer not only to plants but, more significantly, to the polis. The puer's psychological retardation entails political retardation: to fail to become an adult is to fail to become a citizen. A puer is suited for precisely that form of government which involves no responsibility and therefore permits, if not requires, political infancy: tyranny. Adonis's submission to the mother fits a matriarchal society.[20] He lives in a society in which males are neither rulers nor even citizens. Having experienced only smothering females, he projects those qualities onto all females and thereby submits unquestioningly to them. Females are able to tyrannize him because he projects the smothering side of the mother archetype onto them. For Jung, a female tyrant serves as the object for the mother archetype, just as a male tyrant like Hitler serves as the object for the shadow archetype.[21]

The family constitutes the link between personality and the polis. The opposition that Herodotus, among others, draws between the polis of Greece, in which even the ruler is subject to the law, and the tyranny of Persia and the East, in which the ruler is above the law, holds for family life as well.

Herodotus catalogues the violations of familial mores by Eastern potentates to demonstrate their tyranny. King Candaules of Sardis orders Gyges, his bodyguard, to look secretly at the Queen as she disrobes. She then forces Gyges to kill her husband (Herodotus 1.8–13). Solon tells King Croesus of Lydia that the happiest man he has known was an obscure Athenian who had fine sons and lived to see them raise children in turn. Croesus himself has two sons, one deaf and dumb, the other killed—like Adonis, while hunting boar—by a friend who had accidentally killed his brother and been banished by his father for it (Herodotus 1.29–33). King Astyages of Media orders Cyrus, his grandson, killed at birth to prevent his usurpation of the throne. In revenge for Harpagus's failure to carry out the deed,

Astyages serves him up his son. Cyrus subsequently topples, though does not kill, his grandfather (Herodotus 1.117–19). King Cambyses of Persia, Cyrus's son and successor, marries two of his sisters, murders one of them, and murders his brother as well. He goes insane and dies childless (Herodotus 3.31–32). King Xerxes of Persia, having failed to seduce his brother's wife, arranges a marriage between his son and his brother's daughter, whom he then manages to seduce instead. In revenge for her daughter-in-law's getting her robe, Xerxes's wife has the daughter-in-law's mother, her own sister-in-law, mutilated. Xerxes then offers his brother his own daughter in marriage as a substitute for his mutilated wife. Declining the offer, the brother goes off with his sons to foment revolt. Xerxes has all of them killed.

As for the domestic lives of Greek tyrants, whom Herodotus acknowledges but deems an aberration, Periandros of Corinth murders his wife, deposes his father-in-law, and dispossesses his one talented son (Herodotus 3.50.3–3.52.6). Peisistratos of Athens refuses to have "normal" sex with his second wife because he fears a curse upon her family (Herodotus 1.61.1).

Adonis is incapable of citizenship because he, like the tyrants, is incapable of settled family life. On the one hand he fosters no family: he never marries, has no children, and dies young. On the other hand he is born into no family: he is the child of incest, not marriage, and his father tries to kill his mother. He is thus barred doubly from citizenship: he lacks not only maturity but also a pedigree, itself the result of the immaturity of his puellalike mother. If Herodotus testifies to the political necessity of siring a family, the Aristotelian *Constitution of Athens* testifies to the political necessity of descending from one: "the right of citizenship belongs to those whose parents have been citizens" (*Constitution of Athens*, 42).[22]

Until Cleisthenes in 507 B.C. changed the basis of Athenian citizenship from kinship to locale, membership in a phratry was prerequisite. Even after the deme, which was a matter of locale, replaced the phratry as the prime political unit, the phratry remained important. Though a fourth-century Athenian, for example, could be a citizen without belonging to a phratry, his position would be both "uncomfortable and questionable."[23] Moreover, membership in the deme was itself hereditary. Consequently, citizenship remained a matter of birth, as the *Constitution of Athens*, referring to the time after Cleisthenes, states.

The tie between humans and plants itself furnishes a metaphor for the tie between humans and politics. *Hubris,* or "excess," is related to "exuberance in plants." For Hesiod, Theognis, and others, loyalty to the polis yields political fruit and disloyalty political barrenness.[24]

The Greeks link the puer not only to plants and politics but also to hunting. Adonis's haplessness at hunting symbolizes his haplessness at adulthood. He fails utterly as a hunter not just because he becomes the hunted instead but, even more fundamentally, because he has no conception of hunting. He succumbs to the hunt for the same reason that he succumbs to the goddesses: blindness. Just as he thinks that all loving females are the Great Mother, so he thinks that the world itself is. More accurately, he thinks the world loving or at least thinks himself protected from it by the Great Mother. He ignores Aphrodite's warning not because he valiantly dismisses ordinary caution but because he does not comprehend the danger. In Ovid's version, Aphrodite tells him that the dangerous animals respect neither youth nor beauty, but he is deaf to her pleas. He assumes that all animals are either tame or easy prey.

A true hero would be aware of the danger but bold enough to face it. His heroism would *presuppose* his recognition of the true nature of the world. By contrast, the pseudo-hero Adonis is oblivious to any danger and need therefore muster no bravery to face it. He is oblivious to the nature of the world. He is less effeminate than blind—less unwilling or even unable to hunt than unaware of what hunting, of what killing and getting killed, means. He dies not because he is a poor hunter but because he is none at all. Yet his case is even more severe. So enveloped is he in the Great Mother that he actually *wants* to be killed in order to return wholly to her. Consciously, he is blind to the danger of the hunt, but unconsciously he courts it.

To say that Adonis courts danger is certainly to say that he chooses it. Even though he is unaware of the nature of what he is choosing, he still chooses to hunt. He is not, therefore, reducible to an impersonal force like corn for Frazer. He remains a personality, however lopsided a personality. One can, then, invoke him as a model, even if a negative model, for life in society.

Like the tie between human and plant, the tie between human and hunter becomes a metaphor for the tie between human and citizen. Pierre Vidal-Naquet suggests that hunting was a key aspect of the two-year military stint that, according to the *Constitution of Athens* (42), Athenian youths were required to undergo before citizenship. Following not only Lévi-Strauss but even more Arnold van Gennep, Vidal-Naquet argues that those years were a rite of passage that involved a break with the life that the youths, or *ephebes*, both had known until now and would know afterward. The ephebes thus spent their years at the frontier rather than in the city and spent them with one another rather than with their families.[25]

Above all, claims Vidal-Naquet, the ephebes engaged in a brand of hunting that was the opposite of the brand that, as *hoplites*, they would soon be undertaking. As ephebes, they hunted individually, in the mountains, at night, and armed only with nets—thereby relying on trickery to capture their prey. As hoplites, they would be hunting in a group, on the plain, during the day, and armed with spears—thus relying on courage and skill to kill their prey. Vidal-Naquet cites texts in which these two kinds of hunting are sharply contrasted: adult hunting, by day and with the spear (in keeping with the hoplite ethos), and hunting by night, a "black hunt" based on the use of the net. Following again van Gennep and Lévi-Strauss, Vidal-Naquet contends that the contrast between the hunting of ephebes and the hunting of hoplites served to inculcate hoplite values in the ephebes.

Vidal-Naquet's evidence for the link of the *ephebeia* with hunting is twofold. He appeals, first, to the myth associated with the Apatouria, the festival at which Athenian fathers registered their sixteen-year-old sons as citizens, as members of phratries, and as ephebes for two years. Vidal-Naquet asserts that the subject of the myth, the Athenian Melanthos, or "Black One," is—like Adonis—a negative model for the ephebes: he is an ephebe who never becomes a hoplite. Even as an adult he resorts to deceit rather than courage or skill to defeat his opponent, the Boeotian King Xanthos (the "Blond One").

Vidal-Naquet appeals, second, to the figure of Melanion, the Black Hunter, as described by Aristophanes:

> Now to tell a little story
> > Fain, fain I grow,
> One I heard when quite an urchin
> > Long, long ago.
> > How that once
> All to shun the nuptial bed
> From his home Melanion fled,
> To the hills and deserts sped,
> > Kept his dog,
> > Wove his snares,
> > Trapped his hares;
> Home he nevermore would go,
> He detested women so.
> We are of Melanion's mind,
> We detest the womankind.
> > (*Lysistrata* 781–96)[26]

The connection between Melanion and the *ephebeia* is both that Melanion, as a fellow black character, has all of the dark associations of Melanthos and that Melanion is an ephebelike hunter who never marries. To Vidal-Naquet, Aristophanes depicts Melanion "as an ephebe, but a sort of ephebe *manqué*." The chorus provides a version of "the widespread myth of the gloomy solitary hunter who is either a misogynist or who tries to insult Artemis, and who, in either case, flouts the social rules."[27]

The severity of Adonis's failure at hunting makes him truly a *puer* rather than, like Melanthos and Melanion, merely an adolescent. If one extrapolates from

Melanthos as fighter to him as hunter, both he and Melanion succeed at hunting of only an adolescent variety. By contrast, Adonis fails at hunting of any kind. One can scarcely imagine his defeating an animal or human foe not just by courage or skill but even by trickery. One can scarcely imagine his recognizing who his foes are or even what a foe is. Adonis is thus not, like Melanthos and Melanion, just an adolescent who never advances to adulthood but an infant who never advances to adolescence—or even to childhood. His infantilism takes adolescent form, but infantilism rather than adolescence it is. The severity of his failure as a hunter means the severity of his failure as a citizen. The myth of Adonis represents, then, the negation of practices without which the polis cannot be conceived: exogamy and reproduction. The myth dramatizes the consequences of rejecting those practices: barrenness and death. Myth can teach by negative as well as positive models. Its function can still be political.[28]

VIII • IN QUEST OF THE HERO

THE STUDY OF HERO myths goes back at least to 1871, when the English anthropologist Edward Tylor argued that many of them follow a uniform plot, or pattern: the hero is exposed at birth, is saved by other humans or animals, and grows up to become a national hero.[1] Tylor sought only to establish a common pattern, not to analyze its origin, function, or subject matter. He appeals to the uniformity of the pattern to make the standard comparativist claim that whatever the origin, function, or subject matter of hero myths, it must be the same in all hero myths to account for the resulting similarities: "The treatment of similar myths from different regions, by arranging them in large compared groups, makes it possible to trace in mythology the operation of imaginative processes recurring with the evident regularity of mental law; and thus stories of which a single instance would have been a mere isolated curiosity, take their place among well-marked and consistent structures of the human mind."[2] While some theorists are attentive to the differences among hero myths, by definition all seek similarities and so are comparativists.

In 1876 the Austrian scholar Johann Georg von Hahn used fourteen cases to argue that all "Aryan" hero tales follow a more comprehensive "exposure and return" formula.[3] In each case the hero is born illegitimately, out of the fear of the prophecy of his future greatness is abandoned by his father, is saved by animals and raised by a lowly couple, fights wars, returns home triumphant, defeats his persecutors, frees his mother, becomes king, founds a city, and dies young. Though himself a solar mythologist, von Hahn, too, tried only to establish, not to analyze, the pattern.[4]

Similarly, in 1928 the Russian folklorist Vladimir Propp sought to demonstrate that Russian fairy tales follow a common biographical plot, in which the hero goes off on a successful adventure and upon his return marries and gains the throne.[5] Propp's pattern skirts both the birth and the death of the hero. Like von Hahn and Tylor, Propp attempted only to establish, not to analyze, his pattern.

Of the scholars who have analyzed the hero patterns they have delineated, by far the most influential have been the Viennese psychoanalyst Otto Rank (1884–1939), the American mythographer Joseph Campbell (1904–1987), and the English folklorist Lord Raglan (1885–1964). Rank wrote *The Myth of the Birth of the Hero* (1909) as an outright disciple of Sigmund Freud.[6] Campbell wrote *The Hero with a Thousand Faces* (1949) as a kindred soul of C. G. Jung.[7] Raglan wrote *The Hero* (1936) as a theoretical ally of James Frazer.[8]

OTTO RANK

Only in passing does Freud himself analyze myth. Because he always compares myths with dreams, it is fitting as well as notable that his brief interpretation of the myth of Oedipus occurs in *The Interpretation of Dreams* (1900).[9] In *Dreams in Folklore* (1911), written with D. E. Oppenheim, Freud interprets dreams in folklore, but none of the pieces of folklore considered is a myth.[10]

Along with Rank's *Myth of the Birth of the Hero,* the other classic Freudian analysis of myth is Karl Abraham's *Dreams and Myths,* also originally published in 1909.[11] Abraham and Rank alike follow the master in comparing myths with dreams and in deeming both the disguised, symbolic fulfillment of repressed, overwhelmingly Oedipal wishes lingering in the adult myth maker or reader. But Rank's work is by far the richer and sprightlier of the two. He considers more myths, analyzes them in more detail, and above all establishes a common plot for them—a manifest pattern, which he then translates into latent, Freudian terms. Most important, he focuses on hero myths. Rank later broke irrevocably with Freud, but at the time he wrote *The Myth of the Birth of the Hero* he was an apostle and indeed soon emerged as Freud's heir apparent. In fact, Freud himself wrote the section of the work on the "family romance."[12]

The title of Rank's monograph is at once misleading and prescient. It is misleading because Rank's Freudian emphasis is not on the hero's birth but on the hero's later, Oedipal relationship to his parents. The birth is decisive not because of the hero's separation from his mother but because of the parents' attempt to fend off at birth the prophesied parricidal consequences. The title is prescient because Rank, like Sandor Ferenczi, Géza Róheim, and Melanie Klein, came to reject the orthodox Freudian priority of the Oedipal stage over any other. Rank came to view birth rather than the Oedipus complex as the key trauma and so the key source of neurosis.[13] While Freud, at least as early as 1909, was prepared to grant that "the act of birth is the first experience of anxiety, and thus the source and prototype of the affect of anxiety,"[14] he was never prepared to make birth the prime, let alone sole, source of anxiety and neurosis.[15] Freud refused to subordinate the Oedipus complex, which focuses on the father, to the trauma of birth, which necessarily centers on the mother. It is revealing that in Freud's writings on religion even the nurturing and protective god, not just the threatening one, is male rather than female.

The Myth of the Birth of the Hero evinces not only early Rank's but also early Freud's views. Psychoanalytic theory has evolved considerably since 1909. Contemporary Freudians, spurred by the development of ego psychology, regard myth far more positively than early Rank and Freud did. Myths solve problems rather than perpetuate them, are progressive rather than regressive, and abet adjustment to the world rather than flight from it. Myths serve not, or not just, to vent bottled-up drives but also to sublimate them. They are as different from dreams as akin to them. Finally, they serve everyone, not just neurotics.[16] Still, Rank's monograph remains the classic Freudian analysis of hero myths and offers a striking foil to Campbell's largely Jungian analysis.

JOSEPH CAMPBELL

Despite the commonly applied epithet, Joseph Campbell was never a straightforward "Jungian." He did edit both *The Portable Jung* and the six-volume selection from the *Eranos-Jahrbuch,* which, while not uniformly Jungian, is Jungian in spirit. Campbell himself twice gave lectures published in the *Jahrbuch*. Several volumes of his works appear in the Bollingen Series, which is likewise broadly Jungian. Two of Campbell's works even constitute the inaugural and final entries in the series. He also edited other Bollingen volumes. He was both a fellow and a trustee of the Bollingen Foundation.

Still, Campbell was not a Jungian analyst and underwent no analysis. Not only did he never call himself a Jungian, but he even denied that he was: "You know, for some people, 'Jungian' is a nasty word, and it has been flung at me by certain reviewers as though to say, 'Don't bother with Joe Campbell: he's a Jungian.' I'm not a Jungian!"[17] Of all theorists of myth, Campbell does praise Jung the most: "As far as interpreting myths, Jung gives me the best clues I've got."[18] But Campbell, fancying himself a theorist in his own right, refuses to defer to Jung: "he [Jung]'s not the final word—I don't think there is a final word."[19]

Campbell differs most with Jung over the origin and function of myth. Where for Jung the archetypal contents of myth arise out of the unconscious, only in some works of Campbell's do they do so. Even then, sometimes the unconscious for Campbell is, as for Freud, acquired rather than, as for Jung, inherited. Other times the contents of myth—contents that Campbell, like Northrop Frye, calls "archetypal" simply because they are similar worldwide—emerge from the imprint of either recurrent or traumatic experiences. In all of these cases, as for Jung, each society creates its own myths—whatever the source of the material it uses.

Other times, however, Campbell, in blatant contrast to Jung, is a diffusionist: myths for him originate in one society and spread elsewhere.

Where for Jung myth functions to reveal the archetypes of the unconscious and to enable humans to encounter them, for Campbell myth serves additional functions as well. Campbell comes to declare repeatedly that myth serves four distinct functions: to instill and maintain a sense of awe and mystery before the world; to provide a symbolic image for the world such as that of the Great Chain of Being; to maintain the social order by giving divine justification to social practices like the Indian caste system; and above all to harmonize human beings with the cosmos, society, and the parts of themselves. Jung, ever seeking a balance between the internal and the external worlds, would doubtless applaud many of these functions for keeping humans anchored to the outer, everyday, conscious world, but he himself is more concerned with reconnecting humans to the inner, unconscious world, with which they have ordinarily lost contact. While Jung does venture beyond a psychological payoff to an existential one akin to Campbell's fourth function, overall Jung would likely consider Campbell's quaternity of functions askew to his own.

For all Jung's praise of myth, he does not regard it as indispensable. Religion, art, dreams, and what he calls the "active imagination" can work as well, even if at times Jung uses the term "myth" so loosely as to encompass these alternatives to it. For Campbell, by contrast, myth is irreplaceable. Campbell attributes to myth so many disparate functions that it is hard to envision any possible substitute. Moreover, he defines myth so broadly that religion, art, and dreams become instances of myth rather than substitutes for it.

Jung considers myth neither necessary nor sufficient for human fulfillment. Campbell considers it both. Where for Jung therapy supplements myth, for Campbell myth precludes therapy, which is only for those bereft of myth. For Jung, one should reflect on a myth rather than heed it blindly. For Campbell, one should follow a myth—any myth—faithfully. Where for Jung a myth can lead one astray, for Campbell it never can.[20]

Despite these conspicuous differences, Campbell stands close to Jung and stands closest in *The Hero with a Thousand Faces,* which remains the classic Jungian analysis of hero myths. Campbell himself, to be sure, states that he became ever more of a Jungian *after* writing *Hero:* "When I wrote *The Hero with a Thousand Faces* they [Freud and Jung] were equal in my thinking: Freud served in one context, Jung in another. But then, in the years following, Jung became more and more eloquent to me. I think the longer you live, the more Jung can say to you."[21] But Campbell is likely basing this characterization of *Hero* on his reliance on the Freudian Géza Róheim, who, however, strays from Freudian orthodoxy in a manner that Campbell adopts and carries still further to Jung.

LORD RAGLAN

Neither Rank nor Campbell focuses on the relationship between myth and ritual. Campbell would doubtless assume that every ritual has an accompanying myth, but neither he nor Rank assumes that every myth has a ritualistic counterpart. Of the three theorists of hero myths considered here, only Lord Raglan does. He alone therefore qualifies as a myth-ritualist.

The specific connection between myth and ritual varies from myth-ritualist to myth-ritualist. For the Victorian biblicist and Arabist William Robertson Smith, the pioneering myth-ritualist, myth is inferior to ritual. It arises as an explanation of ritual only once the point of a ritual is no longer understood. For the classicist and anthropologist James Frazer, myth is the equal of ritual and arises with it to serve as its script. From the outset, myth explains what ritual magically enacts. The classicist Jane Harrison and the biblicist S. H. Hooke go beyond Frazer in bestowing magical efficacy on myth itself, not just on ritual. The Semiticist Theodor Gaster and the anthropologist Adolf Jensen seek to elevate myth above ritual.[22]

Raglan's brand of myth-ritualism derives ultimately from Frazer: myth for Raglan arises alongside ritual to provide the script and is of equal importance. Yet Frazer himself wavers.[23] On the one hand the heart of especially the second and third editions of *The Golden Bough* is exactly the ritualistic enactment of the myths of dying and rising gods of vegetation. On the other hand Frazer's theoretical statements increasingly detach myth from ritual. Indeed, in the introduction to his translation of the *Library* of Apollodorus, an introduction published only six years after the appearance of the twelfth and final volume of the third edition of *The Golden Bough* in 1915, Frazer attacks, though not by name, the very group of Cambridge classicists who deem him their mentor.[24] The fact that the biblicist counterparts to these classicist myth-ritualists single out Frazer as their anti-ritualist nemesis underscores Frazer's inconsistent stands.[25]

Frazer's ambivalence toward myth-ritualism manifests itself in Raglan, who at once applies Frazer's form of myth-ritualism yet takes it considerably from Hooke, Frazer's self-professed antagonist. Having cited Frazer in support of myth-ritualism, Raglan quietly notes that "Sir James elsewhere expresses views difficult to reconcile with this."[26]

RANK'S FREUDIAN HERO

For Rank, following Freud, heroism deals with what Jungians call the first half of life. The first half—birth, childhood, adolescence, and young adulthood—involves the establishment of oneself as an independent person in the external world. The attainment of independence expresses itself concretely in the securing of a job and a mate. The securing of either requires both separation from one's parents and mastery of one's instincts. Independence of one's parents means not the rejection of them but self-sufficiency. Likewise independence of one's instincts means not the rejection of them but control over them: it means not the denial of instincts but the rerouting of them into socially acceptable outlets. When Freud says that the test of happiness is the capacity to work and love, he is clearly referring to the goals of the first half of life, which for him apply to all of life.

Freudian problems involve a lingering attachment to either parents or instincts. Either to depend on one's parents for the satisfaction of instincts or to satisfy instincts in antisocial ways is to be stuck, or fixated, at childhood.

Rank's pattern, which he applies fully to fifteen hero myths, is limited to the first half of life. Roughly paralleling von Hahn's pattern, of which he was unaware, Rank's goes from the hero's birth to his attainment of a "career":

> The hero is the child of most distinguished parents, usually the son of a king. His origin is preceded by difficulties, such as continence, or prolonged barrenness, or secret intercourse of the parents due to external prohibition or obstacles. During or before the pregnancy, there is a prophecy, in the form of a dream or oracle, cautioning against his birth, and usually threatening danger to the father (or his representative). As a rule, he is surrendered to the water, in a box. He is then saved by animals, or by lowly people (shepherds), and is suckled by a female animal or by an humble woman. After he has grown up, he finds his distinguished parents, in a highly versatile fashion. He takes his revenge on his father, on the one hand, and is acknowledged, on the other. Finally, he achieves rank and honors.[27]

Literally, or consciously, the hero, who is always male, is a historical or legendary figure like Oedipus. The hero is heroic because he rises from obscurity to the throne. Literally, he is an innocent victim of either his parents or, ultimately, fate. While his parents have yearned for a child and abandon him only to save the father, they nevertheless do abandon him. The hero's revenge, if the parricide is even committed knowingly, is, then, understandable: who would not consider killing one's would-be killer?

Symbolically, or unconsciously, the hero is heroic not because he dares to win a throne but because he dares to kill his father. The killing is definitely intentional, and the cause is not revenge but sexual frustration. The father has refused to surrender his wife—the real object of the son's efforts: "the deepest, generally unconscious root of the dislike of the son for the father, or of two brothers for each other, is related to be competition for the tender devotion and love of the mother."[28] Too horrendous to face, the true meaning of the hero myth gets covered up by the concocted story. Rather than the culprit, the hero becomes an innocent victim or at worst a justified avenger: "The fictitious romance is the excuse, as it were, for the hostile feelings which the child harbors against his father, and which in this fiction are projected against the father."[29] What the hero seeks gets masked as power, not incest. Most of all, who the hero is becomes some third party, a historical or legendary figure, rather than either the creator of the myth or anyone stirred by it. Identifying himself with the literal hero, the myth maker or reader vicariously revels in the hero's triumph, which in fact is his own. *He* is the real hero of the myth.

Why the literal hero is usually the son of royalty, Rank never explains. Perhaps the filial clash thereby becomes even more titanic: it is over power as well as revenge. Indeed, when, as in Oedipus's case, the hero kills his father unknowingly, the conscious motive can hardly be revenge, so that ambition or something else non-Freudian is needed as an overt motive.

Literally, the myth culminates in the hero's attainment of a throne. Symbolically, the hero gains a mate as well. One might, then, conclude that the myth fittingly expresses the Freudian goal of the first half of life. In actuality, it expresses the opposite. The wish it fulfills is not for detachment from one's parents and from one's antisocial instincts but, on the contrary, for the most intense possible relationship to one's parents and the most antisocial of urges: parricide and incest, even rape. Taking one's father's job and one's mother's hand does not quite spell independence of them.

The myth maker or reader is an adult, but the wish vented by the myth is that of a child of three to five: "Myths are, therefore, created by adults, by means of retrograde childhood fantasies, the hero being credited with the myth maker's personal infantile history."[30] The fantasy is the fulfillment of the Oedipal wish to kill one's father in order to gain access to one's mother. The myth fulfills a wish never outgrown by the adult who either invents or uses it.[31] That adult is psychologically an eternal child. Having never developed an ego strong enough to master his instincts, he is neurotic: "There is a certain class of persons, the so-called psychoneurotics, shown by the teachings of Freud to have remained children, in a sense, although otherwise appearing grown-up."[32] Since no mere child can overpower his father, the myth maker imagines being old enough to do so. In short, the myth expresses not the Freudian goal of the first half of life but the fixated childhood goal that keeps one from accomplishing it.

To be sure, the Oedipal wish is fulfilled in only a limited fashion. The fulfillment is symbolic rather than literal, disguised rather than overt, unconscious rather than conscious, vicarious rather than direct, and mental rather than physical. By identifying himself with the hero, the creator or reader of the myth acts out in his mind deeds that he would dare not act out in the proverbial real world. Still, the myth does provide fulfillment of a kind and, in light of the conflict between the neurotic's impulses and the neurotic's morals, provides the best possible fulfillment.

As brilliant as it is, Rank's theory can be criticized on multiple grounds. One can grant the pattern while denying the Freudian meaning, which, after all, reverses the manifest one. Or one can deny the pattern itself. Certainly the pattern fits only those hero myths, or the portions of them, that cover heroes in the first half of life. Excluded, for example, would be the bulk of the myths of Odysseus and Aeneas, who are largely adult heroes. Rank's own examples come from Europe, the Near East, and India and may not fit heroes from elsewhere.

Indeed, Rank's pattern does not even fit all of his own examples. Moses, for example, is hardly the son of Pharaoh, does not kill or seek to kill Pharaoh, and does not succeed Pharaoh. Moses is the son of lowly rather than noble parents, is exposed by his parents to save rather than to kill him, and is saved by the daughter of Pharaoh.

Yet far from oblivious to these departures from his scheme, Rank, in defense, appeals both to nonbiblical versions of the Moses saga that come closer to his pattern and, still more, to aspects of the biblical account that hint at the pattern. He appeals above all to Pharaoh's fear of the coming generation of Israelite males and the consequent attempt to have them killed at birth. The mighty Pharaoh's terror before mere newborns parallels that of the hero's father before his infant son.

Still, why is there any disparity between the Moses story itself and the pattern it purportedly typifies? Rank would say that it is for the same reason that there is a disparity between that pattern and the Freudian meaning it purportedly harbors: even the pattern, not just the meaning of it, bears too wrenching a truth for the creator or user of the myth to confront. The disparity keeps the truth sequestered. At the same time Rank assumes that the Moses story is close enough for the pattern to be said to hold. A skeptic might contend that in Moses' case and that of others the divide is so wide that no hero pattern lurks beneath.

Even the case of Oedipus, which should surely be paradigmatic, does not fit fully. Oedipus is not abandoned to the water, is raised by a royal rather than lowly couple, and does not consciously seek revenge on his father.[33] Had he known Laius to be his father, he would have shuddered at the idea of killing him.[34]

CAMPBELL'S JUNGIAN HERO

Where for Freud and Rank heroism is limited to the first half of life, for C. G. Jung it involves the second half even more. For Freud and Rank, heroism involves relations with parents and instincts. For Jung, heroism in even the first half involves, in addition, relations with the unconscious. Heroism here means separation not only from parents and antisocial instincts but even more from the unconscious: every child's managing to forge consciousness is for Jung a supremely heroic feat.

For Freud, the unconscious is the product of the repression of instincts. For

Jung, it is inherited rather than created and includes far more than repressed in-stincts. Independence of the Jungian unconscious therefore means more than in-dependence of instincts. It means the formation of consciousness, the object of which in the first half of life is the external world.

The goal of the uniquely Jungian second half of life is likewise consciousness, but now consciousness of the Jungian unconscious rather than of the external world. One must return to the unconscious, from which one has invariably be-come severed. But the aim is not thereby to sever one's ties to the external world. On the contrary, the aim is still to return to the external world. The ideal is a balance between consciousness of the external world and consciousness of the unconscious. The aim of the second half of life is to supplement, not abandon, the achievements of the first half.

Just as classic Freudian problems involve the failure to establish oneself exter-nally, so distinctively Jungian problems involve the failure to reestablish oneself internally. Freudian problems stem from excessive attachment to the world of childhood. Jungian problems stem from excessive attachment to the world one enters upon breaking free of the childhood world: the external world. To be severed from the internal world is to feel empty and lost.

Jung himself allows for heroism in both halves of life, but Campbell does not.[35] Just as Rank confines heroism to the first half of life, so Campbell restricts it to the second half. Rank's scheme begins with the hero's birth; Campbell's, with his adventure. Where Rank's scheme ends, Campbell's begins: with the adult hero ensconced at home. Rank's hero must be young enough for his father and in some cases even his grandfather still to be reigning. Campbell does not specify the age of his hero, but the hero must be no younger than the age at which Rank's hero myth therefore ends: young adulthood. He must, again, be in the second half of life. Campbell does acknowledge heroism in the first half of life and even cites Rank's monograph, but he demotes this youthful heroism to mere preparation for adult heroism: he calls it the "childhood of the human hero." Birth itself he dismisses as unheroic because it is not done consciously.[36]

Rank's hero must be the son of royal or at least distinguished parents. Camp-bell's need not be, though often he is. Campbell later allows for female heroes,[37] but in *Hero* he, like Rank, limits himself to male ones. More accurately, his scheme necessitates male heroes, even though many of his examples are female! Likewise some of his heroes are young, even though his scheme requires adult heroes! Finally, his scheme commits him to human heroes, even though many of his heroes are divine! Rank's pattern, by contrast, allows for divine as well as human heroes.

Where Rank's hero returns to his birthplace, Campbell's marches forth to a strange, new world, which he has never visited or even known existed: "destiny has summoned the hero and transferred his spiritual center of gravity from within the pale of his society to a zone unknown. This fateful region of both treasure and danger may be variously represented: as a distant land, a forest, a kingdom underground, beneath the waves, or above the sky, a secret island, lofty mountain-top, or profound dream state."[38] This extraordinary world is the world of the gods, and the hero must hail from the human world precisely for the worlds to stand in the proper contrast.

In this exotic, supernatural world the hero encounters above all a supreme female god and a supreme male god. The maternal goddess is loving and caring: "She is the paragon of all paragons of beauty, the reply to all desire, the bliss-bestowing goal of every hero's earthly and unearthly quest."[39] By contrast, the male god is tyrannical and merciless—an "ogre."[40] The hero has sex with the goddess and marries her. He then kills and eats the god. Yet with both, not just the goddess, he becomes mystically one and thereby becomes divine himself.[41]

Where Rank's hero *returns* home to encounter his father and mother, Campbell's hero *leaves* home to encounter a male and a female god, who are neither his parents nor a couple. Yet the two heroes' encounters are remarkably akin: just as Rank's hero kills his father and, if usually only latently, marries his mother, so Campbell's hero, in reverse order, first marries the goddess and then kills the god.

The differences, however, are even more significant. Because the goddess is not the hero's mother, sex with her does not constitute incest. Moreover, the two not only marry but also become mystically one.

Despite appearances, the hero's relationship to the male god is for Campbell no less positive. Seemingly, the relationship is blatantly Oedipal. Campbell even cites Róheim's Freudian analysis of aboriginal myths and rituals of initiation, which evince the son's fear of castration by his father and the father's prior fear of death at the hands of his son: "The native Australian mythologies teach that the first initiation rites were carried out in such a way that all the young men were killed. The ritual is thus . . . a dramatized expression of the Oedipal [counter-] aggression [on the part] of the elder generation; and the circumcision, a mitigated castration. But the rites provide also for the cannibal, patricidal impulse of the younger, rising group of males."[42]

Róheim, however, departs from a strictly Freudian interpretation.[43] The sons seek not sex with their mothers but *reunion* with them. They seek to fulfill not their Oedipal desires but their even earlier, infantile ones—a booming echo of the post-Freudian Rank. Their fathers oppose those desires not because they want to keep their wives for themselves but because they want to break their sons' prenatal ties to their mothers. If the fathers try to break those ties by threatening their sons with castration, they also try to break the ties by offering themselves as substitutes for their wives. The fathers selflessly nourish their sons with their own blood, occasionally dying in the process.

Campbell adopts Róheim's more harmonious, non-Freudian interpretation of the clash between sons and fathers and carries it even further. Since Campbell's hero is in the second half of life, he is not, like Róheim's initiates, seeking separation from his mother—for Róheim, as for the renegade Rank, the central experience of life. He is seeking reintegration with her. Furthermore, he is seeking reintegration with his father as well. Indeed, he is not really fighting with his father over his mother. For again, the two gods are neither his parents nor a couple. The hero is seeking from the god the same love that he has just won from the goddess. To secure it he need not give up the goddess but need only trust in the god, who is symbolized by the father: "One must have a faith that the father is merciful, and then a reliance on that mercy."[44] The father sacrifices himself to his son.

When Campbell says that initiation rituals and myths "reveal the benign self-giving aspect of the *archetypal* father," he is using the term in its Jungian sense.[45] For Freudians, gods symbolize parents. For Jungians, parents symbolize gods, who in turn symbolize father and mother archetypes, which are components of the hero's personality. The hero's relationship to these gods symbolizes not, as for Freud, Rank, and Róheim, a son's relationship to other persons—his parents—but the relationship of one side of a male's personality—his ego—to another side—his unconscious. The father and the mother are but two of the archetypes of which the Jungian, or collective, unconscious is composed. Archetypes are unconscious not because they have been repressed but because they have never been conscious. For Jung and Campbell, myth originates and functions not, as for Freud and Rank, to satisfy neurotic urges that cannot be manifested openly but to express normal sides of the personality that have just not had a chance at realization.

By identifying himself with the hero of a myth, Rank's myth maker or reader vicariously lives out in his mind an adventure that, if ever directly fulfilled, would be acted out on his parents themselves. While also identifying himself with the hero of a myth, Campbell's myth maker or reader vicariously lives out in his mind an adventure that even when directly fulfilled would still be taking place in his mind. For parts of the mind are what he is really encountering.

Having managed to break free of the secure, everyday world and go off to a dangerous new one, Campbell's hero, to complete his journey, must in turn break free of the new world, in which he has by now become ensconced, and return to the everyday one. So enticing is the new world that leaving it proves harder than leaving home was. Circe, Calypso, the Sirens, and the Lotus Eaters thus tempt Odysseus with not just a comfortable, long life but a carefree, immortal one.

Though often misconstrued, Jung no less than Freud opposes a state of sheer unconsciousness. Both strive to make the unconscious conscious. While they differ over the origin of the unconscious and over its capacity to become conscious, the ideal for both remains consciousness. Jung opposes the rejection of ordinary, or ego, consciousness for unconsciousness as vigorously as he opposes the rejection of unconsciousness for ego consciousness. He seeks a balance between ego consciousness and the unconscious, between consciousness of the external world and consciousness of the unconscious. For Jung, the hero's failure to return to the everyday world would spell his failure to resist the allure of the unconscious.

By contrast to Jung, Campbell seeks a state of pure unconsciousness. Campbell's hero never returns to the everyday world. He surrenders to the unconscious. Yet Campbell himself demands the hero's return to the everyday world. How, then, can his hero really be spurning it? The answer is that the world to which Campbell's hero returns is not really the everyday world. It is the strange, new world, which turns out to pervade the everyday one. No separate everyday world exists. The everyday world and the new world are really one: "The two worlds, the divine [i.e., new] and the human [i.e., everyday], can be pictured only as distinct from each other—different as life and death, as day and night. . . . Nevertheless . . . the two kingdoms are actually one. . . . The values and distinctions that in normal life seem important disappear with the terrifying assimilation of [what is now] the self into what formerly was [to the ego] only otherness."[46] The hero need never have left home after all: "Hence separateness, withdrawal, is no longer necessary. Wherever the hero may wander, whatever he may do, he is ever in the presence of his own essence—for he has the perfected eye to see. There is no separateness."[47]

To say that the everyday world and the new world are one is to say that no distinctive everyday world exists. Campbell thus dismisses as illusory the "values and distinctions" of the everyday world. If no everyday world exists, then the hero's apparent return to it is a sham. If no everyday world exists, then the ego, which provides consciousness of it, is itself a sham as well.

By contrast to Campbell, Jung never denies the existence of the everyday world and therefore of the ego. He rejects the everyday world, the object of ego consciousness, as the *sole* reality, not as *a* reality. While he seeks to integrate the everyday world with the new one, ego consciousness with the unconscious, he denies that it is possible to fuse them, at least without thereby dissolving both the everyday world and the ego itself.

Campbell's hero both returns and remains home not only because he finds the new world back home but also because he wants selflessly to save others: "The full round, the norm of the monomyth, requires that the hero shall now begin the labor of bringing the runes of wisdom, the Golden Fleece, or his sleeping princess, back into the kingdom of humanity, where the boon may redound to the renewing of the community, the nation, the planet, or the ten thousand worlds."[48] If the hero's return is selfless, then the everyday world to which he is returning is worthless. Indeed, he is returning only to apprise others of the fact:

whatever the literal "boon," the symbolic one is knowledge, knowledge of the status of the everyday world. To be sure, the everyday world here is distinct from the new one, but for exactly that reason it is no less worthless now than when the two worlds are one. Campbell's chief heroes consequently include the selfless Buddha, Moses, Aeneas, and Jesus.

Campbell's characterization of the hero's return as triumphant reveals another fundamental departure from Jung: Campbell's hero ironically remains bound to the *first* half of life. Even though Campbell's hero has undeniably already accomplished the goals of the first half of life, truly reencounters the unconscious, must even guard against succumbing to it, and returns home transformed, he also returns *triumphant*. He thinks he has tamed the unconscious and can do the same for others.

Jung would say that Campbell's hero has in fact missed the power and depth of the unconscious. A Jungian hero would return home humbled rather than elevated, wary rather than brash, the saved rather than the savior. A Jungian hero would seek only a *modus vivendi* with the unconscious, not control over it. Campbell's hero is, in Jungian lingo, merely an "inflated" ego. Only Jung's is a full-fledged "self." If on the one hand Campbell ventures well beyond Jung in seeing heroism as the transcendence of the ego in mystical oneness with the unconscious, on the other hand he stops far short of Jung in simultaneously seeing heroism as the ego's mastery over the unconscious. Only because Campbell assumes that the ego stays in control can he, without trepidation, espouse the fusion of the ego with the unconscious. Jung would deny that in a deeper encounter with the unconscious the ego either could or should remain in control. To underscore the difference between Campbell's and Jung's notions of heroism, Jungian analyst Joseph Henderson goes as far as to restrict heroism per se to Campbell's variety and to relabel the Jungian ideal "initiation."[49]

Like Rank's theory, Campbell's can be faulted on various grounds. As with Rank's theory, one might grant the pattern but deny the meaning. Or one might question the pattern itself. Since it obviously applies only to myths about heroes in the second half of life, it excludes all of Rank's hero myths, or at least all Rank's portions of them. Whether it even fits Campbell's own examples is not easy to tell, for Campbell, unlike either Rank or Raglan, provides no set of hero myths to accompany the whole of his pattern. While he continually cites scores of hero myths to illustrate individual parts of his pattern, he does not apply his full pattern to even one myth. He acknowledges the point but declares brashly that "should he [the reader] wish to prove whether all [the myths cited merely in part] might have been cited for every section of the monomyth, he need only turn to some of the source volumes enumerated in the footnotes and ramble through a few of the multitude of tales."[50]

Yet one might question even so seemingly transparent a confirmation of Campbell's pattern as the myth of Aeneas, which Campbell names as an example of his pattern.[51] Aeneas's descent to Hades and return does fit Campbell's scheme snugly, but Aeneas's larger itinerary does not. Rather than returning home to Troy upon completion of his journey, he proceeds to Italy to found a new civilization. Similarly, Odysseus's descent to the underworld fits Campbell's pattern, but his larger journey, which Campbell cites,[52] does not. Odysseus, unlike Aeneas, does return home, but also unlike Aeneas, he arrives with no boon in hand. His return is an entirely personal triumph. Since Campbell distinguishes a myth from a fairy tale on exactly the grounds that the triumph of a mythic hero is more than personal,[53] Odysseus's story would thereby fail to qualify as a myth.[54]

RAGLAN'S FRAZERIAN HERO

Rank's hero triumphs at the expense of everyone else; Lord Raglan's, like Campbell's, saves everyone else. Campbell's saving hero need not die; Raglan's must. Campbell's hero undertakes a dangerous journey to aid his community; Raglan's hero in the myth is driven from his community and, in the accompanying ritual, is sacrificed by the community. Campbell's hero can be any adult male; Raglan's must be a king. Campbell's hero must—or should—be human; Raglan's can be divine or human.

Raglan is indebted to the myth-ritualists James Frazer and S. H. Hooke not merely for their link of myth to ritual but also for their identification of the specific ritual involved. That ritual involves the king, but Frazer and, following him, Hooke conflate two distinct forms of the ritual.[55] In one form of the ritual the king is a mere human being and simply plays the role of the god. The dramatic enactment of the death and rebirth of the god, who is the god of vegetation, magically causes the rebirth of the presently dead god and in turn of the presently dead vegetation. The ritual is performed annually at the end—the would-be end—of winter. In the other form of the ritual the king is himself divine: the god of vegetation resides in him. The king is actually killed and the soul of the god transferred to his successor. No magic is involved here. The killing of the king does not induce the killing of the god but instead preserves the health of the god, for the king is killed and replaced at the first sign of weakness or at the end of a fixed term so short as to minimize the chance of illness or death in office. As the king goes, so goes the god and so in turn goes vegetation.

Raglan adopts this second version of the ritual.[56] He attributes it to Hooke rather than to Frazer, but Hooke himself takes it from Frazer.[57] Here the king *is* the god of vegetation rather than playing the part of the god.[58] Consequently, the killing and replacement of the king, which initially is literal but later merely symbolic, does not magically cause the death and rebirth of the god but *is* the death and rebirth—better, the weakening and reinvigoration—of that god and therefore of vegetation.[59] For Raglan, as for Frazer and Hooke, the myth describes the life of the figure and the ritual enacts it. The function of the ritual, which is performed either at the end of the king's fixed term or upon his weakening, is, as for Frazer and Hooke, to aid the community. Besides the fertility of the earth, that aid can take the form of success in war, good health, or human fertility.

Venturing beyond both Frazer and Hooke, Raglan equates the king with the hero. For Frazer and Hooke, the king may in effect be a hero to his community, but only Raglan labels him one. In addition, Raglan introduces his own detailed hero pattern, which he applies to twenty-one hero myths.[60] That pattern extends all the way from the hero's conception to his death. In contrast to Rank's and Campbell's patterns, it therefore covers both halves of life:

1. The hero's mother is a royal virgin;
2. His father is a king, and
3. Often a near relative of his mother, but
4. The circumstances of his conception are unusual, and
5. He is also reputed to be the son of a god.
6. At birth an attempt is made, usually by his father or his maternal grandfather, to kill him, but
7. He is spirited away, and
8. Reared by foster-parents in a far country.
9. We are told nothing of his childhood, but
10. On reaching manhood he returns or goes to his future kingdom.
11. After a victory over the king and/or a giant, dragon, or wild beast,
12. He marries a princess, often the daughter of his predecessor, and
13. Becomes king.
14. For a time he reigns uneventfully, and
15. Prescribes laws, but
16. Later he loses favour with the gods and/or his subjects, and
17. Is driven from the throne and city, after which
18. He meets with a mysterious death,
19. Often at the top of a hill.
20. His children, if any, do not succeed him.
21. His body is not buried, but nevertheless
22. He has one or more holy sepulchres.[61]

Clearly, parts one to thirteen correspond roughly to Rank's entire scheme, though Raglan himself never read Rank.[62] Six of Raglan's cases duplicate Rank's, and the anti-Freudian Raglan nevertheless also takes the case of Oedipus as his standard.[63] The victory that gives the hero the throne is not, however, Oedipal, for the vanquished is not necessarily his father, even if, as for Rank, the father is usually the one who had sought his son's death at birth. Parts fourteen to twenty-two do not correspond at all to Campbell's scheme. The hero's exile is loosely akin to the hero's journey, but for Raglan there is no return. The hero's sepulchres do serve as a kind of boon, but not for his native community. For Rank, the heart of the hero pattern is gaining kingship. For Raglan, the heart is losing it. Wherever Campbell's heroes are kings, the heart is their journey *while* king.

For all Raglan's touting of the symbiosis of myth and ritual, his myth and ritual seem incongruously out of sync. In the myth the protagonist is usually human. In the ritual the protagonist is always divine. The myth runs from the birth of the protagonist to his mysterious death. The ritual enacts only the portion of the myth that corresponds to the replacement of the king: the exile of the incumbent.

Raglan nevertheless equates the hero of the myth with the god of the ritual: "The conclusion that suggests itself is that the god is the hero as he appears in ritual, and the hero is the god as he appears in myth; in other words, the hero and the god are two different aspects of the same superhuman being."[64] But how can a god lose power, let alone die? Raglan's answer is that it is the hero, not the god, who loses power and then dies—even though the hero and the god are identical!

Still, how can the myth that purportedly provides the script for the ritual be so at odds with it? Raglan's rejoinder is that the myth and the ritual are not so far apart. In both, the central figure is the king. Moreover, many of the events in the life of the hero are supernatural, so that the hero must in fact be a god himself. Above all, what Raglan considers the core of the myth—the toppling of the king—corresponds to the undeniable core of the ritual—the killing of the king when he either weakens or finishes his term.

For Rank, heroes are heroic because they dare to serve themselves. For both Campbell and Raglan, heroes are heroic because they willingly or unwillingly serve their communities. For Raglan, heroes in myth serve their communities by their victories over those who threaten their peoples' physical welfare. Hence Oedipus defeats the Sphinx, who is starving Thebes. Heroes in ritual serve their communities by their sacrificial deaths. In both myths and rituals, heroes are really ideal kings. For Campbell, heroes in myth serve their communities by their return home with a boon, typically secured only by defeating or at least taming supernatural entities. Where the boon bestowed by Raglan's hero is entirely material, that bestowed by Campbell's is immaterial: it is not food but, again, wisdom. Without Raglan's hero the community would die; without Campbell's, it would remain benighted.

Like Rank's and Campbell's theories, Raglan's can be questioned on various counts. One might grant the mythic pattern but deny a connection to ritual. One might grant some connection but deny that, in the light of the disparity between the myth and the ritual, it takes Raglan's form. Or one might deny the pattern itself—denying either that it applies worldwide[65] or that it even applies substantially to Raglan's own cases. By Raglan's own tally, none of his examples scores all twenty-two points, and one scores only nine. Rank can at least assert, albeit nonfalsifiably, that hero myths which stray from his scheme are distortions created to keep the true pattern hidden. Raglan can use no comparable ploy: there is nothing in his pattern to be kept a secret. Why, then, one might ask, do not any of his hero myths, if not all hero myths, attain perfect scores?[66]

THE THREE THEORIES COMPARED

The theories of Rank, Campbell, and Raglan typify the array of analyses of hero myths. For Rank, the true subject of hero myths is the family. For Campbell, it is the mind. For Raglan, it is the physical world and, even more, the gods who control that world.

Both Rank and Campbell read myth symbolically. Because the real subject of hero myths for Rank is the family, the figures in a hero myth symbolize the myth maker or reader and his parents. It is, then, confusing for Rank to identify the hero with the ego[67]—as if the hero's parents represent other parts of the mind. Because the real subject of hero myths for Campbell is the mind, the figures in a hero myth symbolize parts of the myth maker's or reader's mind: the ego and the archetypes of the collective unconscious.

By contrast to both Rank and Campbell, Raglan reads myth literally. Stories about heroes are really about heroes. While Raglan relentlessly impugns the historicity of heroes, he takes for granted that stories about them are *meant* literally.[68] While Raglan *equates* heroes with gods, heroes for him do not *symbolize* gods. They *are* gods.

For Rank, hero myths originate and function to fulfill a blocked need: the need to fulfill socially and personally unacceptable impulses. The fulfillment that myth provides is compensatory: it is a disguised, unconscious, and merely fantasized venting of impulses that cannot be vented directly. The meaning of myth is therefore unconscious. One cannot face it openly.

For Campbell, hero myths originate and function to fulfill not a blocked need but, more innocently, a yet unrealized one: the need to discover and nurture a latent side of one's personality. There is nothing socially or personally objectionable about that side, in which, indeed, one comes to revel. Rather than a merely compensatory fulfillment, myth provides a direct and full one—in fact, the best possible one. Wherever the meaning of myth is unconscious, that meaning has not been kept hidden. It has merely gone unrecognized. For Rank, deciphering the meaning is like breaking a code. For Campbell, it is like figuring out the Rosetta stone. Campbell, however, goes beyond even Jung, not merely beyond Rank, when he insists both that, except for literalist moderns, the meaning of myth has always been conscious and that myth works only *when* the meaning is conscious.

For Raglan, hero myths originate and function to fulfill neither a blocked need nor a potential one but an ever-beckoning one: the need for food and other necessities. Myth serves the same function as applied science: controlling the physical world in order to survive. For those without science, myth is not merely a compensatory way or even the best way of serving its function but the sole way. Raglan himself, to be sure, does not assume that adherents to myth would die without it, only that they think they would. Adherents take for granted that myth alone enables them to control the gods who control vegetation.

For Rank and Campbell, hero myths work. For Rank, they provide a partial satisfaction of Oedipal wishes. For Campbell, they reveal an otherwise unknown side of the personality. For Raglan, however, hero myths do nothing: they are an illusory means of delivering the goods. Science provides the only true means. For both Rank and Campbell, hero myths work as long as adherents believe in heroes. For Raglan, hero myths would work only if the heroes were real.

Rank allows for modern as well as primitive hero myths. As long as there are neurotics, there will be hero myths. Because hero myths for Rank can be secular as well as religious, there is no automatic conflict between myth and science and so between myth and modernity. Campbell does not merely allow for modern as well as primitive hero myths but proclaims their existence. All humans for him spontaneously spin myths. Relentlessly pitting religion against science, he not only distinguishes religious hero myths from the rest of religion but also maintains that religious heroes are gradually being superseded by secular ones—most recently, by heroes whose adventures take them to outer space. If myth for Campbell fell within the realm of religion, then myth and science, hence myth and modernity, would stand opposed. But for him myth transcends religion.

By contrast to both Rank and Campbell, Raglan denies the existence of modern hero myths. While he doubtless grants the existence of modern heroes, his equation of heroes in myths with gods of nature commits adherents to hero myths to the belief in one or more gods who are incarnate in humans and who directly determine the course of nature. For Raglan, this belief conflicts with modern science, so that to have science is not to have myth. Adherence to hero myths also commits one to kingship, for gods deign to reside only in royalty, never in commoners. Myth for Raglan, following Frazer, is an exclusively prescientific phenomenon. Where for Rank hero myths will disappear only if neurosis ever does, and where for Campbell hero myths will never disappear, for Raglan hero myths *have* disappeared.

IX • THE ROMANTIC APPEAL OF JOSEPH CAMPBELL

OF ALL THE CHARGES that Brendan Gill lodged in the *New York Review of Books* (September 28, 1989) against the heretofore sacrosanct Joseph Campbell, the most stinging was not that Campbell was either an anti-Semite or a political reactionary but that his work appeals to guilt-ridden yuppies seeking a rationalization for their materialistic narcissism.[1] Campbell's pet litany, "Follow your bliss," purportedly inspires his fans to do whatever makes them happy, including making money.

Gill's cynical evaluation of Campbell's posthumous popularity prompts both logical and factual questions. Gill's argument is based not on any polling of Campbell's devotees but on speculation. The popularity of Campbell's *Hero with a Thousand Faces* (1st ed., 1949), the book that has most spurred fans to pave their own yellow brick road, peaked not in the eighties but in the sixties. Campbell first uttered the phrase "Follow your bliss" to his Sarah Lawrence undergraduates decades earlier. Even if that innocuous slogan bestows carte blanche on all who heed it, it hardly follows that to encourage people to do whatever they most deeply want to do is to encourage them to do any specific thing.

Furthermore, Campbell psychologizes the message that he claims myth tells. For him, true heroism is not external but internal: the hero's literal search for wealth or anything else symbolizes the search for self-knowledge. The land to which the hero treks symbolizes the unconscious. Even if all of Campbell's disciples became investment bankers, their acquisitiveness would, for their master, be merely the outward expression of an inner quest.

Most important, Campbell's message is far more mystical than individualistic. Campbell is an uncompromising world ecumenist. As he declares in the preface to *Hero,* he wants to demonstrate that all myths are one in order to demonstrate that all peoples are one. In *The Power of Myth,* the book based on the television interviews with Bill Moyers, he continues to say that we still "need myths that will identify the individual not with his local group but with the planet."[2]

Gill's assertion, focusing on Campbell's private pronouncements rather than on his writings, is not just silly but shallow. Campbell's inspiration to others has come from his authority as an analyst of myth. His advice carries only as much clout as his insight into myth. Had Gill really wanted to damn his lifelong friend, he would have attacked the man's theory. I suggest that Campbell's appeal derives from the unashamed romanticism of his theory. Campbell's recent popularity reflects no changing ethos of the generations but only the unprecedented publicity given him by Moyers.

RATIONALIST AND ROMANTIC APPROACHES TO MYTH

Campbell's romantic view of myth is the opposite of a rationalist view, as epitomized by Edward Tylor. To rationalists, myth is a wholly primitive explanation of the physical world. It is the primitive counterpart to science, which is exclusively modern. Science makes myth both unnecessary and impossible for moderns, who by definition are scientific. Myth and science are not only redundant in function but also incompatible in content: myth invokes the wills of gods to account for the origin and operation of the physical world; science appeals to the mechanical behavior of impersonal forces like atoms. There are no modern myths. "Modern myth" is a contradiction in terms.

By contrast, Campbell and fellow romantics see myth as an eternal, not merely a primitive, possession. Nothing can supersede it. Where rationalists believe that science better serves its explanatory *function* than myth, romantics believe that nothing duplicates the psychological or metaphysical *content* of myth. Read symbolically rather than, as for many rationalists, literally, myth refers not to the physical world described by science but to either the human mind or ultimate reality. Myth runs askew to science and is therefore still acceptable to moderns, who, like rationalists, are by definition scientific. Some romantics, including Campbell, dare to pronounce science itself mythic. To rationalists, nothing could be more anathema.

Rationalists may grant that the explanatory function served by myth is itself indispensable, but only romantics consider myth indispensable to the serving of its function, which is above all the revelation of the nature of reality. For romantics, moderns as well as "primitives" not merely can have but must have myth. Rationalists contend that without some explanation of the environment, be that explanation mythic or scientific, humans would be perplexed, but romantics assert that without the revelation found exclusively in myth, humans would be unfulfilled. Rationalists acknowledge that myth, like science, can be effective—functional—when it is *believed* to be true, but for them it is in fact false: myth is a cogent but nevertheless incorrect explanation of the world, science providing the correct one. Romantics assume that myth is effective not merely when it is accepted as true but because it *is* true: the wisdom it offers would not be wisdom if it proved false.

CAMPBELL'S ROMANTICISM

The first aspect of Campbell's romantic appeal is the elevated status he accords myth. For him, myth constitutes a collective Bible for all humanity. It alone contains the wisdom necessary for what amounts to salvation. Both the array of functions that Campbell ascribes to myth and the scope of his definition of myth guarantee its irreplaceability. Dreams, art, literature, ideology, and science become *varieties* of myth rather than alternatives to it. An action as well as a belief can be mythic, and the belief need not even take the form of a story, which itself can be of any kind.

Because myth defined so broadly is indispensable to the serving of its indispensable functions, Campbell declares unabashedly that without myth, even myth taken literally, humans are lost:

> For not only has it always been the way of multitudes to interpret their own symbols literally, but such literally read symbolic forms have always been . . . the supports of their civilizations, the supports of their moral orders, their cohesion, vitality, and creative powers. . . . With our old mythologically founded taboos unsettled by our own modern sciences, there is everywhere in the civilized world a rapidly rising incidence of vice and crime, mental disorders, suicides and dope addictions, shattered homes, impudent children, violence, murder, and despair.[3]

Because no other theorist makes myth indispensable on so many fronts, no other theorist, not even C. G. Jung or Mircea Eliade, is as much an evangelist for myth as Campbell.

A second aspect of Campbell's romantic appeal is his esteem for primitives. He maintains that moderns barely equal, let alone surpass, them. Rationalists view primitives as intellectually inferior to moderns: where primitives invent myth, which is a childish as well as false explanation of the world, moderns create science, which is a mature as well as true explanation of the world. Campbell views primitives as wiser than moderns: primitives know intuitively the meaning of myth that moderns need depth psychology to extricate. In fact, primitives know the meaning that moderns have altogether forgotten and need both Freudian and especially Jungian psychology to recollect. Campbell thus claims only to be rediscovering, not discovering, the real meaning of myth—a meaning known fully to our forebears. Jung himself, not to mention Freud, never goes this far. For both of them, moderns alone, thanks to psychology, have the chance to discover the true meaning of myth. Similarly for Rudolph Bultmann and Hans Jonas, moderns alone or at least above all, thanks to existentialist philosophy, have the chance to discover the true meaning of myth.

A third aspect of Campbell's romantic appeal follows from the second: if primitives already know the meaning of myth which moderns are merely recovering, that meaning is always the same. An unbroken tradition binds the hoariest myths to the newest ones. Contrary to the rationalist view, there *are* modern myths. Campbell singles out the distinctively modern myths of space travel, as typified by the "Star Wars" saga. But modern myths have the same meaning as primitive ones.

A fourth aspect of Campbell's romantic appeal parallels the third: not only do all myths bear one message, but the message borne is the oneness of all things. Myths not only assume but outright preach mysticism. Myths proclaim that humans are one with one another, with their individual selves, and with the world. No tenet is more staunchly romantic than the conviction that beneath the apparent disparateness of all things lies oneness.

A fifth and final aspect of Campbell's romantic appeal is his assumption that the mystical message of myth is true. To Campbell, not only is the true message of myth the oneness of all things, but all things are truly one. Myth thus discloses the deepest truth about reality.

CRITICISMS

As fetching as Campbell's theory of myth is, it is flawed. First, Campbell operates dogmatically, asserting rather than proving his theory. Because he analyzes surprisingly few myths, at least few whole ones, he rarely puts his theory to the interpretive test. At the same time he ignores rival theorists. Other theorists define myth more narrowly than Campbell; find in myth functions other than the ones Campbell finds; and consider dreams, ritual, art, literature, ideology, or science equal, even superior, ways of fulfilling those functions. Others interpret the meaning of myth differently from Campbell.

Beginning with the third volume (1964) of the four-volume *The Masks of God,* Campbell dogmatically pronounces the function of myth to be fourfold. Myth instills a sense of awe and mystery toward the world; offers not an explanation of the world, which science provides, but a symbolic image for an explanation—for example, the image of the Great Chain of Being; preserves society by justifying social practices and institutions like the Indian caste system; and harmonizes individuals with society, the cosmos, and themselves. Why these four disparate functions, Campbell never explains.

Similarly, Campbell dogmatically insists that the true meaning of myth is ahistorical rather than historical and symbolic rather than literal. He also insists that the symbolic meaning of myth is at once psychological, metaphysical, and mystical: myth preaches not that all is unconsciousness or all ultimate reality but that unconsciousness and consciousness are one and that ultimate reality and everyday reality are one. Myth finds unconsciousness within, not beyond, consciousness, and finds ultimate reality within, not beyond, everyday reality, which is therefore to be embraced rather than rejected. Why the meaning—the sole meaning—of all myths must be ahistorical, symbolic, psychological, metaphysical, mystical, and world-affirming, Campbell, again, never explains.

Other theorists would demur. Some read myth both literally and historically. Others read myth literally but nonhistorically. Campbell, equating a literal interpretation with a historical one, assumes that to read the Oedipus myth literally is to believe that there was once a king named Oedipus. But Lord Raglan and Vladimir Propp, for example, would suggest that the myth, while rightly read literally, describes the life of a king one by no means thereby assumes to have lived. Still others take myth symbolically but neither psychologically nor metaphysically. Emile Durkheim, for example, contends that myth describes society rather than either the mind or ultimate reality. Freud and Jung take myth psychologically but not metaphysically: myth describes the human world, not the external world. While many theorists of myth assume, like Campbell, that all myths harbor a uniform meaning, only Lucien Lévy-Bruhl, among major theorists, deems that meaning mystical.

Campbell's interpretation of myths differs not only from that of other theorists but also from that of believers. Mainstream Christianity, Judaism, Islam, and ancient Greek and Roman religions do not teach that heaven and earth or soul and body, let alone god and humans, are one. Indeed, the worst sin in Western religions is the attempt to dissolve the divide between god and humanity. Mysticism is a minor strain in the West and more often rejects the world than embraces it. Campbell's unruffled response is that Western religions misunderstand their own myths. How he knows better than believers themselves the meaning of their own myths, Campbell never says.

Second, Campbell contradicts himself on the meaning, function, and origin of myth. On the one hand he regularly interprets the meaning of all myths as mystical. On the other hand he comes to read modern Western myths as espousing self-reliant individualism rather than self-effacing mysticism.

Likewise Campbell does not always say that myth serves the four functions noted. Most often he considers the prime function revelatory: myth discloses a deeper side of both humans and the world. Tied to this function is an experiential one: through myth humans do not merely discover but actually encounter this deeper reality. At other times the function is more mechanical: myth activates the release and even the sublimation of emotions.

Sometimes Campbell says that myth arises out of the unconscious, which itself is alternatively an inherited, Jungian-like entity and a forged, Freudian-like one. Other times he says that myth emerges from the effects of either recurrent or traumatic experiences. In all of these cases, each society invents its own myths. At other times, however, he says that myth originates in one society and spreads elsewhere. Occasionally, Campbell gives these competing explanations in the same book.

Third, Campbell argues circularly. He declares that myth serves foremost to reveal the oneness of all things, but it serves that function only if all things are in fact one. How does he know that they are? Because myth says so! We are to trust myth because myth is trustworthy. Campbell is like a Christian fundamentalist who urges everyone to accept the Bible because it is true. Where other theorists of myth turn to psychology, sociology, history, and other disciplines to evaluate myth, Campbell deems myth self-validating. For example, rather than using history to assess myths of primordial matriarchy, he draws from myths historical conclusions about matriarchy. Myth, proclaims Campbell, is always right. Why? Because it is myth.

Fourth, Campbell is lopsidedly universalistic. Seeking similarities is itself unobjectionable. By definition, all theorists seek similarities among myths, and the quest for similarities is central to the quest for knowledge. But in his search for similarities Campbell brazenly ignores lingering differences. Though he continually professes interest in differences as well as similarities, he finally dismisses all differences as trivial: "Dissolving, the ethnic [i.e., local] ideas become transparent to the archetypes, those elementary ideas of which they [i.e., the ethnic ideas] are no more than the local masks."[4]

In *Masks* Campbell does distinguish among primitive, Eastern, ancient Western, and modern Western mythologies. He further divides primitive mythology into hunting and planting mythologies. Yet he simultaneously asserts that hunters are at heart planters, Westerners at heart Easterners, and modern Westerners like primitive hunters—in which case all peoples and so all myths are really one. And all myths turn out to preach the same mystical homily.

A revealing foil to Campbell's universalism is Jung's approach. To interpret a myth, Campbell simply identifies the archetypes in it. An interpretation of the *Odyssey,* for example, would show how Odysseus's life conforms to a heroic pattern. Jung, by contrast, considers the identification of archetypes merely the first step in the interpretation of a myth. One must also determine the meaning of those archetypes in the specific myth in which they appear and the meaning of that myth in the life of the specific person who is stirred by it. One must analyze the person, not just the myth.

Fifth, Campbell uniformly ignores the adherents of myth. Though he investigates why and how myths originate and function, he never asks who invents and uses myths. He does not care. Hence his insistence that Westerners have systematically miscontrued their own myths. While Campbell's refusal to defer to the actor is refreshing, his indifference to the actor is startling. Few theorists of myth *end* with the actor's point of view—otherwise they would have nothing of their own to offer—but nearly all *start* there. Indeed, that point of view provides the phenomenon to be analyzed.

Sixth, Campbell typically ignores the story in myths—most ironic for someone lauded as a masterly storyteller. With the conspicuous exception of *Hero,* the only place in which he provides a pattern for myths, Campbell ignores the plot and instead isolates either the beliefs underlying the plot or else specific archetypes in the plot. The fact that, in addition, he analyzes few whole myths and includes as myths creeds and even rituals underscores how limited for him is the role of storytelling.

A final weakness is Campbell's pitting of myth against religion. He assumes that in the West, though somehow not in the East, religion inevitably literalizes and historicizes myth. He takes the typical Church Father to be not Augustine but Jimmy Swaggart. Actually, mainstream and not just heretical Christianity and Judaism have traditionally interpreted the Bible symbolically as well as literally. Conversely, some of the most fervent antinomians have been literalists. Campbell's equation of institutionalization with degeneration and of individualism with purity is adolescent. Max Weber noted long ago that the institutionalization of any movement is not only inevitable but also necessary. The alternative is extinction.

Here, too, the difference between Campbell and Jung is acute. Jung is wary of the psychological risks of spontaneous religiosity, praises quintessentially institutionalized Catholicism for its psychological efficacy, nearly equates mainline Protestantism with modern atheism, bemoans the decline of Christianity generally, and turns anxiously to analytical psychology as a modern substitute. By contrast, Campbell, who is far closer to Nietzsche than to Jung, castigates traditional Christianity generally *as* institutionalized and therefore psychologically impotent, damns his own boyhood Catholicism most of all, revels in the anticipated demise of all Christianity, and sees no need for a substitute for it. Jung suggests that psychology at once replaces religion and reinterprets its extant myths. Campbell argues that psychology merely restores the interpretations of myths directly imbibed by earliest humanity but haplessly missed ever since by its "churched" successors.[5]

Despite these many criticisms, Joseph Campbell merits much praise. He, more than anyone else, has helped to revive popular interest in myth. His indefatigable proselytizing for a comparativist, symbolic, psychological, and mystical approach to myth has done much to liberate those raised on a particularistic, literalist, historical, and antimystical approach to the Bible above all. Campbell's work is an important introduction to myth. It is simply not the last word.

X · HANS BLUMENBERG AS THEORIST
OF MYTH

IN HIS CONTEMPORARY CLASSIC, *Work on Myth* (hereafter *WOM*),[1] Hans Blumenberg attacks two leading modern views of myth: that of the Enlightenment and that of Romanticism. Edward Tylor, though cited only once (see *WOM*, 151), and Joseph Campbell, though never cited, are standard exemplars of each view.[2]

Blumenberg sums up the Enlightenment view, which he by no means limits to the eighteenth century, in the familiar phrase "from *mythos* to *logos*."[3] Tylor, epitomizing that view, assumes an evolution from myth, which he subsumes under religion, to philosophy and, more, to science. For him, "primitives" alone have myth and moderns alone have science. Myth and science are not only incompatible in content but also redundant in function: both serve to explain the physical world—myth invoking the decisions of gods, science the mechanical behavior of impersonal forces.

Blumenberg assumes that the contrast between *mythos* and *logos* necessarily makes myth irrational. He thus berates the Enlightenment for failing to see myth "as itself [serving] a rational function" (*WOM*, 48). But his criticism does not hold for all "Enlightened" theorists and certainly not for Tylor. Far from either blind superstition or frivolous storytelling, myth for Tylor is a scrupulously logical and reflective enterprise: "The basis on which such [mythic] ideas as these are built is not to be narrowed down to poetic fancy and transformed metaphor. They rest upon a broad philosophy of nature, early and crude indeed, but thoughtful, consistent, and quite really and seriously meant."[4] Tylor does judge myth false, but not irrational. *As* the primitive counterpart to modern science, it offers a systematic and coherent account of the world.

Having been displaced by science as the explanation of the world, myth, according to Blumenberg, is left by Enlightened theorists with a merely aesthetic role: "In his discussion of myth Fontenelle expressed the Enlightenment's amazement at the fact that the myths of the Greeks had still not disappeared from the world. Religion [i.e., Christianity] and reason had, it is true, weaned people from them, but poetry and painting had given them the means by which to survive. They had known how to make themselves indispensable to these arts" (*WOM,* 263). Ironically, Tylor here goes even further than Blumenberg assumes Enlightened theorists go. In the wake of science, *religion* for him severs itself from myth, which had previously been a part of it. Modern religion secures an ethical, not merely aesthetic, function in place of its explanatory one, but *myth* secures nothing. Bereft of even an aesthetic task, extant myth is a mere relic—in Tylor's terms, a mere "survival." "Modern myth" is a contradiction in terms.

Blumenberg rejects the Enlightenment view of myth on two grounds: first, that myth continues to exist in modernity (see *WOM,* 263–64, 274)—a point conceded by much of the Enlightenment—and, second, that myth was never an explanation of the world. At least once Blumenberg combines these arguments: "That does not yet mean that the *explanation* of phenomena has always had priority and that myths are something like early ways of dealing with the difficulty of lacking theory. If they were an expression of the lack of science or of prescientific explanation, they would have been disposed of automatically at the latest when science . . . made its entrance" (*WOM,* 274). For Blumenberg, the survival of myths in the wake of science proves that their function was never scientific.[5]

By a scientific explanation, Blumenberg means a genetic, or an etiological, one. As he says in criticism of the Enlightenment view, "That the relationship between the 'prejudice' called myth and the new science should [for the Enlightenment] be one of competition necessarily presupposes the interpretation of individual myths as etiological" (*WOM,* 265).

For a number of reasons, asserts Blumenberg, myth is nonetiological. First, even standard creation myths like Hesiod's *Theogony* and Genesis 1–2 give no ultimate origin of the world. Rather, they presuppose the existence of something and explain the creation of the world either by or from it:

> Flaubert noted in his Egyptian diary on June 12, 1850, that during the day his group had climbed a mountain on the summit of which there was a great number of large round stones that almost resembled cannonballs. He was told that these had originally been melons, which God had turned into stones. The story is over, the narrator is evidently satisfied; but not the traveler, who has to ask for the reason why. Because it pleased God, is the answer, and the story simply goes no further. (*WOM,* 257; see also 126–27, 161, 257–59)

Second, myths tell stories rather than give reasons: "In the [erroneous] etiological explanation of myth . . . the recognition of myth as an archaic accomplishment of reason has to be justified by its having initially and especially given answers to questions, rather than having [in actuality] been the implied rejection of those questions by means of storytelling" (*WOM*, 166; see also 184–85, 257–59).

Third, within a myth anything can derive from anything else, in which case there must be scant interest in accurate derivation and therefore in derivation itself: "When anything can be derived from anything, then there just is no explaining, and no demand for explanation. One just tells stories" (*WOM*, 127). Indeed, myth presents mere chronology rather than causality (see *WOM*, 126, 128).

Fourth and most important, myth describes the significance more than the origin of phenomena. Thus the Bible tells not how but why God created the rainbow:

> He [God] gives those who have just escaped the Flood a first specimen of the sequence of agreements and covenants that were to characterize his dealings with his people: "This is the token of the covenant which I make between me and you and every living creature that is with you, for perpetual generations. . . ." One will not want to say that this is an "explanation" of the rainbow, which would have had to be replaced as quickly as possible, with arrival at a higher level of knowledge, by a physical [i.e., scientific] theory. (*WOM*, 265)

Blumenberg asserts not only that myth fails to give the origin of phenomena but also that the origin of myth itself is unknowable: "But theories about the origin of myths are idle. Here the rule is: *Ignorabimus* [We will not know]" (*WOM*, 45; see also 59). If so, then Blumenberg's consequent turning from the origin of myth to the function makes sense. What does not is his seeming additional justification for so doing: the fact that myth itself is not concerned with the origin of things! Surely even if Blumenberg's claim that myth itself scorns the question of the origin of phenomena is correct, a *theory* of myth need not therefore scorn the question of the origin of *myth*. Yet Blumenberg repeatedly implies that the issues that myth itself considers somehow determine the issues that theories of myth should consider.

Blumenberg argues that the function, or "work," of myth is not, as for the Enlightenment, to explain the world but to allay anxiety over the world, to fulfill the need "to be at home in the world" (*WOM*, 113). Like Freud, Blumenberg asserts that humans wish the world were nicer than it is.[6] For Freud, humans fulfill their wish by transforming an indifferent, impersonal world into one ruled by caring, humanlike gods. For Blumenberg, there are many stages in between. First, the still impersonal world gets named—as Fate, for example. Anxiety, which has no object, thereby gets reduced to fear, which does. The impersonal force then gets transformed into animal gods, who in turn become humanlike gods. Initially capricious gods become predictable; initially indifferent gods become just and then merciful; initially implacable gods become appeasable through rituals and ethics. The originally single cosmic force, which is omnipotent, becomes multiple gods, who neutralize one another's power. They in turn ultimately become a single god, but one whose omnipotence is tempered by justice and mercy (see *WOM*, esp. 5–6, 13–14, 18, 22–23, 35–36, 117, 124–25).

For Freud, the transformation of the world under myth serves less to control than to justify the world. For Blumenberg, the transformation serves less to control or even to justify the world than, in a nonetiological sense to be spelled out, to "explain" it. Where James Frazer assumes that an impersonal world is both more readily explained (etiologically) and more readily controlled than a personified one, both Freud and Blumenberg assume the opposite.[7] Freud likely does so because he assumes that humans seek above all to justify the world and that a world ruled by personal agents offers the possibility of a rationale and therefore of a justification. Frazer assumes instead not only that humans seek to explain and thereby control the world but also that an impersonal world offers direct control, unmediated by gods. Blumenberg assumes that a world ruled, like society, by personalities is more familiar and therefore less alien than an impersonal one.[8]

Unlike Freud and Frazer, Blumenberg attributes human helplessness to biology, not to the environment. He is here like Géza Róheim and Peter Berger, among others.[9] Róheim argues that humans are born much too soon and are thus more dependent on their mothers than other animals. Culture, including myth, arises to provide a substitute for the mother and thereby to restore some control over the world. Berger maintains that humans are born less premature than, in existentialist fashion, "unfixed." Culture, again including myth, arises not, as for Róheim, to tame the world but to make sense of it—above all by justifying the experiences that cannot be ameliorated: suffering, especially death. The justification provided gives humans a settled place in the world. While Blumenberg singles out myth, he, too, sees all of culture as serving to compensate for the limits of human biology—but, again, primarily by "explaining" rather than by either controlling or justifying the world.

When Blumenberg says that myth "explains," that it provides "explanations for the inexplicable" (*WOM*, 5), he likely means that myth explains the *operation* rather than the *origin* of the world and in this sense is nonetiological. But myth for Tylor as well explains the operation more than the origin of the world, though Tylor is not, like Blumenberg, preoccupied with the distinction. How much Blumenberg's view of myth therefore really differs from that of his Enlightened nemeses will be considered after considering the view of his other nemeses: the Romantics.

Where the Enlightenment sees myth as superseded by science, Romanticism, itself no more restricted to the nineteenth century than the Enlightenment is to the eighteenth, sees myth as eternal. Where the Enlightenment believes that myth gets superseded by something that better serves the same *function,* Romanticism believes that myth can never be superseded because nothing else bears the same *content.* As representative romantic, Campbell thus applauds the view of fellow romantic Jung that myths "are telling us in picture language of powers of the psyche to be recognized and integrated in our lives, powers that have been common to the human spirit forever, and which represent that wisdom of the species by which man has weathered the millenniums. Thus they have not been, and can never be, displaced by the findings of science."[10]

Tylor does argue that science functions better than myth *because* of its content: science provides a true explanation of the world, myth a false one. Conversely, Campbell does argue that humans *need* the message found only in myth, which therefore serves an irreplaceable function. Still, Tylor is far more concerned with the efficacy of myth as an explanation than with the specifics of the explanation, and Campbell is at least as interested in the archetypal contents of myth as in the use of myth.

Romanticism argues that myth not only offers eternal wisdom but also has always offered it. Moderns thus lack not only a superior successor to myth but also superior myths: ancient myths contain all the wisdom to be had. But moderns are not bereft of myths of their own. For Campbell, all humans are continuously spinning them. He cites the distinctively modern myths of space travel, as typified by the "Star Wars" saga. Moderns harbor no superior myths because there are none: all myths are the same because all say the same. "Romanticism," says Blumenberg, "set up the more or less distinct idea of a substance of tradition that changes only in form" (*WOM,* 49; see also 130–31). Not coincidentally, Campbell is an arch-comparativist, seeking only similarities among myths and dismissing all differences as trivial.

For romantics, moderns no more possess superior interpretations of traditional myths than possess superior myths: ancients already intuited the deepest meanings of their own myths. Only obtuse moderns need sophisticated theories to extricate those meanings. Romanticism, says Blumenberg, "attaches the seriousness of the conjecture that in it [myth] there is hidden [to moderns] the unrecognized, smuggled contents of an earliest revelation to mankind, perhaps of the recollection of Paradise, which was so nicely interchangeable with Platonic anamnesis" (*WOM,* 48; see also 273–74).

To be sure, Blumenberg may not be saying that for romantics ancients themselves were conscious of this revelation, only that it was present in their myths. But at least for Campbell they were fully conscious of it. Hence he employs Freud and Jung alike to raise to modern consciousness the meaning of which our forebears were fully aware: "The old teachers knew what they were saying. Once we have learned to read again their symbolic language, it requires no more than the talent of an anthologist [i.e., Campbell] to let their teaching be heard. But first we must learn the grammar of the symbols, and as a key to this mystery I know of no better tool than psychoanalysis."[11] Freud and Jung themselves never credit early humanity with superior consciousness.

Against Romanticism, Blumenberg argues, first, that new myths are not constantly being created. Rather, old myths are continually getting reworked, and by a Darwinian competition only the most effective myths or versions of myths survive. Blumenberg argues, second, that the meaning of myths changes. If, then, on the one hand there are no new myths, on the other hand there are new meanings to old ones—a process of reinterpretation that Blumenberg calls "work on" myth.

Blumenberg is consequently a staunch particularist rather than a comparativist. Echoing R. G. Collingwood, he goes as far as to say that reinterpretations of myths broach new questions rather than merely give new answers to perennial ones.[12] At the same time new interpreters feel obliged to answer old questions in order to prove their worth—a process that Blumenberg calls "reoccupation" (see *WOM*, 27–28).[13] The effort of new interpreters to meet their predecessors on their predecessors' home grounds bolsters the false, romantic view that there is nothing new under the sun.[14]

Blumenberg's arguments against both Romanticism and the Enlightenment are moot. Even though he traces brilliantly the sharply shifting meanings of the Prometheus myth, his romantic adversaries would surely emphasize the persistence of the myth itself. The debate between comparativists and particularists seems unresolvable. Just as particularists can always point to differences between one myth and another or between one interpretation of a myth and another, so comparativists can always point to similarities. More accurately, each side need deny only the importance, not the existence, of the other's emphasis. Particularists maintain that the similarities deciphered by comparativists are vague and superficial. Comparativists contend that the differences etched by particularists are trivial and incidental.

So what, say Campbell's critics, if all heroes undertake a dangerous trek to a distant world and return to spread the word? The differences between one heroic quest and another count more. Where, for example, Odysseus is seeking to return home, Aeneas is seeking a new home. Where Odysseus is at least eventually eager to reach Ithaca, Aeneas must relentlessly be prodded to proceed to Italy. Where Odysseus encounters largely supernatural entities along the way, Aeneas encounters largely human ones. Where Odysseus's triumph is entirely personal, Aeneas's is that of a whole people. Campbell would retort that, as different as Odysseus and Aeneas are, both are heroes. Blumenberg's appeal to the differences thus convinces only confirmed particularists.

As for Blumenberg's arguments against the Enlightenment, first, the undeniable survival of myth in modernity does not prove that its function must be nonscientific. Surely myth and science can simultaneously serve the same function, compatibly or not. Blumenberg wrongly assumes that myth is compatible with science only when it cedes to science all explanation rather than just direct explanation. Like Rudolf Bultmann, he wrongly assumes as well that myth actually does yield explanation to science. Fundamentalists are not the only ones who espouse both mythic and scientific explanations.[15]

Second, even if science does preclude a mythic explanation of the world, *prior* to science myth might have functioned as an explanation. So says Tylor. Or myth might have functioned concurrently as both explanation and something else—the nonexplanatory function alone now remaining. So says Bultmann. To make his case, Blumenberg must rebut these alternatives.

It would be one thing for Blumenberg, like numerous other theorists, to deny that myth is primitive science on the grounds that its real subject is human nature (Freud, Jung), society (Emile Durkheim, A. R. Radcliffe-Brown, Bronislaw Malinowski), or ultimate reality (Bultmann, Campbell) *rather than* the physical world (Tylor, Frazer). It is another thing for him to deny that myth is primitive science *even though* its subject matter is the physical world. That Blumenberg deems the subject matter of myth the physical world is clear from his criticism of Freud for rooting myth in pleasure—the "absolutism of images and wishes"—rather than in "reality" (*WOM*, 8). It is even clearer from his castigation of the Enlightenment for contrasting *logos,* which deals with physical reality, to myth, which supposedly does not: "The boundary line between myth and logos is imaginary and does not obviate the need to inquire about the logos of myth in the process of working free of the absolutism of reality" (*WOM*, 12). Blumenberg insists that myth helps humans master the physical world and is itself "a piece of high-carat 'work of logos'" (*WOM*, 12; see also 3ff., 26, 27, 48). Yet he continues to deny that myth is primitive science.

Certainly, myth can refer to the physical world and still not be primitive science. For Samuel Noah Kramer, for example, myth is merely a metaphorical description of the physical world: stripped of the metaphor, myth is not primitive but *modern* science—observationally, even if not theoretically.[16] Where for Frazer the metaphor is taken literally by adherents, for Kramer it is recognized as a metaphor. For Lucien Lévy-Bruhl, myth functions to unite primitives mystically with the physical world rather than to explain the world.[17] For Claude Lévi-Strauss, whom Blumenberg berates on other grounds, myth *is* primitive science, but it is not, as for the Enlightenment, inferior science.[18] Whether or not these strategies succeed in reconciling myth with science without sacrificing a common subject matter, they at least confront the problem. Blumenberg evades it: he says *that,* never *how,* myth and science manage to deal compatibly with the same subject.

Blumenberg himself waxes ambivalent about the relationship between myth and science. In faulting the Enlightenment for failing to give myth credit for

beginning the process of mastering the physical world—of overcoming the "absolutism of reality" (see *WOM*, 3ff.)—he surely implies that science continues the
process. In that case myth must be serving the same function as science:

> Theory [i.e., science] is the better adapted mode of mastering the episodic *tremenda*
> [terrors] of recurring world events. But leisure and dispassion in viewing the world,
> which theory presupposes, are already results of that millenniums-long work of myth
> itself. . . . [T]he antithesis between myth and reason [i.e., science] is a late and a poor
> invention, because it forgoes seeing the function of myth, in the overcoming of that
> archaic unfamiliarity of the world, as itself a rational function, however due for expira-
> tion its means may seem after the event. (*WOM*, 26, 48)

Even in asserting that science can never fully master the world, so that a place for
myth always remains, Blumenberg must still mean that the two serve the same
function: science cannot be merely "reoccupying" the position of myth.

Blumenberg's other arguments for myth as nonetiological are even more tenuous. First, if creation myths provide no etiology because they presuppose the
existence of something, then science provides no etiology either, as Blumenberg
himself concedes. Explaining the origin of anything means explaining out of
what it came (see *WOM*, 126–27). Ironically, science often gets faulted for failing
to do what religion, including myth, purportedly does: explaining "where it all
began."[19]

Second, myths undeniably tell stories rather than give arguments. But this
difference in form need scarcely mean a difference in function. Plato, Plotinus,
and other ancient critics of myth *as* story take for granted that the function of
myth is the same as that of philosophy, which Blumenberg rightly associates with
science. Insofar as Thales and other Presocratics succeed Homer and Hesiod,
Homer and especially Hesiod must be providing etiologies of their own. Again,
philosophy cannot be merely reoccupying the place vacated by myth.

Third, undeniably in myth anything can derive from anything else. Indeed,
nearly anything at all can happen. But even the most fantastic etiologies are not
therefore less etiological. Even if anything can happen in myth, myth is still re-
porting how it did happen.

Fourth, even if one grants that myth provides above all the significance, not
the origin, of the world, the significance still depends on the origin. The Bible
may not explain how God created the rainbow, but only the divine origin of the
rainbow gives it its clout. As a merely natural occurrence, the rainbow would not
quite represent God's covenant with future humanity. The status of woman in the
Theogony and in Genesis 2 stems considerably from the circumstances of her origin. All of the world in Genesis 1 is good in no small part because God created
it. For theorists of myth like Bronislaw Malinowski and Mircea Eliade, the sig-

nificance of the phenomena considered by myth stems entirely, not just partly, from their primordial lineage.[20]

Blumenberg declares that myths, as stories, block, not merely ignore, etiological questions: "The stories that it is our purpose to discuss here simply weren't told in order to answer questions, but rather in order to dispel uneasiness and discontent, which have to be present in the beginning for questions to be able to form themselves" (*WOM*, 184; see also 127, 166). Augustine, he says, asks why God created the world not "in order to give an answer, but rather in order simply to discredit inquiry" (*WOM*, 258). Hence Augustine's sole answer: "Because he wanted to" (*WOM*, 258).

If, however, myth gives either arbitrary answers to etiological questions or none at all, how is it managing to quell anxiety? How is it "a way of expressing the fact that the world and the powers that hold sway in it are not abandoned to pure arbitrariness, . . . a system of the elimination of arbirariness" (*WOM*, 42–43)? Blumenberg never says. Perhaps he would reply that myth eliminates arbitrariness by cogently explaining the operation rather than the origin of the world. But myth typically explains how things *are* by explaining how they *came to be*. Hesiod provides no cosmology in *addition* to his cosmogony. From his cosmogony *comes* the cosmology. The same is true of the Bible. Even if, contrary to Aristotle, Thales is offering a cosmology *rather than* a cosmogony, Hesiod and the Bible are not.

Blumenberg boasts that the meaning myth provides rests on no scientific grounds: "No one will want to maintain that myth has better arguments than science. . . . Nevertheless it has something to offer that—even with reduced claims to reliability, certainty, faith, realism, and intersubjectivity—still constitutes satisfaction of intelligent expectations. The quality on which this depends can be designated by the term *significance* [*Bedeutsamkeit*], taken from Dilthey" (*WOM*, 67). But if neither evidence nor etiology supports mythic pronouncements of significance, what does? Blumenberg never says.

Blumenberg contends that classical, not biblical, myths are the ones that survive (see *WOM*, 215–18, 238–40). The use of biblical myths by modern writers like Thomas Mann is presumably an exception. Blumenberg's justification for nevertheless claiming that mythology generally did not die out with science must be his argument that the Bible remained tied to a fixed text and to adherents controlling its interpretation: "What prevents the [modern] poet from making use of the figures in the Bible . . . is the way they are fixed in a written book, and the incomparable presence of this book in people's memories" (*WOM*, 216). In proceeding to say that classical mythology was free of not only a single text and disciples but also a priesthood and dogma, Blumenberg is really saying that it was free of religion (see *WOM*, 237–40). But is classical mythology thereby typical of mythology worldwide? Does, then, mythology generally survive science? If only because of the presence in myths of gods and other supernatural elements, many theorists subsume myth under religion. The Enlightenment shift from myth to science is thus, as for Tylor, a shift from religion as well.

Let's even suppose that Enlightened theorists wrongly assume that myth survives only as literature or art. By contrasting the survival of classical mythology to the demise of its biblical counterpart, Blumenberg himself appears to be agreeing with them that the survival of myth in any form requires its severance from religion. Whether a state exists for myth between religion and aesthetics is the question. Truncated from Greek religion, Prometheus ceases to be an actual entity and becomes only a symbol of something else, human or cosmic. Is he not thus reduced to a literary or artistic figure?

Blumenberg is far from the first theorist of myth to abandon the question of origin for the question of function or significance. Indeed, the quest for function or significance is as characteristic of twentieth-century theorists as the quest for origin was of nineteenth-century ones. Tylor is thereby the quintessential nineteenth-century theorist of myth. The quintessential twentieth-century ones are A. R. Radcliffe-Brown and Malinowski, who pursue function, and Bultmann and Hans Jonas, who pursue significance.[21]

Yet Blumenberg, despite his peremptory dismissal of the quest for origin, does not himself forsake the quest. He may refuse to speculate on *how* myth arose, but he certainly hypothesizes *why* and even *when*.[22] He denies both the Enlightenment view that myth arose to satisfy intellectual curiosity and the romantic view that myth simply arose spontaneously. Rather, he says, myth arose to cope with the anxiety felt by those who had ventured from the shelter and security of the forest to the expanse and uncertainty of the savanna:

> It was a situational leap, which made the unoccupied distant horizon into the ongoing expectation of hitherto unknown things. What came about through the combination of leaving the shrinking forest for the savanna and settling in caves was a combination of the meeting of new requirements for performance in obtaining food outside the living places and the old advantage of undisturbed reproduction and rearing of the next generation. (*WOM*, 4)

Is grander speculation imaginable?

NOTES

1. TYLOR'S THEORY OF MYTH AS PRIMITIVE SCIENCE

1. Tylor discusses only the historicity and diffusion of myth in *Researches into the Early History of Mankind*, 1st ed. (London: Murray, 1865), chs. 11–12. His full theory of myth is presented in *Primitive Culture*, 1st ed. (London: Murray, 1871), 1: chs. 8–10. He sums up his views in *Anthropology*, 1st ed. (London: Macmillan; New York: Appleton, 1881), ch. 15. Citations to *Primitive Culture* (hereafter *PC*) are to the 1958 Harper reprint of the final, 5th ed. (1913). In this reprint (New York: Harper Torchbooks, 1958) the last chapter of volume 1 is moved to volume 2. Volume 1, now given the separate title *The Origin of Culture*, contains chs. 1–10 of all earlier editions of *Primitive Culture*; volume 2, now titled *Religion in Primitive Culture*, contains chs. 11–19 of all earlier editions of *Primitive Culture*. The 1970 Peter Smith edition is a reprint in turn of the Harper edition. Citations to *Anthropology* are to the abridged edition, ed. Leslie A. White (Ann Arbor: University of Michigan Press, 1960). Tylor does not discuss myth in his first book, *Anahuac* (London: Longmans, Green, 1861).

2. See my "Paralleling Religion and Science: The Project of Robin Horton," *Annals of Scholarship* 10 (1993): 177–98.

3. See Carl G. Hempel, *Aspects of Scientific Explanation and Other Essays in the Philosophy of Science* (New York: Free Press, 1965), 463–87; Adolf Grünbaum, *The Foundations of Psychoanalysis* (Berkeley: University of California Press, 1984), 69–94.

4. See Wesley C. Salmon, "Determinism and Indeterminism in Modern Science," in *Reason and Responsibility*, ed. Joel Fineberg, 2d ed. (Encino, Calif.: Dickenson, 1971), 321–26.

5. For the classic statement of this view of science vis-à-vis myth, see Karl R. Popper, *Conjectures and Refutations*, 5th ed. (London: Routledge & Kegan Paul, 1974 [1962]), esp. 38, 50–51, 126–30. At the same time Popper, antithetically to Tylor, allows for scientific myths as well as religious ones and, more, argues that "historically speaking all—or very nearly all—scientific theories originate from myths" (ibid., 38). The classical philosopher F. M. Cornford also holds this view.

6. To be sure, Tylor sometimes contrasts myth, together with religion, to *modern* science (see, for example, *PC*, 2:31), in which case myth and religion are scientific, just primitively so.

But more often Tylor contrasts myth, together with religion, to science per se (see, for example, *PC,* 2:29), in which case myth and religion are merely scientificlike.

7. To be accurate, Tylor, following Müller, does allow for "myths based on realization of fanciful metaphor" (*PC,* 1:368), but these myths constitute only one, minor category of myth. For Müller, all myths are the realization of fanciful metaphor.

8. Says Campbell: "Wherever the poetry of myth is interpreted [literally] as biography, history, or science, it is killed. The living images become only remote facts of a distant time or sky. Furthermore, it is never difficult to demonstrate that as science and history mythology is absurd. When a civilization begins to reinterpret its mythology in this way, the life goes out of it, temples become museums, and the link between the two perspectives is dissolved" (*Hero with a Thousand Faces,* 2d ed. (Princeton, N.J.: Princeton University Press, 1968 [1949], 249).

9. While Tylor dismisses as "euhemerists" those who interpret gods as mere metaphors for human beings, euhemerists themselves conventionally grant that gods, once postulated, are interpreted as gods. Instead, they merely argue that gods *arise* from the magnification of humans, as Tylor himself allows. Strictly speaking, ancient euhemerists maintained that the first gods were really great kings, who were deified after their deaths. Euhemerus himself maintained that the first gods were living kings, who were deified during their lives. On the term, see Joseph Fontenrose, *The Ritual Theory of Myth,* Folklore Studies, no. 18 (Berkeley: University of California Press, 1966), 20–23.

10. At his most dismissive, Tylor says against the moral allegorizers what Claude Lévi-Strauss says against Freudians: that they so misconstrue the nature of myth as in effect to invent new versions of old myths rather than to decipher existing versions. Says Tylor: "For here, where the interpreter believed himself to be reversing [i.e., by interpreting] the process of myth-making, he was in fact only carrying it a stage further in the old direction" (*PC,* 1:277). Says Lévi-Strauss: "Under the pretense of going back to the original myth, all Freud did—all he ever did—was to produce a modern version" (*The Jealous Potter,* trans. Bénédicte Chorier [Chicago: University of Chicago Press, 1988], 189). See also Lévi-Strauss, "The Structural Study of Myth" (1955), in *Myth,* ed. Thomas A. Sebeok (Bloomington: Indiana University Press, 1965 [1958]), 92–93.

11. For another set of divisions of myth, see Tylor, *PC,* 1:7–8.

12. See Lévi-Strauss, "The Structural Study of Myth," 83; *The Raw and the Cooked,* trans. John and Doreen Weightman (New York: Harper Torchbooks, 1970 [1969]), 10.

13. On history as narrative, see W. B. Gallie, "The Historical Understanding," *History and Theory* 3 (1964): 149–202; *Philosophy and the Historical Understanding* (New York: Schocken, 1964), chs. 2–5; Morton White, "The Logic of Historical Narration," in *Philosophy and History,* ed. Sidney Hook (New York: New York University Press, 1963), 3–31; *Foundations of Historical Knowledge* (New York: Harper & Row, 1965), ch. 6; Arthur C. Danto, *Analytical Philosophy of History* (Cambridge: Cambridge University Press, 1965), chs. 7, 8, 11; Louis O. Mink, *Historical Understanding,* ed. Brian Fay, Eugene O. Golob, and Richard T. Vann (Ithaca, N.Y.: Cornell University Press, 1987). The four differ on the compatibility of narrative with causal explanation and specifically with causal explanation of a Popperian or Hempelian kind. On history as explanation, see Maurice Mandelbaum, "A Note on History as Narrative," *History and Theory* 6 (1967): 413–19. On the debate, see also Richard G. Ely, Rolf Gruner, and William H. Dray, "Mandelbaum on Historical Narrative: A Discussion," *History and Theory* 8 (1969): 275–94.

14. See Richard Chase, "Notes on the Study of Myth," *Partisan Review* 13 (1946): 338–46; "Myth as Literature," *English Institute Essays 1947* (New York: Columbia University Press, 1948), 3–22; *Quest for Myth* (New York: Greenwood, 1969 [1949]), v–vii, 73–74, 80–81, 110–31.

15. On these issues, see, classically, Percy Lubbock, *The Craft of Fiction* (London: Jonathan Cape; New York: Scribner, 1921); E. M. Forster, *Aspects of the Novel* (New York: Harcourt, Brace, 1927). See, more recently, Wayne C. Booth, *The Rhetoric of Fiction* (Chicago: University of Chicago Press, 1961); Wolfgang Iser, *The Implied Reader* (Baltimore: Johns Hopkins University Press, 1974); Seymour Chatman, *Story and Discourse* (Ithaca, N.Y.: Cornell University Press, 1978); Meir Sternberg, *Expositional Modes and Temporal Ordering in Fiction* (Baltimore: Johns Hopkins University Press, 1978); Gérard Genette, *Narrative Discourse,* trans. Jane E. Lewin (Ithaca, N.Y.: Cornell University Press, 1980); Shlomith Rimmon-Kenan, *Narrative Fiction* (London and New York: Routledge, 1983); Mieke Bal, *Narratology,* trans. Christine van Boheemen (Toronto: University of Toronto Press, 1985).

II. DOES MYTH HAVE A FUTURE?

1. See Marcel Detienne, *The Creation of Mythology,* trans. Margaret Cook (Chicago: University of Chicago Press, 1986), chs. 3–5.

2. On Frazer's inconsistent views, see Robert Ackerman, "Frazer on Myth and Ritual," *Journal of the History of Ideas* 36 (1975): 115–34; *J. G. Frazer* (Cambridge: Cambridge University Press, 1987), 231–35, 253–55, 282–83; *The Myth and Ritual School,* Theorists of Myth Series, vol. 3 (New York: Garland Publishing, 1991), 55–60. See also my introduction to *The Myth and Ritual Theory* (Oxford and Malden, Mass.: Blackwell, 1998), 3–5; reprinted in *Theorizing about Myth,* ch. 3

3. On Tylor's assumption that personal causation is unscientific, see my "Tylor's Theory of Myth as Primitive Science," in *The Sum of Our Choices: Essays in Honour of Eric J. Sharpe,* ed. Arvind Sharma (Atlanta: Scholars Press, 1996), 70–72; reprinted in *Theorizing about Myth,* ch. 1.

4. See E. B. Tylor, *Primitive Culture,* 5th ed., vol. 1 (retitled *The Origins of Culture*) (New York: Harper Torchbooks, 1958 [1913, 1st ed. 1871]), 277–78, 408–15.

5. Ibid., 277, 278.

6. Ibid., 285.

7. Mircea Eliade, *Myth and Reality,* trans. Willard R. Trask (New York: Harper Torchbooks, 1968 [1963]), 5–6.

8. Ibid., 11.

9. Ibid., 92.

10. Eliade, *The Sacred and the Profane,* trans. Willard R. Trask (New York: Harvest Books, 1968 [1959]), 82.

11. Ibid.

12. Ibid., 205.

13. Rudolf Bultmann, "New Testament and Mythology," in *Kerygma and Myth,* ed. Hans-Werner Bartsch, trans. Reginald H. Fuller, vol. 1 (London: SPCK, 1953), 10.

14. Ibid., 1.

15. Bultmann, *Jesus Christ and Mythology* (New York: Scribner's, 1958), 19, 21.

16. Bultmann, "New Testament and Mythology," 4.

17. Ibid., 10.

18. Bultmann, "Bultmann Replies to His Critics," in *Kerygma and Myth*, ed. Bartsch, 1:203.

19. Bultmann, "New Testament and Mythology," 16.

20. Hans Jonas, *The Gnostic Religion*, 2d ed. (Boston: Beacon, 1963 [1958]), 322.

21. Ibid., 324.

22. Ibid., 329.

23. Ibid., 326–27.

24. Jonas, "Delimitation of the Gnostic Phenomenon—Typological and Historical," in *Le Origini dello Gnosticismo*, ed. Ugo Bianchi, Supplements to *Numen*, vol. 12 (Leiden: Brill, 1967), 107.

25. See Jonas, *Gnosis und spätantiker Geist*, 1st ed., vol. 2, pt. 1 (Göttingen: Vandenhoeck & Ruprecht, 1954), 122–70; "Myth and Mysticism: A Study of Objectification and Interiorization in Religious Thought," *Journal of Religion* 49 (1969): 315–29.

26. Jonas is not the only philosopher to "update" Gnosticism. The other preeminent figure is the political philosopher Eric Voegelin. Voegelin, however, is interested less in myth than in ideology and, more important, is interested in showing only the Gnostic nature of modernity and not also, like Jonas, the modern nature of Gnosticism. He seeks to show how modern movements like positivism, Marxism, communism, fascism, and psychoanalysis evince what he calls "the Gnostic attitude." See esp. his *Science, Politics and Gnosticism* (Chicago: Regnery Gateway Editions, 1968) and *The New Science of Politics* (Chicago: University of Chicago Press, 1952).

27. One might add Freud to the duo, but Freud hardly sees himself as a defender of myth.

28. See my *Joseph Campbell: An Introduction*, rev. ed. (New York: Penguin/New American Library, 1990 [1987]; reprinted Meridian Books, 1997). On Jung, see my introduction to *Jung on Mythology* (Princeton, N.J.: Princeton University Press; London: Routledge, 1998), 3–45; reprinted in *Theorizing about Myth*, ch. 6

29. C. G. Jung, "The Psychology of the Child Archetype," in *Collected Works of C. G. Jung*, ed. Sir Herbert Read et al., trans. R. F. C. Hull et al., vol. 9, pt. 1, *The Archetypes and the Collective Unconscious*, 2d ed. (Princeton, N.J.: Princeton University Press, 1968 [1959]), 154–55.

30. Jung, "The Spiritual Problem of Modern Man," in *Collected Works*, vol. 10, *Civilization in Transition*, 2d ed. (Princeton, N.J.: Princeton University Press, 1970 [1964]), 83–84.

31. Ibid., 83.

32. See Jonas, *The Gnostic Religion*, 320–21.

33. Ibid., 325.

34. Jung, "The Spiritual Problem of Modern Man," 83.

35. Jung writes about Gnosticism throughout his corpus. See esp. his "Gnostic Symbols of the Self," in *Collected Works*, vol. 9, pt. 2, *Aion*, 2d ed. (Princeton, N.J.: Princeton University Press, 1968 [1959]), ch. 13.

36. Jung, "The Spiritual Problem of Modern Man," 84.

37. For a criticism of Jung's interpretation of Gnosticism, see my introduction to *The Gnostic Jung* (Princeton, N.J.: Princeton University Press; London: Routledge, 1992), 23–27, 31–32; "Jung and Gnosticism: A Reply to Matthew Brewer," *Harvest* 44 (1988): 126–49; Michael Howard, "The Jungian Reading of Gnosticism—An Interview with Robert Segal," *San Francisco Jung Institute Library Journal* 13 (1994): 51–65.

38. Jung, "The Structure and Dynamics of the Self," in *Aion*, 222.

39. On the limitations of myth for Jung, see my *Joseph Campbell*, 259–62. On Campbell's skewed interpretation of Gnosticism, see ibid., 126–27, 134–37.

III. THE MYTH AND RITUAL THEORY

1. See William Robertson Smith, *Lectures on the Religion of the Semites*, First Series, 1st ed. (Edinburgh: Black, 1889).

2. See E. B. Tylor, *Primitive Culture*, 1st ed. (London: Murray, 1871), 1: chs. 8–10. On Tylor, see my "Tylor's Theory of Myth as Primitive Science," in *The Sum of Our Choices: Essays in Honour of Eric J. Sharpe*, ed. Arvind Sharma (Atlanta: Scholars Press, 1996), 70–84; reprinted in *Theorizing about Myth*, ch. 1.

3. See J. G. Frazer, *The Golden Bough*, 1st ed., 2 vols. (London: Macmillan, 1890); 2d ed., 3 vols. (London: Macmillan, 1900); 3d ed., 12 vols. (London: Macmillan, 1911–15); abridged ed. (London: Macmillan, 1922). Citations are to the abridged edition.

4. Frazer, *The Golden Bough*, 377.

5. Ibid., 312–13.

6. See J. G. Frazer, introduction to Apollodorus, *The Library*, trans. Frazer, Loeb Classical Library (London: Heinemann; New York: Putnam, 1921), 1: esp. xxvii–xxviii.

7. See Jane Ellen Harrison, *Themis*, 1st ed. (Cambridge: Cambridge University Press, 1912); *Alpha and Omega* (London: Sidgwick & Jackson, 1915), ch. 6; *Epilegomena to the Study of Greek Religion* (Cambridge: Cambridge University Press, 1921); S. H. Hooke, "The Myth and Ritual Pattern of the Ancient East," in *Myth and Ritual*, ed. Hooke (London: Oxford University Press, 1933), ch. 1; introduction to *The Labyrinth*, ed. Hooke (London: SPCK; New York: Macmillan, 1935), v–x; *The Origins of Early Semitic Ritual*, Schweich Lectures 1935 (London: Oxford University Press, 1938); "Myth, Ritual and History" and "Myth and Ritual Reconsidered," in Hooke, *The Siege Perilous* (London: SCM, 1956), chs. 3 and 12; "Myth and Ritual: Past and Present," in *Myth, Ritual, and Kingship*, ed. Hooke (Oxford: Clarendon Press, 1958), ch. 1.

8. Hooke, "The Myth and Ritual Pattern of the Ancient East," 2–3.

9. Harrison, *Epilegomena to the Study of Greek Religion*, 32.

10. Hooke, "The Myth and Ritual Pattern of the Ancient East," 3.

11. Harrison, *Themis*, 328.

12. Harrison, *Epilegomena to the Study of Greek Religion*, 27.

13. Hooke, "The Myth and Ritual Pattern of the Ancient East," 3.

14. Harrison, *Themis*, 330.

15. See Gilbert Murray, "Excursis on the Ritual Forms Preserved in Greek Tragedy," in Harrison, *Themis*, 341–63; *Euripides and His Age*, 1st ed. (New York: Holt; London: Williams and Norgate, 1913), 60–68; *Aeschylus* (Oxford: Clarendon Press, 1940); "Dis Geniti," *Journal of Hellenic Studies* 71 (1951): 120–28; F. M. Cornford, "The Origin of the Olympic Games," in Harrison, *Themis*, ch. 7; *The Origin of Attic Comedy* (London: Arnold, 1914); "A Ritual Basis for Hesiod's *Theogony*" (1941), in Cornford, *The Unwritten Philosophy and Other Essays*, ed. W. K. C. Guthrie (Cambridge: Cambridge University Press, 1950), 95–116; *Principium Sapientiae*, ed. W. K. C. Guthrie (Cambridge: Cambridge University Press, 1952), 191–256; A. B. Cook, *Zeus*, 3 vols. in 5 (Cambridge: Cambridge University Press, 1914–40).

16. See Ivan Engnell, *Studies in Divine Kingship in the Ancient Near East*, 1st ed. (Uppsala:

Almqvist & Wiksells, 1943); *A Rigid Scrutiny,* ed. and trans. John T. Willis (Nashville: Vanderbilt University Press, 1969) (retitled *Critical Essays on the Old Testament* [London: SPCK, 1970]); Aubrey R. Johnson, "The Role of the King in the Jerusalem Cultus," in *The Labyrinth,* ed. Hooke, 73–111; "Hebrew Conceptions of Kingship," in *Myth, Ritual, and Kingship,* ed. Hooke, 204–35; *Sacral Kingship in Ancient Israel,* 1st ed. (Cardiff: University of Wales Press, 1955); Sigmund Mowinckel, *The Psalms in Israel's Worship,* trans. D. R. Ap-Thomas, 2 vols. (New York: Abingdon, 1962); *He That Cometh,* trans. G. W. Anderson (Nashville: Abingdon, 1954), ch. 3.

17. See A. M. Hocart, *The Life-giving Myth and Other Essays,* ed. Lord Raglan (London: Methuen, 1952; New York: Grove Press, 1953), chs. 1, 4, 5; *Kingship* (Oxford: Oxford University Press, 1927); *The Progress of Man* (London: Methuen, 1933), chs. 13, 19; *Social Origin* (London: Watt, 1954), chs. 2, 8; *Imagination and Proof,* ed. Rodney Needham (Tucson: University of Arizona Press, 1987), ch. 4; E. O. James, *Christian Myth and Ritual* (London: Murray, 1933); *Comparative Religion,* 1st ed. (London: Methuen, 1938), ch. 4; *The Beginnings of Religion* (London: Hutchinson, 1948), ch. 7; "Myth and Ritual," *Eranos-Jahrbuch* 17 (1949): 79–120; *Myth and Ritual in the Ancient Near East* (London: Thames and Hudson, 1958), esp. ch. 9.

18. See Bronislaw Malinowski, *Myth in Primitive Psychology* (London: Routledge & Kegan Paul; New York: Norton, 1926) (reprinted in his *Magic, Science and Religion and Other Essays* [Glencoe, Il.: Free Press, 1948], 72–124); "Magic, Science and Religion," in *Science, Religion and Reality,* ed. Joseph Needham (London: Sheldon Press; New York: Macmillan, 1925), esp. 76–78 (reprinted in *Magic, Science and Religion and Other Essays,* 1–71); "The Role of Myth in Life," *Psyche* 6 (1926): 29–39; *Malinowski and the Work of Myth,* ed. Ivan Strenski (Princeton, N.J.: Princeton University Press, 1992).

19. See Mircea Eliade, *The Sacred and the Profane,* trans. Willard R. Trask (New York: Harcourt, Brace, 1959), ch. 2; *Myth and Reality,* trans. Willard R. Trask (New York: Harper & Row, 1963); *Patterns in Comparative Religion,* trans. Rosemary Sheed (London: Sheed and Ward, 1958), esp. ch. 15; "The Prestige of the Cosmogonic Myth," trans. Elaine P. Halperin, *Diogenes* 23 (1958): 1–13.

20. See Jane Ellen Harrison, *Ancient Art and Ritual* (New York: Holt; London: Williams and Norgate, 1913); in addition to the references in note 15 above, see Gilbert Murray, "Hamlet and Orestes: A Study in Traditional Types," Annual Shakespeare Lecture, 1914, *Proceedings of the British Academy* 6 (1913–14): 389–412 (reprinted in his *The Classical Tradition in Poetry* [Cambridge, Mass.: Harvard University Press; London: Oxford University Press, 1927], ch. 8).

21. See Jessie L. Weston, *From Ritual to Romance* (Cambridge: Cambridge University Press, 1920); E. M. Butler, *The Myth of the Magus* (Cambridge: Cambridge University Press; New York: Macmillan, 1948); C. L. Barber, *Shakespeare's Festive Comedy* (Princeton, N.J.: Princeton University Press, 1959); Herbert Weisinger, *Tragedy and the Paradox of the Fortunate Fall* (London: Routledge & Kegan Paul; East Lansing: Michigan State College Press, 1953); "The Myth and Ritual Approach to Shakespearean Tragedy," *Centennial Review* 1 (1957): 142–66; "An Examination of the Myth and Ritual Approach to Shakespeare," in *Myth and Mythmaking,* ed. Henry A. Murray (New York: Braziller, 1960), ch. 8; *The Agony and the Triumph* (East Lansing: Michigan State University Press, 1964); Francis Fergusson, *The Idea of a Theater* (Princeton, N.J.: Princeton University Press, 1949); "'Myth' and the Literary Scruple," *Sewanee Review* 64 (1956): 171–85; Lord Raglan, "The Hero of Tradition," *Folk-Lore* 45 (1934): 212–31; *The Hero* (London: Methuen, 1936); *Death and Rebirth* (London: Watts, 1945); *The Origins of Religion* (London:

Watts, 1949), esp. chs. 9–10; "Myth and Ritual," *Journal of American Folklore* 68 (1955): 454–61; C. M. Bowra, *Primitive Song* (London: Weidenfeld and Nicolson, 1962), ch. 9; Stanley Edgar Hyman, "Myth, Ritual, and Nonsense," *Kenyon Review* 11 (1949): 455–75; "The Ritual View of Myth and the Mythic," *Journal of American Folkore* 68 (1955): 462–72; *The Promised End* (Cleveland: World Publishing, 1963), 198–212, 249–70, 278–94, 356–67; *The Critic's Credentials,* ed. Phoebe Pettingell (New York: Atheneum, 1978), 284–97, 298–304; Northrop Frye, "The Archetypes of Literature," *Kenyon Review* 13 (1951): 92–110; *Anatomy of Criticism* (Princeton, N.J.: Princeton University Press, 1957), 131–239; "Myth, Fiction, and Displacement," *Daedalus* 90 (1961): 587–605; "Literature and Myth," in *Relations of Literary Study,* ed. James Thorpe (New York: Modern Language Association, 1967), 27–55; "Myth," *Antaeus* 43 (1981): 64–84.

22. See René Girard, *Violence and the Sacred,* trans. Patrick Gregory (London: Athlone Press; Baltimore: Johns Hopkins University Press, 1977); *"To double business bound"* (London: Athlone Press; Baltimore: Johns Hopkins University Press, 1978); *The Scapegoat,* trans. Yvonne Freccero (London: Athlone Press; Baltimore: Johns Hopkins University Press, 1986); *Things Hidden since the Foundation of the World,* trans. Stephen Bann and Michael Metteer (London: Athlone Press; Stanford, Calif.: Stanford University Press, 1987); *Job, the Victim of his People,* trans. Yvonne Freccero (London: Athlone Press; Stanford, Calif.: Stanford University Press, 1987).

23. See Theodor H. Gaster, "Divine Kingship in the Ancient Near East: A Review Article," *Review of Religion* 9 (1945): 267–81; *Thespis,* 1st ed. (New York: Schuman, 1950); "Myth and Story," *Numen* 1 (1954): 184–212; *The New Golden Bough* (New York: Criterion, 1959), 462–64; *Myth, Legend, and Custom in the Old Testament* (New York: Harper & Row, 1969), xxv–xxxvii; Adolf E. Jensen, *Myth and Cult among Primitive Peoples,* trans. Marianna Tax Choldin and Wolfgang Weissleder (Chicago: University of Chicago Press, 1963).

24. See Clyde Kluckhohn, "Myths and Rituals: A General Theory," *Harvard Theological Review* 35 (1942): 45–79; "Recurrent Themes in Myth and Mythmaking," in *Myth and Mythmaking,* ed. Murray, ch. 2; Kluckhohn and Dorothea Leighton, *The Navaho,* rev. ed. (Cambridge, Mass.: Harvard University Press, 1974 [1946]), 229–40.

25. See Walter Burkert, *Structure and History in Greek Mythology and Ritual,* Sather Classical Lectures, vol. 47 (Berkeley: University of California Press, 1979), esp. 56–58, 99–101; *Homo Necans,* trans. Peter Bing (Berkeley: University of California Press, 1983), esp. 29–34; *Ancient Mystery Cults* (Cambridge, Mass.: Harvard University Press, 1987), 73–78; "The Problem of Ritual Killing," in *Violent Origins,* ed. Robert G. Hamerton-Kelly (Stanford, Calif.: Stanford University Press, 1987), 149–76; *Creation of the Sacred* (Cambridge, Mass.: Harvard University Press, 1996), chs. 2–3.

26. See Claude Lévi-Strauss, "The Structural Study of Myth," *Journal of American Folklore* 68 (1955): 428–44 (reprinted in his *Structural Anthropology,* trans. Claire Jacobson and Brooke Grundfest Schoepf [New York: Basic Books, 1963], ch. 11); "Structure and Dialectics," in his *Structural Anthropology,* ch. 12; "Comparative Religions of Nonliterate Peoples," in his *Structural Anthropology II,* trans. Monique Layton (New York: Basic Books, 1976), ch. 5.

27. Lévi-Strauss, "The Structural Study of Myth," 443.

28. Lévi-Strauss, "Comparative Religions of Nonliterate Peoples," 65–66.

29. To cite a single example of the influence of the theory on specialists: "Modern research stresses the connection between myth and ritual. The myths are stories explaining the rites enacted in the sacred dramas of the great festivals. Above all the creation drama of the New

Year Festival has been of great importance in the whole Ancient Near East, and through the medium of Canaan it has also gained a firm footing in Israel" (Aage Bentzen, *Introduction to the Old Testament,* 5th ed. [Copenhagen: Gad, 1959], 1:242).

30. Criticisms of the myth-ritualist theory abound. In addition to Frazer's criticism cited in note 6 above, see esp. William Ridgeway, *The Dramas and Dramatic Dances of Non-European Races* (Cambridge: Cambridge University Press, 1915), 41–64; Norman H. Snaith, *The Jewish New Year Festival* (London: SPCK, 1947); Henri Frankfort, *Kingship and the Gods* (Chicago: University of Chicago Press, 1948); *The Problem of Similarity in Ancient Near Eastern Religions,* Frazer Lecture 1950 (Oxford: Clarendon Press, 1951); Haskell M. Block, "Cultural Anthropology in Contemporary Literary Criticism," *Journal of Aesthetics and Art Criticism* 11 (1952): 46–54; Wallace W. Douglas, "The Meanings of 'Myth' in Modern Criticism," *Modern Philology* 50 (1953): 232–42; Stith Thompson, "Myths and Folktales," *Journal of American Folklore* 68 (1955): 482–88; William Bascom, "The Myth-Ritual Theory," *Journal of American Folklore* 70 (1957): 103–14; S. G. F. Brandon, "The Myth and Ritual Position Critically Examined," in *Myth, Ritual, and Kingship,* ed. Hooke, 261–91; H. J. Rose, "The Evidence for Divine Kings in Greece," in *The Sacral Kingship/La Regalità Sacra,* 8th International Congress for the History of Religions (Leiden: Brill, 1959), 371–78; Joseph Fontenrose, *Python* (Berkeley: University of California Press, 1959), ch. 15; *The Ritual Theory of Myth,* Folklore Studies, no. 18 (Berkeley: University of California Press, 1966); Francis Lee Utley, "Folklore, Myth, and Ritual," in *Critical Approaches to Medieval Literature,* ed. Dorothy Bethurum (New York: Columbia University Press, 1960), 83–109; A. N. Marlow, "Myth and Ritual in Early Greece," *Bulletin of the John Rylands Library* 43 (1961): 373–402; G. S. Kirk, *Myth,* Sather Classical Lectures, vol. 40 (Berkeley: University of California Press, 1966), 12–31; *The Nature of Greek Myths* (Harmondsworth, Middlesex: Penguin, 1974), ch. 10; Hans H. Penner, "Myth and Ritual: A Wasteland or a Forest of Symbols?" *History and Theory* Beiheft 8 (1968): 46–57.

31. The fullest presentations of the myth-ritualist theory are to be found in Richard F. Hardin, "'Ritual' in Recent Criticism: The Elusive Sense of Community," *PMLA* 98 (1983): 846–62; H. S. Versnel, "What's Sauce for the Goose Is Sauce for the Gander: Myth and Ritual, Old and New," in *Approaches to Greek Myth,* ed. Lowell Edmunds (Baltimore: Johns Hopkins University Press, 1990), ch. 1 (revised version in Versnel, *Transition and Reversal in Myth and Ritual* [Leiden: Brill, 1993], ch. 1); Robert Ackerman, *The Myth and Ritual School,* Theorists of Myth Series, vol. 3 (New York: Garland Publishing, 1991).

IV. THE GRAIL LEGEND AS FRAZERIAN MYTH AND RITUAL

1. See Marylyn J. Parins, "Scholarship, Modern Arthurian," in *The New Arthurian Encyclopedia,* ed. Norris J. Lacy (New York: Garland Publishing, 1991 [1986]), 402–11.

2. Northrop Frye, "The Archetypes of Literature," *Kenyon Review* 13 (1951): 105.

3. On Weston's development into a Frazerian see Stanley Edgar Hyman, "Jessie Weston and the Forest of Broceliande," *Centennial Review* 9 (1966): 509–21.

4. J. G. Frazer, *The Golden Bough,* abridged ed. (London: Macmillan, 1922), 377.

5. Frazer actually kept changing his mind about myth. He was a myth-ritualist most fully in the first edition of *The Golden Bough* and was least so by the third. On Frazer's changing views, see Robert Ackerman, "Frazer on Myth and Ritual," *Journal of the History of Ideas* 36 (1975):

115–34; J. G. *Frazer* (Cambridge: Cambridge University Press, 1987), 231–35, 253–55, 282–83; *The Myth and Ritual School,* Theorists of Myth Series, vol. 3 (New York: Garland Publishing, 1991), 55–60. Nonetheless, Weston and the Cambridge Ritualists take him as a myth-ritualist.

6. Frazer, *The Golden Bough,* 392, 378.

7. Ibid., 391.

8. On Frazer's skewed interpretation of the myth of Adonis, see my "Adonis: A Greek Eternal Child," in *Myth and the Polis,* ed. Dora C. Pozzi and John M. Wickersham (Ithaca, N.Y.: Cornell University Press, 1991), 65–68; reprinted in *Theorizing about Myth,* ch. 7.

9. Frazer, *The Golden Bough,* 312–13.

10. Ibid., 309.

11. On the complications in Frazer's myth-ritualist theory, see my introduction to *The Myth and Ritual Theory* (Oxford and Malden, Mass.: Blackwell, 1998), 3–5; reprinted in *Theorizing about Myth,* ch. 3.

12. See Hippolytus, *The Refutation of All Heresies,* trans. J. H. MacMahon, in *Ante-Nicene Christian Library,* ed. Alexander Roberts and James Donaldson, vol. 6, pt. 1 (Edinburgh: T. & T. Clark, 1868), bk. 5, chs. 1–5.

13. See, for example, Kurt Rudolph, *Gnosis,* trans. Robert McLachlan Wilson et al. (San Francisco: Harper & Row, 1983), 214–15, 285–87.

14. It is surprising that Weston, in making her case for a Gnostic dimension to the Grail legend, ignores the often suggested association of Wolfram von Eschenbach's version of the story, *Parzival,* with the medieval variety of Gnosticism known as Catharism.

15. Roger Sherman Loomis, *Celtic Myth and Arthurian Romance* (New York: Columbia University Press, 1927), 261.

16. Roger Sherman Loomis, *The Grail* (Princeton, N.J.: Princeton University Press, 1991 [1963]), ix.

V. FAIRY TALES SÍ, MYTHS NO: BRUNO BETTELHEIM'S ANTITHESIS

1. Alan Dundes, "The Psychological Study of Folklore in the United States, 1880–1980," *Southern Folklore* 48 (1991): 115.

2. Dundes, *Folklore Matters* (Knoxville: University of Tennessee Press, 1989), 120–22.

3. Ibid. On the psychoanalytic study of folklore, see Dundes's various surveys and applications: "Fairy Tales from a Folkoristic Perspective," in *Fairy Tales and Society,* ed. Ruth B. Bottigheimer (Philadelphia: University of Pennsylvania Press, 1986), ch. 17; *Parsing through Customs* (Madison: University of Wisconsin Press, 1987), ch. 1; *Folklore Matters,* 112–50; "The Psychological Study of Folklore in the United States, 1880–1980," 97–120.

4. Bruno Bettelheim, *The Uses of Enchantment* (hereafter *UOE*)(New York: Vintage Books, 1977 [1976]). See also his foreword to Jakob and Wilhelm Grimm and Others, *German Fairy Tales,* ed. Helmut Brackert and Volkmar Sander (New York: Continuum, 1985), ix–xvi.

5. Dundes, "The Psychological Study of Folklore in the United States, 1880–1980," 116. On Bettelheim, see Dundes, *Parsing through Customs,* 29–32; "Bruno Bettelheim's Uses of Enchantment and Abuses of Scholarship," *Journal of American Folklore* 104 (1991): 74–83.

6. Similarly, Bettelheim sees circumcision rituals as means of maturation rather than, like

early Freudians, as expressions of neuroses: see his *Symbolic Wounds,* rev. ed. (New York: Collier Books, 1962 [1954]).

7. For a comparable pair of criticisms, see Robert A. Paul, "Bettelheim's Contribution to Anthropology," in *The Psychoanalytic Study of Society,* vol. 15, ed. L. Bryce Boyer and Simon A. Grolnick (Hillsdale, N.J.: Analytic Press, 1990), 314–15.

8. See Franz Ricklin, *Wishfulfillment and Symbolism in Fairy Tales,* trans. William A. White, Nervous and Mental Disease Monograph Series, no. 21 (New York: Nervous and Mental Disease Publishing, 1915); Géza Róheim, "Psycho-Analysis and the Folk-Tale," *International Journal of Psycho-Analysis* 3 (1922): 180–86; *The Riddle of the Sphinx,* trans. R. Money-Kyrle (New York: Harper Torchbooks, 1974 [1934]); "Myth and Folk-Tale," *American Imago* 2 (1941): 266–79; *The Eternal Ones of the Dream* (New York: International Universities Press, 1945); *Psychoanalysis and Anthropology* (New York: International Universities Press, 1950); *The Gates of the Dream* (New York: International Universities Press, 1952); *Fire in the Dragon and Other Psychoanalytic Essays on Folklore,* ed. Alan Dundes (Princeton, N.J.: Princeton University Press, 1992).

9. Dundes, "Bruno Bettelheim's Uses of Enchantment and Abuses of Scholarship," 76–77.

10. Ibid., 80.

11. See, for example, Otto Rank and Hans Sachs, *The Significance of Psychoanalysis for the Mental Sciences,* trans. Charles R. Payne, Nervous and Mental Disease Monograph Series, no. 23 (New York: Nervous and Mental Disease Publishing, 1916), ch. 2.

12. See Sigmund Freud, *The Interpretation of Dreams,* trans. James Strachey (New York: Avon Books, 1965 [1953]), 294–98; "The Occurrence of Dreams in Material from Fairy Tales," in *The Standard Edition of the Complete Psychological Works of Sigmund Freud,* trans. James Strachey et al., vol. 12 (London: Hogarth Press, 1958), 281–87.

13. Róheim, "Myth and Folk-Tale," 279.

14. Róheim, "Psycho-Analysis and the Folk-Tale," 181.

15. See Róheim, *Psychoanalysis and Anthropology,* 225–26.

16. Róheim, "Myth and Folk-Tale," 275.

17. Ibid., 277–78.

18. Róheim, *The Riddle of the Sphinx,* 252.

19. Ibid., 251.

20. Ibid., 260.

21. See Jacob A. Arlow, "Ego Psychology and the Study of Mythology," *Journal of the American Psychoanalytic Association* 9 (1961): 371–93.

22. Ibid., 382–83.

23. Ibid., 381.

24. Ibid., 382.

25. See Dundes, "Bruno Bettelheim's Uses of Enchantment and Abuses of Scholarship," 79; Róheim, "Myth and Folk-Tale," 276.

26. See Freud, *The Interpretation of Dreams,* 294–98; Otto Rank, *The Myth of the Birth of the Hero,* 1st ed., trans. F. Robbins and Smith Ely Jelliffe, Nervous and Mental Disease Monograph Series, no. 18 (New York: Journal of Nervous and Mental Disease Publishing, 1914); reprinted in Rank et al., *In Quest of the Hero* (Princeton, N.J.: Princeton University Press, 1990), 3–86; *Psychoanalytische Beiträge zur Mythenforschung,* Internationale Psychoanalytische Bibliothek, no.

4, 1st ed. (Leipzig and Vienna: Internationaler Psychoanalytischer Verlag, 1919); Rank and Sachs, *The Significance of Psychoanalysis for the Mental Sciences;* Ricklin, *Wishfulfillment and Symbolism in Fairy Tales;* Karl Abraham, *Dreams and Myths,* trans. William A. White, Nervous and Mental Disease Monograph Series, no. 15 (New York: Journal of Nervous and Mental Disease Publishing, 1913).

27. Where Dundes stresses the similarities that Bettelheim draws between fairy tales and dreams ("Bruno Bettelheim's Uses of Enchantment and Abuses of Scholarship," 74), Bettelheim himself, anxious to make fairy tales more than dreamlike fulfillments of fantasies, emphasizes the differences at least as much: "To a considerable degree, dreams are the result of inner pressures which have found no relief, of problems which beset a person to which he knows no solution and to which the dream finds none. The fairy tale does the opposite: it projects the relief of all pressures and not only offers ways to solve problems but promises that a 'happy' solution will be found" (*UOE,* 36). By contrast, early Freudians view both fairy tales and dreams as wish fulfillments: see, for example, Freud, "The Occurrence of Dreams in Material from Fairy Tales"; Freud and D. E. Oppenheim, *Dreams in Folklore,* trans. A. M. O. Richards (New York: International Universities Press, 1958); Ricklin, *Wishfulfillment and Symbolism in Fairy Tales,* 1; Róheim, "Psycho-Analysis and the Folk-Tale," 181.

28. See Róheim, *The Riddle of the Sphinx,* 251–61.

29. See, for example, Freud, *The Interpretation of Dreams,* 294–98; Rank, *The Myth of the Birth of the Hero,* in *In Quest of the Hero,* 13–15.

30. Arlow, "Ego Psychology and the Study of Mythology," 375. See also Sidney Tarachow et al., "Mythology and Ego Psychology," in *The Psychoanalytic Study of Society,* vol. 3, ed. Warner Muensterberger and Sidney Axelrad (New York: International Universities Press, 1964), 10–11, 13–14, 23–24, 31–32, 73–74, 94–97; Martin S. Bergman, "The Impact of Ego Psychology on the Study of the Myth," *American Imago* 23 (1966): 257–64. Even when Arlow says that myths originate out of childhood wishes, he deems their function adaptive rather than maladaptive: "The mythology of religion fosters social adaptation of the individual and integration with the community" ("Scientific Cosmogony, Mythology, and Immortality," *Psychoanalytic Quarterly* 51 [1982]: 188). Róheim, once again the prescient exception among early Freudians, similarly characterizes "myths of transition" as "functioning socially in harmony with initiation rites: the mythological material helps the young men to grow up, and to make the transition from the Oedipus situation to marriage" (*The Eternal Ones of the Dream,* 17).

31. See Arlow, "Ego Psychology and the Study of Mythology," 387, 388.

32. Tarachow et al., "Mythology and Ego Psychology," 32.

33. Arlow, "Ego Psychology and the Study of Mythology," 373. On fairy tales and dreams see Simon A. Grolnick, "Fairy Tales and Psychotherapy," in *Fairy Tales and Society,* ed. Bottigheimer, 205–6.

VI. JUNG ON MYTHOLOGY

1. C. G. Jung, "The Psychology of the Child Archetype," in *The Collected Works of C. G. Jung,* ed. Sir Herbert Read et al., trans. R. F. C. Hull et al., vol. 9, pt. 1, *The Archetypes and the Collective Unconscious,* 2d ed. (Princeton, N.J.: Princeton University Press, 1968 [1959]), 154.

2. J. G. Frazer, *The Golden Bough*, abridged ed. (London: Macmillan, 1922), 392.

3. Jung, *Psychological Types, Collected Works*, vol. 6 (Princeton, N.J.: Princeton University Press, 1971), 193.

4. Jung's reverence for the hiatus between the divine and the human is not always shared by his followers. For example, Jean Shinoda Bolen breezily effaces the line between the two, as her titles declare: *Goddesses in Everywoman* (New York: Harper & Row, 1984) and *Gods in Everyman* (New York: Harper & Row, 1989).

5. Jung, *Psychological Types*, 193–94.

6. Jung, "On the Psychology of the Unconscious," in *Collected Works*, vol. 7, *Two Essays on Analytical Psychology*, 2d ed. (Princeton, N.J.: Princeton University Press, 1966 [1953]), 69.

7. E. B. Tylor, *Primitive Culture*, 1st ed. (London: Murray, 1871), 1:262.

8. Jung, "On Psychic Energy," in *Collected Works*, vol. 8, *The Structure and Dynamics of the Psyche*, 2d ed. (Princeton, N.J.: Princeton University Press, 1969 [1960]), 37–38.

9. Jung, *Psychological Types*, 444.

10. Jung, "The Structure of the Psyche," in *The Structure and Dynamics of the Psyche*, 152. For Jung, heroes are mythical because they are more than human. For Lord Raglan, who extends Frazer's theory of myth to heroes, heroes are mythical because they are not historical. That is, Raglan concentrates on disproving the historicity of hero stories in order to make them mythical, where Jung takes for granted that heroes cannot be historical because they are quasi-divine. See Lord Raglan, *The Hero* (London: Methuen, 1936), pt. 2; reprinted in Otto Rank et al., *In Quest of the Hero* (Princeton, N.J.: Princeton University Press, 1990), 89–175.

11. Jung, *Symbols of Transformation, Collected Works*, vol. 5, 2d ed. (Princeton, N.J.: Princeton University Press, 1967 [1956]), 391.

12. Jung, "On the Psychology of the Unconscious," 95.

13. Jung, "The Psychology of the Child Archetype," 155.

14. Ibid.

15. Ibid.

16. Jung, "Introduction to Kraenfeldt's 'Secret Ways of the Mind,'" in *Collected Works*, vol. 4, *Freud and Psychoanalysis* (Princeton, N.J.: Princeton University Press, 1961), 330.

17. Jung, "On the Nature of the Psyche," in *The Structure and Dynamics of the Psyche*, 227.

18. Jung, "The Concept of the Collective Unconscious," in *The Archetypes and the Collective Unconscious*, 44–45. On the case of Leonardo, see also, for example, "On the Psychology of the Unconscious," 65; "Concerning the Archetypes, with Special Reference to the Anima Concept," in *The Archetypes and the Collective Unconscious*, 68 n. 27.

19. Jung, "Archetypes of the Collective Unconscious," in *The Archetypes and the Collective Unconscious*, 156.

20. Ibid.

21. Jung, "Psychology and Literature," in *Collected Works*, vol. 15, *The Spirit in Man, Art, and Literature* (Princeton, N.J.: Princeton University Press, 1966), 96–97.

22. Jung, "Introduction to the Religious and Psychological Problems of Alchemy," in *Collected Works*, vol. 12, *Psychology and Alchemy*, 2d ed. (Princeton, N.J.: Princeton University Press, 1968 [1953]), 25.

23. Jung, "Archetypes of the Collective Unconscious," 160.

24. Ibid., 157.

25. Ibid., 160.

26. Jung, *Psychological Types,* 120–21.

27. Jung, "The Psychological Aspects of the Kore," in *The Archetypes and the Collective Unconscious,* 189.

28. While not in fact a Jungian, Campbell is often deemed one, and not merely because he interprets myths psychologically but also because he usually stresses only the similarities among myths. See my *Joseph Campbell: An Introduction,* rev. ed. (New York: Penguin/New American Library, 1990 [1987]; reprinted Meridian Books, 1997), chs. 9, 12.

29. Jung, "The Significance of Constitution and Heredity in Psychology," in *The Structure and Dynamics of the Psyche,* 111.

30. Jung, *Symbols of Transformation,* 157–58. See also Jung, "The Structure of the Psyche," 150–51; "The Concept of the Collective Unconscious," 50–52; "The Tavistock Lectures" [*Analytical Psychology: Its Theory and Practice*], in *Collected Works,* vol. 18, *The Symbolic Life* (Princeton, N.J.: Princeton University Press, 1976), 41–42; "The 'Face to Face' Interview," in *C. G. Jung Speaking,* ed. William McGuire and R. F. C. Hull (Princeton, N.J.: Princeton University Press, 1977), 434–35. Sonu Shamdasani coined the term "Solar Phallus Man" in his "A Woman Called Frank," *Spring* 50 (1990): 40. The first challenge to Jung's assumption that this patient could not previously have known of the idea of the sun's having a phallus is to be found in Henri F. Ellenberger, *The Discovery of the Unconscious* (New York: Basic Books, 1970), 743 n. 140. For a more recent challenge, see Richard Noll, "Jung the Leontocephalus," *Spring* 53 (1992): 17–18, 48 n. 15; Noll, *The Jung Cult* (Princeton, N.J.: Princeton University Press, 1994), 181–84.

31. Jung, *Symbols of Transformation,* 158.

32. Frazer, *The Golden Bough,* 448.

33. See Otto Rank, *The Myth of the Birth of the Hero,* trans. F. Robbins and Smith Ely Jelliffe (New York: Journal of Nervous and Mental Disease Publishing, 1914); reprinted in Rank et al., *In Quest of the Hero,* 3–86.

34. See, for example, Melanie Klein, *Narrative of a Child Analysis* (London: Hogarth, 1975 [1961]).

35. Jung, "The Psychology of the Child Archetype," 154.

36. Jung, "The Tavistock Lectures," 82–83. See also Jung, *Memories, Dreams, Reflections,* recorded and edited by Aniela Jaffé, trans. Richard and Clara Winston (New York: Vintage Books, 1962), 161–62.

37. Jung, "Paracelsus as a Spiritual Phenomenon," in *Collected Works,* vol. 13, *Alchemical Studies* (Princeton, N.J.: Princeton University Press, 1968), 162–63.

38. Jung, "Background to the Psychology of Christian Alchemical Symbolism," in *Collected Works,* vol. 9, pt. 2, *Aion,* 2d ed. (Princeton, N.J.: Princeton University Press, 1968 [1959]), 180.

39. Jung, "Archetypes of the Collective Unconscious," 6.

40. Jung, "Approaching the Unconscious," in Jung et al., *Man and His Symbols* (New York: Dell Laurel Editions, 1968 [1964]), 76.

41. Ibid., 84.

42. Jung, *Symbols of Transformation,* 231.

43. Jung, *Letters,* ed. Gerhard Adler and Aniela Jaffé, trans. R. F. C. Hull, vol. 2 (Princeton, N.J.: Princeton University Press, 1976), 495.

44. Ibid., 541.

45. On synchronicity, see above all Jung, "Synchronicity: An Acausal Connecting Principle" and "On Synchronicity," in *The Structure and Dynamics of the Psyche,* 417–519 and 520–31. Of the many books on Jung's concept of synchronicity, see esp. Robert Aziz, C. G. *Jung's Psychology of Religion and Synchronicity* (Albany: State University of New York Press, 1990), and Roderick Main, introduction to *Jung on Synchronicity and the Paranormal* (London: Routledge, 1997), 17–36.

46. Jung, "The Aims of Psychotherapy," in *Collected Works,* vol. 16, *The Practice of Psychotherapy,* 2d ed. (Princeton, N.J.: Princeton University Press, 1966 [1954]), 45.

47. Jung, "The Houston Films," in *C. G. Jung Speaking,* 292–93.

48. Bronislaw Malinowski, "Myth in Primitive Psychology" [1926], in his *Magic, Science and Religion and Other Essays* (Garden City, N.Y.: Doubleday/Anchor Books, 1954[1948]), 107.

49. Jung, *Symbols of Transformation,* 24.

50. Jung, "The Psychology of the Child Archetype," 154.

51. Jung, "On Psychic Energy," 38.

52. Jung, "Archetypes of the Collective Unconscious," 5.

53. Jung, "The Psychology of the Child Archetype," 153.

54. Jung, "Analytical Psychology and Education," in *Collected Works,* vol. 17, *The Development of Personality* (Princeton, N.J.: Princeton University Press, 1964 [1954]), 117–19.

55. Jung even states that "archetypes were originally derived, not from dreams, but from mythological material, like fairy tales, legends, and religious forms of thought" (*Dream Analysis,* ed. William McGuire [Princeton, N.J.: Princeton University Press, 1983], 550).

56. See Rudolf Bultmann, "New Testament and Mythology," in *Kerygma and Myth,* ed. Hans-Werner Bartsch, trans. Reginald H. Fuller, vol. 1 (London: SPCK, 1953), 1–44; Hans Jonas, *Gnosis und spätantiker Geist,* 1st ed., vol. 2, pt. 1 (Göttingen: Vandenhoeck & Ruprecht, 1954).

57. See Lucien Lévy-Bruhl, *How Natives Think,* trans. Lilian A. Clare (London: Allen & Unwin, 1926).

58. See Claude Lévi-Strauss, *Introduction to a Science of Mythology,* trans. John and Doreen Weightman, 4 vols. (New York: Harper & Row, 1969–81).

59. See Sigmund Freud, *The Interpretation of Dreams,* trans. James Strachey (New York: Avon Books, 1965 [1953]), ch. 6.

60. Jung, *Symbols of Transformation,* 17.

61. Ibid., 11.

62. Jung, "On Psychic Energy," 38.

63. Jung, *Symbols of Transformation,* 21.

64. Ibid., 23.

65. Ibid., 22–23.

66. Jung, "The Psychology of the Child Archetype," 164.

67. See Mircea Eliade, *The Sacred and the Profane,* trans. Willard R. Trask (New York: Harcourt, Brace, 1959), ch. 2.

68. See Rank, *The Myth of the Birth of the Hero.*

69. See Jacob A. Arlow, "Ego Psychology and the Study of Mythology," *Journal of the American Psychoanalytic Association* 9 (1961): 371–93.

70. See Alan Dundes, "Earth-Diver: Creation of the Mythopoeic Male," *American Anthropologist* 64 (1962): 1032–51.

71. Jung, "The Fish in Alchemy," in *Aion*, 148.

72. Jung, *Memories, Dreams, Reflections*, 3.

73. Ibid.

74. Jung, "The Psychology of the Child Archetype," 162.

75. Ibid., 162–63.

76. Ibid., 153.

77. Ibid., 154.

78. Jung, "Archetypes of the Collective Unconscious," 6.

79. Jung, *Symbols of Transformation*, 24–25.

80. Jung, "The Philosophical Tree," in *Alchemical Studies*, 300.

81. Ibid.

82. Jung, "Philosophy and Literature," 97.

83. Ibid.

84. Jung, "Wotan," in *Collected Works*, vol. 10, *Civilization in Transition*, 2d ed. (Princeton, N.J.: Princeton University Press, 1970 [1964]), 180. For a less negative, more balanced view of Wotan, who turns out to have traditionally been a god of life and not just of death, see Margrit Burri, "Repression, Falsification, and Bedeviling of Germanic Mythology," trans. Wolfgang Giegerich, *Spring* (1978): 88–104.

85. Jung, "Flying Saucers," in *Civilization in Transition*, 328.

86. See ibid., 413–17; "Letter to Keyhoe," in *The Symbolic Life*, 632.

87. Jung, *Symbols of Transformation*, 25.

88. Jung, "The Personification of the Opposites," in *Collected Works*, vol. 14, *Mysterium Coniunctionis*, 2d ed. (Princeton, N.J.: Princeton University Press, 1970 [1963]), 142.

89. Jung, "Gnostic Symbols of the Self," in *Aion*, 184, 190. On Gnostic self-consciousness, see my introduction to *The Gnostic Jung* (Princeton, N.J.: Princeton University Press; London: Routledge, 1992), 33–35.

90. Jung, "The Conjunction," in *Mysterium Coniunctionis*, 475.

91. Jung, "Rex and Regina," in *Mysterium Coniunctionis*, 336 n. 297.

92. Jung, "The Undiscovered Self," in *Civilization in Transition*, 265.

93. Ibid., 285.

94. Ibid.

95. Jung, "The Conjunction," 528.

96. Jung, "The Undiscovered Self," 266.

97. Jung, "Psychology and Religion," in *Collected Works*, vol. 11, *Psychology and Religion: West and East*, 2d ed. (Princeton, N.J.: Princeton University Press, 1969 [1958]), 88–89. Like a child in myth, Christ symbolizes at once an archetype—the self—and the developing ego. On Christ as a symbol of the self, see Jung, "Christ, a Symbol of the Self," in *Aion*, ch. 5. On Christ as a symbol of the ego in relation to the self, see Edward F. Edinger, *Ego and Archetype* (Baltimore: Penguin, 1973 [1972]), ch. 5.

98. Jung, "Psychology and Religion," 88.

99. Jung, *Memories, Dreams, Reflections*, 332.

100. Ibid.

101. Jung's ambiguous position on Christianity has spawned contrary interpretations. Some maintain that Jung seeks to replace dying Christianity with psychology: see esp. Raymond

Hostie, *Religion and the Psychology of Jung,* trans. G. R. Lamb (New York: Sheed and Ward, 1957); Howard L. Philp, *Jung and the Problem of Evil* (London: Rockliff, 1958). Others contend that Jung seeks to resurrect Christianity through psychology: see esp. Hans Schaer, *Religion and the Cure of Souls in Jung's Psychology,* trans. R. F. C. Hull (New York: Pantheon, 1950); David Cox, *Jung and Saint Paul* (London: Longmans, Green; New York: Association Press, 1959); Victor White, *God and the Unconscious* (London: Collins, 1952); Murray Stein, *Jung's Treatment of Christianity* (Chicago: Chiron, 1985). Still others argue for a middle ground: see esp. Peter Homans, *Jung in Context,* 2d ed. (Chicago: University of Chicago Press, 1995 [1979]).

102. Jung, "Approaching the Unconscious," 58, 67.

103. Jung, "Psychological Aspects of the Mother Archetype," in *The Archetypes and the Collective Unconscious,* 79.

104. Jung, "The Psychology of the Child Archetype," 161 n. 21.

105. Jung, "The Concept of the Collective Unconscious," 48.

106. Jung, "Archetypes of the Collective Unconscious," 6 n. 10.

107. Jung, *Symbols of Transformation,* 222.

108. Jung, "The Psychology of the Child Archetype," 153.

109. Ibid.

VII. ADONIS: A GREEK ETERNAL CHILD

1. See Apollodorus, *Library,* 1.116, 3.182, 183–85; Ovid, *Metamorphoses* 10.708–39. On both the myth and the cult of Adonis, see Deborah Dickmann Boedeker, *Aphrodite's Entry into Greek Epic* (Leiden: Brill, 1974), 64–67; Walter Burkert, *Greek Religion,* trans. John Raffan (Cambridge, Mass.: Harvard University Press, 1985), 176–77; *Structure and History in Greek Mythology and Ritual,* Sather Classical Lectures, vol. 47 (Berkeley: University of California Press, 1979), 105–11.

2. See J. G. Frazer, *The Golden Bough,* abridged ed. (London: Macmillan, 1922), chs. 29–33.

3. See Marcel Detienne, *The Gardens of Adonis,* trans. Janet Lloyd (Atlantic Highlands, N.J.: Humanities Press, 1997).

4. See ibid., 1–4, 101–2. See also J.-P. Vernant, introduction to ibid., ii–iv.

5. See Marcel Detienne, *The Creation of Mythology,* trans. Margaret Cook (Chicago: University of Chicago Press, 1986), esp. 114–16.

6. See Mary Douglas, *Purity and Danger* (Baltimore: Penguin Books, 1970 [1966]), esp. chs. 2–3.

7. On Adonis, see esp. C. G. Jung, *Symbols of Transformation, The Collected Works of C. G. Jung,* ed. Sir Herbert Read et al., trans. R. F. C. Hull et al., vol. 5, 2d ed. (Princeton, N.J.: Princeton University Press, 1967 [1956]), 219, 223 n. 32, 258–59, 343 n. 79; "Answer to Job," in *Collected Works,* vol. 11, *Psychology and Religion: West and East,* 2d ed. (Princeton, N.J.: Princeton University Press, 1969 [1958]), 442–43.

8. On the archetype of the *puer aeternus,* see esp. Jung, *Symbols of Transformation,* 257–59, 340; "Psychological Aspects of the Mother Archetype," in *Collected Works,* vol. 9, pt 1, *The Archetypes and the Collective Unconscious,* 2d ed. (Princeton, N.J.: Princeton University Press, 1968 [1959]), 106; *Letters,* ed. Gerhard Adler and Aniela Jaffé, trans. R. F. C. Hull, vol. 1 (Princeton, N.J.: Princeton University Press, 1973), 82. See also Erich Neumann, *The Origins and History of Con-*

sciousness, trans. R. F. C. Hull (Princeton, N.J.: Princeton University Press, 1970 [1954]), 88–101 (Neumann himself using the term "son-lover" for puer).

9. On the archetype of the Great Mother, see esp. Jung, "Psychological Aspects of the Mother Archetype," 75–110; *Symbols of Transformation,* 207–444. See also Erich Neumann, *The Great Mother,* trans. Ralph Manheim, 2d ed. (Princeton, N.J.: Princeton University Press, 1972 [1955]); *The Origins and History of Consciousness,* 39–101, 152–69.

10. See Marie-Louise von Franz, *Puer Aeternus,* 2d ed. (Santa Monica, Calif.: Sigo, 1981 [1970]).

11. Jung, *Symbols of Transformation,* 258.

12. Ibid., 259.

13. See Giacomo Casanova, *History of My Life,* trans. Willard R. Trask, 12 vols. (New York: Harcourt, Brace, 1966–71); Israel Regardie and P. R. Stephensen, *The Legend of Aleister Crowley,* 3d ed. (Phoenix: Falcon Press, 1983 [1930]).

14. See Albert Goldman, *Elvis* (New York: McGraw-Hill, 1981).

15. On the hero archetype, see esp. Jung, *Symbols of Transformation,* 171–444; "The Psychology of the Child Archetype," in *The Archetypes and the Collective Unconscious,* 151–81; "Religious Ideas in Alchemy," in *Collected Works,* vol. 12, *Psychology and Alchemy,* 2d ed. (Princeton, N.J.: Princeton University Press, 1968 [1953]), 333–39; "The Tavistock Lectures" [*Analytical Psychology: Its Theory and Practice*], in *Collected Works,* vol. 18, *The Symbolic Life* (Princeton, N.J.: Princeton University Press, 1976), 105–10. See also Neumann, *The Origins and History of Consciousness,* 131–256; *The Great Mother,* 203–8. On Jungian heroism, see my *Joseph Campbell: An Introduction,* rev. ed. (New York: Penguin/New American Library, 1990 [1987]; reprinted Meridian Books, 1997), chs. 2–3; my introduction to *Jung On Mythology* (Princeton, N.J.: Princeton University Press; London: Routledge, 1998), 16–17, 28–29; reprinted in *Theorizing about Myth,* ch. 6. On the hero as the opposite of the puer, see Edward Whitmont, *The Symbolic Quest* (New York: Putnam, 1969), 182–83.

16. On the puella archetype, see von Franz, *Puer Aeternus,* 81–84, 150–51, 152–54; Whitmont, *The Symbolic Quest,* 178–80.

17. See Lucien Lévy-Bruhl, *How Natives Think,* trans. Lilian A. Clare (London: Allen & Unwin, 1926), chs. 1–2; Jung, "Archaic Man," in *Collected Works,* vol. 10, *Civilization in Transition,* 2d ed. (Princeton, N.J.: Princeton University Press, 1970 [1964]), 50–73.

18. Jung, *Symbols of Transformation,* 343 n. 79.

19. To be sure, this negative interpretation of the puer archetype and therefore of Adonis represents only the classical Jungian view. The post-Jungian, archetypal view of James Hillman and his followers interprets the puer archetype positively and would therefore applaud rather than castigate Adonis for his identification with that archetype. Where for Jung and von Franz the life of a puer ends tragically, if not pathetically, in premature death, for Hillman it ends triumphantly, in a refusal to compromise with the everyday world. The behavior that for Jung and von Franz is childish would for Hillman be childlike: see Hillman, ed., *Puer Papers* (Dallas: Spring Publications, 1979).

20. On matriarchy in Greece and elsewhere, see, classically, J. J. Bachofen, *Myth, Religion, and Mother Right,* trans. Ralph Manheim (Princeton, N.J.: Princeton University Press, 1967).

21. See Jung, "Diagnosing the Dictators," in *C. G. Jung Speaking,* ed. William McGuire and R. F. C. Hull (Princeton, N.J.: Princeton University Press, 1977), 118–20.

22. Aristotle, *Constitution of Athens and Related Texts,* trans. Kurt von Fritz and Ernst Kapp, Hafner Library of Classics (New York: Hafner Press, 1974 [1950]), 114.

23. Antony Andrewes, *The Greeks* (New York: Knopf, 1967), 84. Andrewes points out that, despite the territorial basis of the system instituted by Cleisthenes, an Athenian who went to live elsewhere did not change his deme. On the importance of kinship, see ibid., ch. 5.

24. See Gregory Nagy, *The Best of the Achaeans* (Baltimore: Johns Hopkins University Press, 1985), 60–63.

25. See Pierre Vidal-Naquet, "The Black Hunter and the Origin of the Athenian Ephebeia," in *Myth, Religion and Society,* ed. R. L. Gordon (Cambridge: Cambridge University Press, 1981), 147–62.

26. Aristophanes, *Lysistrata,* trans. Benjamin Bickley Rogers, Loeb Library (London: Heinemann; New York: Harvard University Press, 1924, 3:79–80.

27. Vidal-Naquet, "The Black Hunter and the Origin of the Athenian Ephebeia," 161.

28. On political myth, see Christopher G. Flood, *Political Myth,* Theorists of Myth Series, vol. 8 (New York: Garland Publishing, 1996).

VIII. IN QUEST OF THE HERO

1. See E. B. Tylor, *Primitive Culture,* 1st ed. (London: Murray, 1871), 1:254–55. In an earlier essay Tylor amasses stories of children raised by beasts, but only in passing does he connect them to myths of future heroes: see "Wild Men and Beast-Children," *Anthropological Review* 1 (1863): 21–32. For a superb overview of the history of hero patterns, beginning with Tylor's, see Alan Dundes, *The Hero Pattern and the Life of Jesus,* Protocol of the Twenty-fifth Colloquy, The Center for Hermeneutical Studies in Hellenistic and Modern Culture, 12 December 1976 (Berkeley: The Center for Hermeneutical Studies in Hellenistic and Modern Culture, 1977); reprinted in Dundes, *Interpreting Folklore* (Bloomington: Indiana University Press, 1980), 223–61; reprinted in Otto Rank et al., *In Quest of the Hero,* Mythos Series (Princeton, N.J.: Princeton University Press, 1990), 179–223. Citations are to the reprint in *In Quest of the Hero.*

2. Tylor, *Primitive Culture,* 1:255–56.

3. See Johann Georg von Hahn, *Sagwissenschaftliche Studien* (Jena: Mauke, 1876), 340. Trans. Henry Wilson in John C. Dunlop, *History of Prose Fiction,* rev. Wilson (London: Bell, 1888), in an unnumbered attachment to the last page of vol. 1.

4. For an application of von Hahn's otherwise neglected pattern, see Alfred Nutt, "The Aryan Expulsion-and-Return-Formula in the Folk and Hero Tales of the Celts," *Folk-lore Record* 4 (1881): 1–44.

5. See Vladimir Propp, *Morphology of the Folktale,* trans. Laurence Scott, 2d ed., rev. and ed. Louis A. Wagner, Publications of the American Folklore Society Bibliographical and Special Series, vol. 9; Indiana University Research Center in Anthropology, Folklore, and Linguistics Publication 10 (Austin: University of Texas Press, 1968 [1958]). For Propp's later, more historical work, see his *Theory and History of Folklore,* ed. Anatoly Liberman, trans. Ariadna Y. Martin and Richard P. Martin, *Theory and History of Literature,* vol. 5 (Minneapolis: University of Minnesota Press, 1984), esp. ch. 5; "Oedipus in the Light of Folklore," trans. Polly Coote, in *Oedipus: A Folklore Casebook,* Folklore Casebooks, no. 4, ed. Lowell Edmunds and Alan Dundes (New York: Garland Publishing, 1983), 76–121. On Propp, see Alan Dundes's introduction to

Morphology of the Folktale; Anatoly Liberman's introduction to *Theory and History of Literature;* Archer Taylor, "The Biographical Pattern in Traditional Narrative," *Journal of the Folklore Institute* 1 (1964): 121–29; Isidor Levin, "Vladimir Propp: An Evaluation on His Seventieth Birthday," *Journal of the Folklore Institute* 4 (1967): 32–49; Robert Scholes, *Structuralism in Literature* (New Haven, Conn.: Yale University Press, 1974), 59–69; Walter Burkert, *Structure and History in Greek Mythology and Ritual,* Sather Classical Lectures, vol. 47 (Berkeley: University of California Press, 1979), 5–11, 15–17, 20–22; *Creation of the Sacred* (Cambridge, Mass.: Harvard University Press, 1996), 58–63, 65–66, 71–72.

6. Otto Rank, *The Myth of the Birth of the Hero,* 1st ed., trans. F. Robbins and Smith Ely Jelliffe, Nervous and Mental Disease Monograph Series, no. 18 (New York: Journal of Nervous and Mental Disease Publishing, 1914); reprinted (New York: Brunner, 1952); reprinted in Rank, *The Myth of the Birth of the Hero and Other Writings,* ed. Philip Freund (New York: Vintage Books, 1959), 3–96; reprinted in Rank et al., *In Quest of the Hero,* 3–86. Citations are to the reprint in *In Quest of the Hero.* The second, enlarged, 1922 edition of *Der Mythus von der Geburt des Helden* has never been translated into English.

7. Joseph Campbell, *The Hero with a Thousand Faces* (New York: Pantheon Books, 1949); 2d ed. (Princeton, N.J.: Princeton University Press, 1972); reprinted in Mythos Series (Princeton, N.J.: Princeton University Press, 1990). Citations are to the second edition.

8. Lord Raglan, *The Hero* (London: Methuen, 1936); reprinted (New York: Vintage Books, 1956); part 2, which is on myth, reprinted in Rank et al., *In Quest of the Hero,* 89–175. Citations are to the reprint in *In Quest of the Hero.* Chs. 16–17 of *The Hero* were originally published, with minor differences, as "The Hero of Tradition," *Folk-Lore* 45 (1934): 212–31.

9. See Sigmund Freud, *The Interpretation of Dreams,* trans. James Strachey (New York: Avon Books, 1965 [1953]), 294–98.

10. Sigmund Freud and D. E. Oppenheim, *Dreams in Folklore,* trans. A. M. O. Richards (New York: International Universities Press, 1958).

11. Karl Abraham, *Dreams and Myths,* trans. William A. White, Nervous and Mental Disease Monograph Series, no. 15 (New York: Journal of Nervous and Mental Disease Publishing, 1913); rev. trans. in Abraham, *Clinical Papers and Essays on Psycho-Analysis,* ed. Hilda C. Abraham, trans. Hilda C. Abraham and D. R. Ellison (London: Hogarth, 1955), 151–209. Other early Freudian works on myth and kindred literature include Rank, *Der Künstler,* 1st ed. (Vienna: Heller, 1907); *The Incest Theme in Literature and Legend,* trans. Gregory C. Richter, ed. Peter L. Rudnytsky (Baltimore: Johns Hopkins University Press, 1992); *The Double,* ed. and trans. Harry Tucker, Jr. (Chapel Hill: University of North Carolina Press, 1971); *Psychoanalytische Beiträge zur Mythenforschung,* Internationale Psychoanalytische Bibliothek, no. 4, 1st ed. (Leipzig and Vienna: Internationaler Psychoanalytischer Verlag, 1919), esp. chs. 1, 7; *The Don Juan Legend,* ed. and trans. David G. Winter (Princeton, N.J.: Princeton University Press, 1975); "Dreams and Myths"—an appendix to ch. 6 of the 4th through the 7th and penultimate edition of *The Interpretation of Dreams;* Rank and Hanns Sachs, *The Significance of Psychoanalysis for the Mental Sciences,* trans. Charles R. Payne, Nervous and Mental Disease Monograph Series, no. 23 (New York: Nervous and Mental Disease Publishing, 1916), ch. 2; Franz Ricklin, *Wish-fulfillment and Symbolism in Fairy Tales,* trans. William A. White, Nervous and Mental Disease Monograph Series, no. 21 (New York: Nervous and Mental Disease Publishing, 1915); Herbert Silberer, "Phantasie und Mythos," *Jahrbuch für psychoanalytische und psychopathologische Forschungen*

2 (1910): 541–652; Ernest Jones, *Hamlet and Oedipus* (New York: Norton, 1949 [1910]), ch. 7; Karl Johan Karlson, "Psychoanalysis and Mythology," *Journal of Religious Psychology* 7 (1914): esp. 182–206; Clarence O. Cheney, "The Psychology of Mythology," *Psychiatric Quarterly* 1 (1927): 198–209. See also Norman O. Brown, "Psychoanalysis and the Classics," *Classical Journal* 52 (1957): 241–45; Joseph R. Cautela, "Use of Psychoanalysis in the Study of the Classics," *Psychoanalysis and the Psychoanalytic Review* 47 (1960): 117–19; Justin Glenn, "Psychoanalytic Writings on Greek and Latin Authors, 1911–1960," *Classical World* 66 (1972): 129–45; "Psychoanalytic Writings on Classical Mythology and Religion: 1909–1960," *Classical World* 70 (1976–77): 225–47; Richard S. Caldwell, "Selected Bibliography on Psychoanalysis and Classical Studies," *Arethusa* 7 (1974): 115–34; "The Psychoanalytic Interpretation of Greek Myth," in *Approaches to Greek Myth*, ed. Lowell Edmunds (Baltimore: Johns Hopkins University Press, 1990), ch. 7; Marilyn Arthur, "Classics and Psychoanalysis," *Classical Journal* 73 (1977): 56–68; Lowell Edmunds and Richard Ingber, "Psychoanalytical Writings on the Oedipus Legend: A Bibliography," *American Imago* 34 (1977): 374–86.

12. See Rank, *The Myth of the Birth of the Hero*, 59–62; Freud, "Family Romances," *The Standard Edition of the Complete Psychological Works of Sigmund Freud*, trans. James Strachey et al., vol. 9 (London: Hogarth, 1959), 237–41. See also Ernest Jones, *Sigmund Freud*, vol. 2 (London: Hogarth, 1955), 273, 332.

13. See Otto Rank, *The Trauma of Birth*, trans. not given (London: Kegan Paul; New York: Harcourt, Brace, 1929).

14. Freud, *The Interpretation of Dreams*, 436 n. 2.

15. For Freud's view of the significance of birth in the wake of the break with Rank, see his *The Problem of Anxiety*, trans. Henry Alden Bunker (New York: Psychoanalytic Press and Norton, 1936), chs. 8–10; *New Introductory Lectures on Psychoanalysis*, trans. James Strachey (New York: Norton, 1965 [1933]), 87–88, 143–44. At the same time Freud employs Rank's analysis of hero myths as late as his *Moses and Monotheism* (trans. Katherine James [New York: Vintage Books, 1965 (1939)], pt. 1).

16. For contemporary Freudian approaches to myth, see Jacob A. Arlow, "Ego Psychology and the Study of Mythology," *Journal of the American Psychoanalytic Association* 9 (1961): 371–93; Sidney Tarachow et al., "Mythology and Ego Psychology," in *The Psychoanalytic Study of Society*, vol. 3, ed. Warner Muensterberger and Sidney Axelrad (New York: International Universities Press, 1964), 9–97; Martin S. Bergman, "The Impact of Ego Psychology on the Study of the Myth," *American Imago* 23 (1966): 257–64. Ironically, contemporary Freudian Bruno Bettelheim says roughly the same as Arlow and others of fairy tales *rather than* myths, where he is more like early Rank: see his *The Uses of Enchantment* (New York: Vintage Books, 1977 [1976]), 35–41, 194–99. On Freudian approaches to myth, see my "Fairy Tales Sí, Myths No: Bruno Bettelheim's Antithesis," *The Psychoanalytic Study of Society* 18 (1993): 381–90; reprinted in *Theorizing about Myth*, ch. 5.

17. Joseph Campbell, *An Open Life*, with Michael Toms, ed. John M. Maher and Dennie Briggs (Burdett, N.Y.: Larson, 1988), 123.

18. Ibid.

19. Ibid., 121.

20. On the differences between Campbell and Jung, see, more fully, my *Joseph Campbell: An*

Introduction, rev. ed. (New York: Penguin/New American Library, 1990 [1987]; reprinted Meridian Books, 1997), ch. 12.

21. Campbell, *An Open Life*, 121.

22. On myth-ritualism, see my introduction to *The Myth and Ritual Theory* (Oxford and Malden, Mass.: Blackwell, 1998), 1–13; reprinted in *Theorizing about Myth*, ch. 3.

23. See Robert Ackerman, "Frazer on Myth and Ritual," *Journal of the History of Ideas* 36 (1975): 115–34; *J. G. Frazer* (Cambridge: Cambridge University Press, 1987), 231–35, 253–55, 282–83; *The Myth and Ritual School*, Theorists of Myth Series, vol. 3 (New York: Garland Publishing, 1991), 55–60.

24. See J. G. Frazer, introduction to Apollodorus, *The Library*, trans. Frazer, Loeb Classical Library (London: Heinemann; New York: Putnam's, 1921), I:xxviii n. 1.

25. See S. H. Hooke, "The Myth and Ritual Pattern of the Ancient East," in *Myth and Ritual*, ed. Hooke (London: Oxford University Press, 1933), 1. Even more confusingly, Hooke's critics castigate him for employing Frazer's myth-ritualism: see Henri Frankfort, *The Problem of Similarity in Ancient Near Eastern Religions*, Frazer Lecture 1950 (Oxford: Clarendon Press, 1951), 6–7; S. G. F. Brandon, "The Myth and Ritual Position Critically Examined," in *Myth, Ritual, and Kingship*, ed. S. H. Hooke (Oxford: Clarendon Press, 1958), 263. See, in reply, Hooke, "Myth and Ritual: Past and Present," in *Myth, Ritual, and Kingship*, ed. Hooke, 4–5.

26. Raglan, *The Hero*, 98 n. 19.

27. Rank, *The Myth of the Birth of the Hero*, 57.

28. Ibid., 66.

29. Ibid., 63.

30. Ibid., 71.

31. Still following Freud, Rank introduces a second, non-Oedipal, nonsexual wish that likewise arises in childhood and continues in adult neurotics: a wish for perfect parents. "The entire endeavor to replace the real father by a more distinguished one is merely the expression of the child's longing for the vanished happy time, when his father still appeared to be the strongest and greatest man, and the mother seemed the dearest and most beautiful woman" (ibid., 62). The child invents the "family romance," and the adult invents the full-fledged myth to satisfy both wishes. Rank never tries to reconcile these seemingly incompatible wishes. On the contrary, he, like Freud, thinks that the two wishes work in tandem: both get rid of the father. But the Oedipal aim is to get rid of the real, noble father; the non-Oedipal one, to get rid of the adopted, lowly father—and of the mother as well.

32. Ibid., 58.

33. Contrary to Rank (ibid., 17), Cithaeron is a mountain rather than a river. After all, why pierce Oedipus's ankles if he is to be shipped out to sea?

34. On Rank's theory of hero myths, see William Bascom, "The Myth-Ritual Theory," *Journal of American Folklore* 70 (1957): 109–12; Melville J. and Frances S. Herskovits, *Dahomean Narrative*, Northwestern University African Studies (Evanston, Il.: Northwestern University Press, 1958), 85–95; Clyde Kluckhohn, "Recurrent Themes in Myths and Mythmaking," in *Myth and Mythmaking*, ed. Henry A. Murray (New York: Braziller, 1960), 53–58; Taylor, "The Biographical Pattern in Traditional Narrative," 117, 128–29; Dundes, *Interpreting Folklore*, 51–52; "The Hero Pattern and the Life of Jesus," 186, 187–90, 194–200. See also *Minutes of the Vienna*

Psychoanalytic Society, ed. Herman Nunberg and Ernst Federn, trans. M. Nunberg, vol. 2 (New York: International Universities Press, 1967), 65–72. On Rank's overall psychology, both before and long after his split with Freud, see Fay B. Karpf, *The Psychology and Psychotherapy of Otto Rank* (New York: Philosophical Library, 1953); Ruth L. Munroe, *Schools of Psychoanalytic Thought* (New York: Holt, Rinehart, 1955), ch. 14; Ira Progoff, *The Death and Rebirth of Psychology* (New York: Julian Press, 1956), ch. 7; Ernest Jones, *Sigmund Freud,* vol. 3 (London: Hogarth, 1957), ch. 2; Jessie Taft, *Otto Rank* (New York: Julian Press, 1958); W. H. Werkmeister, "The Symbolism of Myth," *Personalist* 39 (1958): 120–22; Jack Jones, "Otto Rank: A Forgotten Heresy," *Commentary* 30 (1960): 219–29; Samuel Eisenstein, "Otto Rank: The Myth of the Birth of the Hero," in *Psychoanalytic Pioneers,* ed. Franz Alexander, Eisenstein, and Martin Grotjahn (New York: Basic Books, 1966), 36–50; Paul Roazen, *Freud and His Followers* (New York: Knopf, 1975), ch. 8; Dennis B. Klein, *Jewish Origins of the Psychoanalytic Movement* (New York: Praeger, 1981), ch. 4; Esther Menaker, *Otto Rank* (New York: Columbia University Press, 1982); *Separation, Will, and Creativity,* ed. Claude Barbre (Northvale, N.J.: Jason Aronson, 1996); "Otto Rank: A Centennial Tribute," ed. Peter L. Rudnytsky, *American Imago* 41 (1984): 323–87; E. James Lieberman, *Acts of Will* (Amherst: University of Massachusetts Press, 1993 [1985]); Peter Gay, *Freud* (New York: Norton, 1988), 470–89; Peter L. Rudnytsky, *The Psychoanalytic Vocation* (New Haven, Conn.: Yale University Press, 1991); Robert Kramer, Introduction to Otto Rank, *A Psychology of Difference* (Princeton, N.J.: Princeton University Press, 1996), 3–47.

35. For Jung's interpretation of heroism in both halves of life, see C. G. Jung, "The Psychology of the Child Archetype," in *The Collected Works of C. G. Jung,* ed. Sir Herbert Read et al., trans. R. F. C. Hull et al., vol. 9, pt. 1, *The Archetypes and the Collective Unconscious,* 2d ed. (Princeton, N.J.: Princeton University Press, 1968 [1959]), 151–81; *Symbols of Transformation, Collected Works,* vol. 5, 2d ed. (Princeton, N.J.: Princeton University Press, 1967 [1956]), 171–444; *Psychology and Alchemy, Collected Works,* vol. 12, 2d ed. (Princeton, N.J.: Princeton University Press, 1968 [1953]), 333–39; "The Tavistock Lectures" [*Analytical Psychology*], in *Collected Works,* vol. 18, *The Symbolic Life* (Princeton, N.J.: Princeton University Press, 1976), 105–10. On Jungian heroism, see Erich Neumann, *The Origins and History of Consciousness,* trans. R. F. C. Hull (Princeton, N.J.: Princeton University Press, 1970 [1954]), 131–256; *The Great Mother,* trans. Ralph Manheim, 2d ed. (Princeton, N.J.: Princeton University Press, 1972 [1955]), 203–8; Joseph L. Henderson, "Ancient Myths and Modern Man," in Jung et al., *Man and His Symbols* (New York: Dell Laurel Editions, 1968 [1964]), 103–25; Marie-Louise von Franz, *An Introduction to the Psychology of Fairy Tales,* 1st ed. (New York: Spring, 1970), 41–46; M. Esther Harding, *Psychic Energy,* 2d ed. (Princeton, N.J.: Princeton University Press, 1963 [1948]), ch. 9; Jolande Jacobi, *The Way of Individuation,* trans. R. F. C. Hull (New York: Harcourt, Brace, 1967), 60–78; John Weir Perry, "The Messianic Hero," *Journal of Analytical Psychology* 17 (1972): 184–98; my introduction to *Jung on Mythology* (Princeton, N.J.: Princeton University Press; London: Routledge, 1998), 16–17, 28–29; reprinted in *Theorizing about Myth,* ch. 6.

36. See Campbell, *The Hero with a Thousand Faces,* 318–34; *The Power of Myth,* with Bill Moyers, ed. Betty Sue Flowers (New York: Doubleday, 1988), 124–25. On Rank's view of heroism, see also Campbell, *The Masks of God: Occidental Mythology* (New York: Viking, 1964), 73–74, 77.

37. See Campbell, *The Power of Myth,* 125. On female Jungian heroes, see Coline Covington, "In Search of the Heroine," *Journal of Analytical Psychology* 34 (1989): 243–54.

38. Campbell, *The Hero with a Thousand Faces,* 58.

39. Ibid., 110–11.

40. Ibid., 126.

41. To be sure, Campbell, in his second, longer summary of his pattern (ibid., 246), makes these specific relationships to gods optional.

42. Ibid., 139.

43. See my *Joseph Campbell,* 48–50, 222–29.

44. Campbell, *The Hero with a Thousand Faces,* 130.

45. Ibid., 139–40.

46. Ibid., 217.

47. Ibid., 386.

48. Ibid., 193.

49. See Joseph L. Henderson, *Thresholds of Initiation* (Middletown, Conn.: Wesleyan University Press, 1967), esp. 101–2, 134–35, 151–52, 159, 178–80; "Ancient Myths and Modern Man," esp. 101–25; introduction to Henderson and Maud Oakes, *The Wisdom of the Serpent* (New York: Braziller, 1963), esp. ch. 5. See also John Beebe, introduction to *Aspects of the Masculine,* (Princeton, N.J.: Princeton University Press, 1989), esp. xi–xiii.

50. Campbell, *The Hero with a Thousand Faces,* 58 n. 10.

51. Ibid., 30.

52. Ibid., 58.

53. Ibid., 37–38.

54. On Campbell's theory of hero myths, see Dundes, "The Hero Pattern and the Life of Jesus," 180, 187–88; Dundes's headnotes to my "Joseph Campbell's Theory of Myth," in *Sacred Narrative,* ed. Dundes (Berkeley: University of California Press, 1984), 256–57; my *Joseph Campbell,* chs. 2–3; Taylor, "The Biographical Pattern in Traditional Narrative," 119–21, 128–29; Jean Dalby Clift and Wallace B. Clift, *The Hero's Journey in Dreams* (New York: Crossroad, 1988), chs. 2–3. On Campbell's theory of myth as a whole, see, in addition to my *Joseph Campbell,* Stanley Edgar Hyman, "Myth, Ritual, and Nonsense," *Kenyon Review* 11 (1949): 455–56, 470–75; Richard Chase, *The Democratic Vista* (Garden City, N.Y.: Doubleday Anchor Books, 1958), 74–86; Florence Sandler and Darrell Reeck, "The Masks of Joseph Campbell," *Religion* 11 (1981): 1–20; M. C. D'Arcy, "God and Mythology," *Heythrop Journal* 1 (1960): 95–104; Richard M. Dorson, "Current Folklore Theories," *Current Anthropology* 4 (1963): 107–8; "Mythology and Folklore," *Annual Review of Anthropology* 2 (1973): 108–9; William Kerrigan, "The Raw, the Cooked and the Half-Baked," *Virginia Quarterly Review* 51 (1975): 646–56; Alfred Sundel, "Joseph Campbell's Quest for the Holy Grail," *Sewanee Review* 78 (1970): 211–16; *Paths to the Power of Myth,* ed. Daniel C. Noel (New York: Crossroad, 1990); *Uses of Comparative Mythology,* ed. Kenneth L. Golden (New York: Garland Publishing, 1992).

55. See J. G. Frazer, *The Golden Bough,* 3d ed., 12 vols. (London: Macmillan, 1911–15); abridged ed. (London: Macmillan, 1922); S. H. Hooke, "The Myth and Ritual Pattern of the Ancient East," and "Traces of the Myth and Ritual Pattern in Canaan," in *Myth and Ritual,* ed. Hooke, chs. 1, 4; introduction and "The Myth and Ritual Pattern in Jewish and Christian

Apocalyptic," in *The Labyrinth*, ed. Hooke (London: SPCK; New York: Macmillan, 1935), v–x and ch. 6; *The Origins of Early Semitic Ritual*, Schweich Lectures 1935 (London: Oxford University Press, 1938); "Myth, Ritual and History" and "Myth and Ritual Reconsidered," in his *The Siege Perilous* (London: SCM Press, 1956), chs. 3, 12; "Myth and Ritual: Past and Present," in *Myth, Ritual, and Kingship*, ed. Hooke, ch. 1. On the different versions of the ritual presented in Frazer and Hooke, see my introduction to *The Myth and Ritual Theory*, 4–6; reprinted in *Theorizing about Myth*, ch. 3.

56. See Raglan, *The Hero*, 89–136; *Death and Rebirth* (London: Watts, 1945); *The Origins of Religion* (London: Watts, 1949), esp. chs. 9–10.

57. See Frazer, *The Golden Bough*, abridged ed., chs. 24–26.

58. Going beyond both Frazer and Hooke, Raglan speculates that in the earliest form of the ritual the victim was not the king and that in the next stage of the ritual the king was not the god: see *The Origins of Religion*, chs. 9–10. By contrast, in "Myth and Ritual" (*Journal of American Folklore* 68 [1955]: 459) Raglan places divine kingship in the *first* stage of the ritual.

59. Strictly speaking, the chief god for Raglan is of the sky rather than, as for Frazer and Hooke, of vegetation.

60. Raglan, *The Hero*, 137–56. Raglan claims to be following Hooke but actually devises his own pattern.

61. Ibid., 138.

62. Raglan, "Notes and Queries," *Journal of American Folklore* 70 (1957): 359. Elsewhere Raglan ironically scorns what he assumes to be "the Freudian explanation" as "to say the least inadequate, since it only takes into account two incidents out of at least [Raglan's] twenty-two and we find that the rest of the story is the same whether the hero marries his mother, his sister or his first cousin" ("The Hero of Tradition," 230—not included in *The Hero*). Raglan disdains psychological analyses of all stripes: in response to the Jungian H. G. Baynes, "On the Psychological Origins of Divine Kingship," *Folk-Lore* 47 (1936): 74–104, see his "Psychology and the Divine Kingship," *Folk-Lore* 47 (1936): 340–44.

63. For Raglan's own ritualist analysis of the Oedipus myth, see his *Jocasta's Crime* (London: Methuen, 1933), esp. ch. 26.

64. Raglan, *The Hero*, 162.

65. See Victor Cook, "Lord Raglan's Hero—A Cross Cultural Critique," *Florida Anthropologist* 18 (1965): 147–54.

66. On Raglan's theory of hero myths and of myths as a whole, see, in addition to Cook's "Lord Raglan's Hero," Dundes, "The Hero Pattern and the Life of Jesus," 187–93; Dundes's headnotes to Raglan, "The Hero of Tradition," in *The Study of Folklore*, ed. Dundes (Englewood Cliffs, N.J.: Prentice-Hall, 1965), 142–44; Joseph Fontenrose, *The Ritual Theory of Myth*, Folklore Studies, no. 18 (Berkeley: University of California Press, 1966), ch. 1; William Bascom, "The Myth-Ritual Theory," 103–14; "Notes and Queries," *Journal of American Folklore* 71 (1958): 79–80; Stanley Edgar Hyman, "Notes and Queries," *Journal of American Folklore* 71 (1958): 152–55; Bascom, "Notes and Queries," *Journal of American Folklore* 71 (1958): 155–56; Kluckhohn, "Recurrent Themes in Myths and Mythmaking," 53–58; Herskovitses, *Dahomean Narrative*, 104–5, 111–16; Taylor, "The Biographical Pattern in Traditional Narrative," 118–19, 128–29; Francis Lee Utley, *Lincoln Wasn't There, or Lord Raglan's Hero*, CEA Chap Book (Washington, D.C.: College English Association, 1965); F A. de Caro, "The Chadwicks and Lord

Raglan: A Retrospective Analysis," *Folklore Forum* 6 (1973): 75–86; Scholes, *Structuralism in Literature,* 65–66; Edmund Leach, "Testament of an English Eccentric," *New York Review of Books* 5 (Sept. 16, 1965): 16–17. See Raglan's response to Bascom: "Notes and Queries," *Journal of American Folklore* 70 (1957): 359–60. For applications of Raglan's pattern, see Alwyn D. Rees, "The Divine Hero in Celtic Hagiology," *Folk-Lore* 47 (1936): 30–41; Mary Ann Jezewski, "Traits of the Female Hero: The Application of Raglan's Concept of Hero Trait Patterning," *New York Folklore* 10 (1984): 55–73.

67. See Rank, *The Myth of the Birth of the Hero,* 62, 70–71.

68. On the distinction between a literal and a historical interpretation, see my *Joseph Campbell,* 198–201.

IX. THE ROMANTIC APPEAL OF JOSEPH CAMPBELL

1. See my "Joseph Campbell on Jews and Judaism," *Religion* 22 (1992): 151–70.

2. Joseph Campbell, *The Power of Myth,* with Bill Moyers, ed. Betty Sue Flowers (New York: Doubleday, 1988), 24.

3. Campbell, *Myths to Live By* (New York: Bantam 1973 [1972]), 8–9.

4. Campbell, *Historical Atlas of World Mythology,* vol. 2, pt. 1 (New York: Alfred van der Marck Editions, 1988), 111.

5. On the differences between Campbell and Jung, see, more fully, my *Joseph Campbell: An Introduction,* rev. ed. (New York: Penguin/New American Library, 1990 [1987]; reprinted Meridian Books, 1997), ch. 12; my introduction to Otto Rank et al., *In Quest of the Hero* (Princeton, N.J.: Princeton University Press, 1990), xix–xxii; reprinted in *Theorizing about Myth,* ch. 8.

X. HANS BLUMENBERG AS THEORIST OF MYTH

1. Hans Blumenberg, *Work on Myth* (hereafter *WOM*), trans. Robert M. Wallace (Cambridge, Mass.: MIT Press, 1985).

2. See E. B. Tylor, *Primitive Culture,* 1st ed. (London: Murray, 1871), esp. 1: chs. 8–10; Joseph Campbell, *The Hero with a Thousand Faces,* 1st ed. (New York: Pantheon Books, 1949). On Tylor's and Campbell's theories, see *Theorizing about Myth,* chs. 1 and 9.

3. Indeed, Blumenberg singles out Ernst Cassirer as epitomizing the Enlightenment view. As Blumenberg rightly notes, Cassirer on the one hand says that myth is irreducible to science or any other symbolic form but on the other hand says that myth is incompatible with science, which succeeds it (see *WOM,* 168). See Cassirer, *The Philosophy of Symbolic Forms,* trans. Ralph Manheim, vol. 2 (New Haven: Yale University Press, 1955), 21 (on the one hand), xvii (on the other).

4. Tylor, *Primitive Culture* 1: 285.

5. Similarly, Mary Douglas argues that among primitives the survival of not myths but rituals even after the introduction of science proves that the prime, though not sole, function of rituals was nonscientific from the outset: see Douglas, *Purity and Danger* (Baltimore: Penguin Books, 1970 [1966]), 73.

6. See Sigmund Freud, *The Future of an Illusion,* trans. W. D. Robson-Scott, rev. James Strachey (Garden City, N.Y.: Doubleday Anchor Books, 1964).

7. See J. G. Frazer, *The Golden Bough,* abridged ed. (London: Macmillan, 1922), chs. 3–4.

8. On the reduction of the unfamiliar to the familiar, see Blumenberg, *WOM,* 5, 25.

9. See Géza Róheim, *The Origin and Function of Culture,* Nervous and Mental Disease Monograph Series, no. 69 (New York: Journal of Nervous and Mental Disease Publishing, 1943); Peter L. Berger, *The Sacred Canopy* (Garden City, N.Y.: Doubleday, 1967).

10. Joseph Campbell, *Myths to Live By* (New York: Bantam Books, 1973 [1972]), 13.

11. Campbell, *The Hero with a Thousand Faces,* vii.

12. See R. G. Collingwood, *An Autobiography* (London: Oxford University Press, 1939), ch. 5. See also Blumenberg, *WOM,* 182–84.

13. On "reoccupation," see also Blumenberg, *The Legitimacy of the Modern Age,* trans. Robert M. Wallace (Cambridge, Mass.: MIT Press, 1983), esp. 48–50 and pt. 1, ch. 6.

14. If in *Work on Myth* Blumenberg rails more fervently against the Enlightenment belief in progress than against the romantic belief in continuity, in *The Legitimacy of the Modern Age* (pt. 1, esp. chs. 3–4) he rails against Romanticism almost exclusively: he denies that the modern, Enlightened notion of progress is merely traditional religious eschatology in secular guise.

15. See Rudolf Bultmann, "New Testament and Mythology," in *Kerygma and Myth,* ed. Hans-Werner Bartsch, trans. Reginald H. Fuller, vol. 1 (London: SPCK, 1953), 1–44.

16. See Samuel Noah Kramer, *Sumerian Mythology,* rev. ed. (New York: Harper Torchbooks, 1961 [1944]), 73.

17. See Lucien Lévy-Bruhl, *How Natives Think,* trans. Lilian A. Clare (New York: Washington Square Press, 1966 [1926]), 330–32.

18. See Claude Lévi-Strauss, *The Savage Mind,* trans. not given (Chicago: University of Chicago Press, 1966), esp. ch. 1.

19. See Carl G. Hempel, "Science Unlimited?" *Annals of the Japan Association for Philosophy of Science* 4 (1973): 38–40.

20. See Bronislaw Malinowski, *Myth in Primitive Psychology* (London: Routledge & Kegan Paul; New York: Norton, 1926); Mircea Eliade, *The Sacred and the Profane,* trans. Willard R. Trask (New York: Harcourt, Brace, 1959), ch. 2.

21. See Hans Jonas, *Gnosis und spätantiker Geist,* 1st ed., vol. 2, pt. 1 (Göttingen: Vandenhoeck & Ruprecht, 1954).

22. In his introduction to *Work on Myth* Wallace defends Blumenberg's claim that he is skirting the issue of origin by restricting origin to "how" and categorizing "why" under function (xvii). But by that criterion many theorists of myth ignore the issue of origin—among them Eliade, Bultmann, Jonas, Radcliffe-Brown, and Malinowski. Only the last two of these theorists *profess* to be doing so.

ACKNOWLEDGMENTS

The chapters in this book originally appeared in somewhat different form in the following places. They are reprinted with the permission of the original publishers.

1. "Tylor's Theory of Myth as Primitive Science," from *The Sum of Our Choices: Essays in Honour of Eric J. Sharpe,* ed. Arvind Sharma (Atlanta: Scholars Press, 1996), 70–84.
2. "Does Myth Have a Future?" from *Myth and Method,* ed. Laurie L. Patton and Wendy Doniger (Charlottesville: University Press of Virginia, 1996), 82–106.
3. "The Myth and Ritual Theory": Introduction to *The Myth and Ritual Theory,* ed. Robert A. Segal (Oxford and Malden, Mass.: Blackwell, 1998), 1–13.
4. "The Grail Legend as Frazerian Myth and Ritual": Foreword to Jessie L. Weston, *From Ritual to Romance* (Princeton, N.J.: Princeton University Press, 1993), xix–xxxv.
5. "Fairy Tales Sí, Myths No: Bruno Bettelheim's Antithesis," from *Psychoanalytic Study of Society* 18 (1993): 381–90.
6. "Jung on Mythology": Introduction to *Jung on Mythology,* ed. Robert A. Segal (Princeton, N.J.: Princeton University Press; London: Routledge, 1998), 3–45.
7. "Adonis: A Greek Eternal Child," from *Myth and the Polis,* ed. Dora C. Pozzi and John M. Wickersham (Ithaca, N.Y.: Cornell University Press, 1991), ch. 4.
8. "In Quest of the Hero": Introduction to Otto Rank et al., *In Quest of the Hero* (Princeton, N.J.: Princeton University Press, 1990), vii–xli.
9. "The Romantic Appeal of Joseph Campbell," from *The Christian Century* 107 (Apr. 4, 1990): 332–35.
10. "Hans Blumenberg as Theorist of Myth," from *Annals of Scholarship* 5 (1987): 83–95.

Index